THE **WOMAN** IN THE **ZOOT** SUIT

THE **WOMAN** IN THE **ZOOT** SUIT

Gender, Nationalism,

and the Cultural

Politics of Memory

CATHERINE S. RAMÍREZ

DUKE UNIVERSITY PRESS   DURHAM AND LONDON   2009

© 2009 Duke University Press

All rights reserved

Designed in Scala by Heather Hensley

Typeset by Achorn International

Printed in the United States of America on
acid-free paper ∞

Library of Congress Cataloging-in-Publication
data and republication acknowledgments
appear on the last printed pages of this book.

For my parents,

Vince and Edna Ramírez

And for my children,

Carmen and Omar Ramírez y Porter

CONTENTS

> Pero lo más sura was
> that in all their
> SOCIOLOGICAL
> ANTHROPOLOGICAL
> PSYCHOLOGICAL
> & HISTORICAL
> heaps & piles of bogus bullshit,
> our sister—La Pachuca—of the
> equal sufrimientos;
> aquella carnalita que también
> who also bore the brunt
> de toda la carilla
> remained in their textbooks
> ANONYMOUS.[1]

In his poem "Homenaje al Pachuco (Mirrored Reflections)" (1973), raúlsalinas, one of the more prolific and well-known pachuco poets of the Chicano movement, pays homage to *el pachuco*, the zoot-clad, Mexican American homeboy of the 1940s and 1950s.[2] He also acknowledges this figure's female counterpart, *la pachuca*, and laments her erasure from official accounts of the Mexican American zoot subculture and infamous Zoot Suit Riots.

Although there were few reported serious injuries and property damage was minimal relative to other major twentieth-century civil disturbances, the Zoot Suit Riots represent a critical violent episode in Mexican American and U.S. history. During the riots, white servicemen, some of whom were accompanied by civilians, attacked "zooters," youths wearing zoot suits. In particular, they targeted zoot-clad Mexican Americans. For at least ten days in June of 1943, servicemen from across Southern California and some

* el Moy atuna + friend.*
Civic Auditorium in 1944.

1. A young couple sporting the zoot look, 1944. *Lowrider* magazine, copyright 1978–79. REPRINTED BY PERMISSION OF MCMULLEN ARGUS PUBLISHING, INC., COPYRIGHT 1978, 1979, 2007.

from as far away as Las Vegas poured into Los Angeles and roamed the streets of downtown, Chinatown, Chavez Ravine, East Los Angeles, and Watts in search of their prey. In some instances, they stopped and boarded streetcars, burst into businesses and private homes, and set upon people of color regardless of their attire. When they apprehended zooters, they frequently sheared their hair and stripped them of their distinctive clothing.

Even though the zoot suit was popular among working-class youths of various races and ethnicities in cities across the United States during the early 1940s, *The Woman in the Zoot Suit* focuses on Mexican Americans in Los Angeles, site of not only the Zoot Suit Riots but the Sleepy Lagoon incident as well. Like the riots, the so-called "zoot suit" murder case, as the Sleepy Lagoon incident was also known, drew attention to Mexican Americans' clothing, hair, and makeup.[3] In brief, both events expressed

2. Young Mexican American women on a street in San Fernando, 1943. Note the high pompadour, V-neck sweater, and bobby socks—all characteristics of the wartime zoot look in Los Angeles—on the woman on the far left. SHADES OF L.A. COLLECTION, LOS ANGELES PUBLIC LIBRARY.

3. Hallmarks of pachuca style: up-do, plucked brows, and dark lips, 1941. *Lowrider* magazine, copyright 1978–79. REPRINTED BY PERMISSION OF MCMULLEN ARGUS PUBLISHING, INC., COPYRIGHT 1978, 1979, 2007.

4. A Mexican American youth modeling *el tacuche*, 1942. *Lowrider* magazine, copyright 1978–79. REPRINTED BY PERMISSION OF MCMULLEN ARGUS PUBLISHING, INC., COPYRIGHT 1978, 1979, 2007.

5. A Mexican American man strikes a pose in a zoot suit, 1942. SHADES OF L.A. COLLECTION, LOS ANGELES PUBLIC LIBRARY.

anxiety over Mexican Americans' bodies and their place in a rapidly changing social order.

For young Mexican American women in wartime Los Angeles, the zoot look generally consisted of a cardigan or V-neck sweater and a long, broad-shouldered "finger-tip" coat; a knee-length (and therefore relatively short) pleated skirt; fishnet stockings or bobby socks; and platform heels, saddle shoes, or *huarache* sandals. Many also wore dark lipstick and used foam inserts called "rats" to lift their hair into a high bouffant. For extra panache, some lightened their hair with peroxide, sported tattoos, or wore the masculine version of the zoot suit. Also known as "drapes" or *el tacuche*, this outfit consisted of the "finger-tip" coat, which sometimes extended to the knee, and a pair of billowing "Punjab" pants that tapered at the ankle. Some Mexican American male zooters added a long watch chain and hat (called a *tando*) to the ensemble, but many abandoned the latter in favor of combing

6. A young Mexican American man sporting a pompadour.
Lowrider magazine, copyright 1978–79. REPRINTED BY
PERMISSION OF MCMULLEN ARGUS PUBLISHING, INC.,
COPYRIGHT 1978, 1979, 2007.

their relatively long hair into a pompadour on top and what was known as an "Argentine ducktail" or "duck's ass" ("D. A.") in back. *Calcos* or thick-soled shoes often punctuated the look.[4]

Mexican American women who wore zoot suits during World War II were known as *"pachucas," "chukas," "pachuco women," "women zoot suiters," "lady zoot suiters," "zooter girls," "zoot suit gangsterettes," "zooterinas," "cholitas,"* "slick chicks," and *"malinches."* Their male counterparts were sometimes called *"pachucos"* or *"chukos,"* among other labels. Simply put, pachucas and pachucos were Mexican Americans who produced and took part in *pachuquismo,* a youth subculture whose most salient identifying feature was the zoot suit during the 1930s, 1940s, and 1950s. Many were working-class and second-generation Americans whose parents had emigrated from Mexico to urban centers in California and the Southwest, including Los Angeles and El Paso, the latter of which is often looked to as the birthplace of *pachuquismo.* Many were bilingual and some spoke a distinct vernacular known as *caló* or pachuco slang. Some were also members of youth gangs.

In World War II–era Los Angeles, the zoot suit and its wearer had multiple meanings. For some, the look symbolized youthful insouciance and nothing more. But for many others, it signified rebellion, difference, and even un-Americanism—hence the violence to which its wearers were subjected during the Zoot Suit Riots. With the Chicano movement of the 1960s, 1970s, and 1980s, a number of Chicana and Chicano writers and artists—among them, raúlsalinas—began to ascribe new significance to the zoot suit, *el pachuco*, the Zoot Suit Riots, and the Sleepy Lagoon incident and trial. "Homenaje al Pachuco," for example, invokes the Zoot Suit Riots, during which Mexican Americans confronted physical violence, as represented by a blow to the face (*"la carilla"*). At the same time, this poem points to the discursive forms of violence to which pachucas and pachucos have been subjected by the state and its apparatuses, including academia, the dominant press, and judicial and penal institutions.[5]

Yet, where *el pachuco* was made the object of courtroom testimonies and academic treatises from the 1940s on, *la pachuca* has been ignored. By and large, pachucas are absent in much Chicano cultural production, such as film, literature, scholarship, theater, and visual art. Indeed, when I began this study as a graduate student in the late 1990s, more than one faculty mentor discouraged me from focusing on women zooters because they were convinced that they simply did not exist. Thus, in addition to being omitted from "their textbooks," *la pachuca* has been excluded from most Chicano accounts of what is generally deemed a watershed moment in Mexican American history. Like *el pachuco*'s distortion in scholarly "heaps & piles of bogus bullshit," pachucas' absence in narratives of Mexican American history, cultural identity, and community constitutes epistemic violence.

In this book, I recenter pachucas as agents and *la pachuca* as icon. I show the ways in which both have been excluded from or included in World War II–era conceptions of the American homefront, the Chicano movement's *familia de la raza* (family of the race), and a late-twentieth-century coalition of Chicana feminists. My main argument is twofold. First, I maintain that pachucas have been invisible in most narrations of twentieth-century Mexican American history. Then, as I locate *la pachuca* in a historical and cultural landscape, as defined in great part by literature and visual art, I demonstrate that this seemingly unimportant and often overlooked figure has much to teach us about nationalisms, about citizenship, and about resistant cultural, gender, and sexual identities and their contradictions. Yet, more than simply inserting pachucas into narratives of nation and cultural identity, this book asks what their absence reveals about nationalisms and the ways in which Chicano history and resistance have been conceived of and represented. Ultimately, it shows how their inclusion shifts our understanding of these narratives by exposing new social relationships and subjects.

An interdisciplinary endeavor, *The Woman in the Zoot Suit* excavates pachucas' agency and perspectives and, at the same time, explores the discursive ways in which these young women have been enabled and disabled as historical actors. As I place the archival document, such as a trial transcript or newspaper article from the early 1940s, in dialogue with a visual or literary text—for example, a painting or poem from the 1970s—I hope to underscore the value and limitations of both artifacts to scholars who study the past, be they historians or critics. While I do not care to privilege one type of method or source over another, I wish to throw into question what counts as history, historiography, and evidence. I reject the concept of the *definitive* history for its arrogant attempt to monologize. Although I value other scholarly and personal accounts about pachucas, pachucos, the zoot subculture, the Sleepy Lagoon incident, the Zoot Suit Riots, the World War II period, and the Chicano movement, I also wish to dialogize these stories. And I acknowledge the power of literary and artistic works—culture, in other words—not only to reflect but to produce history, narrative, and meaning.

This book is not only about the past, but about interpretations of it. A self-conscious recovery project, it excavates the overlooked participation of young Mexican American women in events deemed significant to twentieth-century Mexican American history and culture and, at the same time, attempts to make sense of these events, their actors, and the meanings ascribed to them by a later generation of Chicana and Chicano cultural workers. Its scope encompasses World War II, the instant when the figures of the pachuca and pachuco were catapulted into an imagined national community, and the Chicano movement, a period spanning approximately three decades when these figures took on new significance in Chicano cultural production. I link these moments because both were characterized in great part by heightened nationalist consciousness, either statist or insurgent.[6] The former saw widespread patriotism, if not jingoism, and an imperative for racial-ethnic minorities, including Mexican Americans, to assimilate or be assimilated as either loyal citizens or dangerous aliens. During the latter, cultural nationalist dissidence and militancy loomed large.

The Woman in the Zoot Suit is divided into two main sections. The first focuses on American national identity during World War II, while the second emphasizes movement-era Chicano cultural nationalism. Rather than championing one nationalism over another, this dual perspective offers a critique of both. By juxtaposing official and unofficial nationalisms, I not only show what they share in common; I also decenter them. In other words, I use one nationalism to relativize and to shed light on another.

In the introductory chapter, "A Genealogy of *Vendidas*," I present *la pachuca* and *el pachuco* as archetypes or icons and briefly describe the events that first brought them notoriety: the Sleepy Lagoon incident and the Zoot Suit Riots. Then I outline the book's historical span and introduce the theoretical concepts that undergird it, including *malinchismo*, nationalism, and citizenship. I argue that these concepts inform and have been informed by narrow definitions of home and family.

Home and family are the subject of chapter 1, "Domesticating the Pachuca." This chapter draws from archival sources and oral history for evidence of the participation of Mexican American girls and women in the Sleepy Lagoon incident and trial, Zoot Suit Riots, and wartime zoot subculture. Additionally, it begins to explore the myriad meanings that Mexican American women have ascribed to *la pachuca* and *el pachuco* and the events with which these figures have been associated. Yet, as it renarrates the familiar tales of Sleepy Lagoon and the Zoot Suit Riots, it removes Mexican American women, particularly pachucas, from the margins of Chicano historiography and foregrounds their redefinitions of contested cultural categories, such as "American," "lady," and "pachuca."

While chapter 1 emphasizes Mexican American women's agency, chapter 2, "Black Skirts, Dark Slacks, and Brown Knees: Pachuca Style and Spectacle during World War II," takes a closer look at the World War II–era social structures that helped to produce and to shape their actions. In this chapter, I scrutinize the iconic or discursive pachuca as produced by newspaper articles and academic treatises. Treating the zoot suit as a text, image, representation, and social relationship, I posit that this ensemble was construed as a sign of an aberrant femininity, competing masculinity, and homosexuality during the Second World War.[7] As a non-white, working-class, and queer signifier, it was perceived as un-American.

With its emphasis on both social structures and signs, chapter 2 serves as a bridge between the first and second halves of this book. Chapters 3 and 4 offer close readings of representations of *la pachuca* in a variety of texts and contexts. In chapter 3, "Saying Nothin': Pachucas and the Languages of Resistance," I study women speakers of pachuco slang. Moving from the visual to the oral, I examine the relationship of resistance to gender and style, specifically coolness. In order to better understand the linguistic varieties of pachucos and pachucas in the 1940s and the ways their utterances were recuperated by a later generation of Chicana and Chicano cultural workers, I draw upon an eclectic array of sources, including a poem, short story, *corrido* (ballad), trial transcript, and play. I contend that, while male speakers of pachuco slang have been upheld as icons of resistance and cultural affirmation, female, Mexican American speakers have been mocked, punished, or silenced for failing to reproduce the ideal subjects of U.S. nationalism, of an oppositional Chicano cultural identity, and of normative femininity.

Then, in chapter 4, "*La Pachuca* and the Excesses of Family and Nation," I study representations of *la pachuca* in works from the Chicano movement by the visual artist Judith F. Baca, the poet Inés Hernández, and the poet and playwright Cherríe Moraga. I locate these works against the backdrop of the Chicano movement and Chicano cultural nationalism. Paying close attention to their portrayals of relationships between women and their depictions of female masculinity, I probe the ways they express, distort, and exceed the cultural nationalist concept of *la familia de raza* and imagine new subjects and communities.

Last, in the epilogue, "Homegirls Then and Now, from the Home Front to the Frontline," I briefly discuss more recent representations of *la pachuca*'s successor: the war on terror's Latina GI. This project was nearly derailed by the events of September 11, 2001, and their aftermath, including the attack on and ongoing occupation of Afghanistan and Iraq by the United States. Why write about pachucas in the midst of war? I asked myself. What can a book about coats, skirts, trousers, pompadours, and lipstick tell us about the contested meanings of citizenship and the fragility of civil rights in and beyond the United States after 9/11?

In fact, the figure of the pachuca shows us that the World War II period and the post-9/11 moment share more than a few things in common. As a *New York Times* fashion critic recently quipped, "In a crisis, fashion produces a crisis of its own."[8] Since 9/11, the *hijab*, the head covering worn by some Muslim women, has taken on new significance, especially in Western Europe. For some, it is a symbol of piety, pride, or defiance; for others, it signifies fundamentalism and the oppression of Muslim women. In either case, the *hijab*, like the zoot suit before it, is a mark of difference. More than a simple "bit of cloth," it functions as both a metaphor and metonym as it prompts complex questions concerning citizenship, difference, and the particular roles racialized women play in (dis)articulating the two.[9]

Because of its focus on the war on terror and Latina servicewomen, the epilogue may at first appear incongruous in relation to the rest of this book. However, it strives to bring the seemingly distant and disparate into greater proximity by highlighting what they share in common. It also shows how the moment in which I have written *The Woman in the Zoot Suit* (the early twenty-first century) differs from the moments that I study (the World War II period and the Chicano movement of the late 1960s, 1970s, and early 1980s). By carefully examining the figure of the pachuca, the previous chapters stress the ways nations have violently excluded Mexican American women. The epilogue, in contrast, looks at the violence of *inclusion* in the nation and empire by focusing on the Latina GI, a figure relatively new to the American cultural landscape. Moreover, it seeks to acknowledge some of the women who are currently making history with the hope that they, like raúlsalinas's pachuca, are not rendered anonymous or forgotten altogether.

The seeds for this project are numerous. I have been inspired not only by raúlsalinas's "Homenaje al Pachuco" but by Luis Valdez's play and film *Zoot Suit* and Judith F. Baca's multimedia triptych *Las Tres Marías* (1976). Like these works, *The Woman in the Zoot Suit* is an intervention. By presenting an alternative interpretation of events and their actors, it offers a new, albeit familiar, story, one that I hope will prompt us to rethink older narratives.

7. Judith F. Baca, *Las Tres Marías*, 1976. Copyright SPARC, www.sparcmurals.org.

I first encountered *Las Tres Marías* when I attended the retrospective "Chicano Art: Resistance and Affirmation" at the San Francisco Museum of Modern Art in 1990. This important work features a pachuca from the 1950s and a chola from the 1970s.[10] As I stood before it for the first time, *la pachuca*'s absence in Chicano cultural production became visible to me. I am a native of Southern California's predominately Asian and Hispanic San Gabriel Valley, and although I was born long after the era of the zoot suit—the 1940s and 1950s—I grew up with women who resembled those in Baca's triptych. My father, who was born in 1924 and raised in East Los Angeles, familiarized me with *la pachuca* when I was a teenager in the 1980s. He likened my friends and me to the formidable girls of his youth as he complained about our tall, teased hair, thick eyeliner, dark lipstick, and oversized earrings. On Friday and Saturday nights, a friend sometimes joined me at my house or, more often than not, I went to her house, where we consulted each other about what to wear and how to wear it, swapped clothes and accessories, and helped each other with our hair and makeup before heading to a house party, school dance, *quinceañera*, or nightclub, like the Quiet Cannon, Marilyn's Backstreet, or Florentine Gardens. On more than one occasion, my parents and I argued over my appearance. Invariably, my father called out to me, "*Esa*, you look like a pachuca!" and grumbled that I reminded him of the girls he used to fear when he was growing up in East L.A. Indeed, the tough, urban pachuca of the 1940s was very present during my suburban, Reagan-era adolescence; I grew up surrounded not only by her ghost but by her late-twentieth-century heirs as well: cholas and cha-chas.[11] Yet, as a college student in the late 1980s and early 1990s, I found that there was a discrepancy between the historical actors I had encountered while growing up in Southern California and the subject of the narratives I was reading in school. *Las Tres Marías* prompted me to ask why pachucas were virtually invisible, while representations of *el pachuco* abounded in Chicano cultural production, from scholarly articles and books to the pages of *Lowrider* magazine.

I also credit many of the girls with whom I attended high school for inspiring this project. During the week, my classmates and I wore a drab uniform that consisted of a pleated, plaid skirt, white oxford shirt, cardigan sweater and/or vest, and a pair of anachronistic black-and-white saddle shoes that—no matter the size—made everyone's feet look abnormally large. School rules banned earrings bigger than a quarter and skirt hems more than two inches above the knee. On weekends, however, my friends and I happily petrified our hair with Aqua Net, darkened our lips with Wet 'n' Wild, and sported fluorescent lace and black spandex, often while listening to a mix tape with Debbie Deb's cha-cha anthem "Look Out Weekend." Meanwhile, many of the young men with whom we associated aspired to look "GQ"—an adjective taken from the title of the men's fashion magazine—by slicking their hair back and donning suits they had purchased at the Montebello Town Center. Like the pachucas of the 1940s and 1950s, many of the young women with whom I grew up negotiated rigid and oppressive conceptions of feminine decency as they cultivated a distinctive style, one that sought to infuse beauty, dignity, and more than a little glamour into their working- and lower-middle-class lives. I did not have the ability to articulate this when I was a teenager, but I was keenly aware of the difference—racial, class, and sexual—their look made. This book is also for them.

ACKNOWLEDGMENTS

This project has numerous inspirations and supporters and an equal number of debts. As an English major at the University of California, Berkeley, I took a circuitous path to Chicano studies and entered this scholarly field via African American and postcolonial studies. I'm grateful to my undergraduate faculty mentors, Professors Alfred Arteaga, Barbara Christian, and David Lloyd, for sparking my interest in Chicana feminism, literature, and history and encouraging me to pursue a career in academia. As a graduate student in ethnic studies at UC Berkeley, I benefited from the support of Professors Norma Alarcón, Judith Butler, Waldo Martin, Michael Rogin, Mary Ryan, and José David Saldívar. Berkeley is a big school, but the wonderful friends I made there made it more intimate and exciting. I thank Rob Avila, Mary Pat Brady, Glenda Carpio, Christina Civantos, Davina Chen, David Eng, Jill Gurvey, Eungie Joo, Josh Kun, David Hernández, Ellie Hernández, Amy Lonetree, Donna Murch, Rhacel Parreñas, Charlie Sciammas, Sarita See, Caroline Streeter, and Matt Wray for their encouragement, advice, and invaluable companionship. And I thank Rosa Johnson and Barbara Quan for steering me through Berkeley's bureaucratic maze.

At the University of New Mexico, I was surrounded by smart and supportive friends, colleagues, and mentors, among them Beth Bailey, Adriana Estill, David Farber, Eric-Christopher García, Teresa Márquez, Vera Norwood, Tey Marianna Nunn, Adriana Ramírez, Barbara Reyes, Diana Robin, Sam Truett, Hector Torres, and Claire Waters. I'm especially grateful to Tey Diana Rebolledo for her guidance, to Minrose Gwin and Ruth Salvaggio for their affirmation, and to Jesse Alemán for his relentless wit and refreshing perspective.

This project blossomed at the University of California, Santa

Cruz, where I've prospered from the friendship, direction, and, on more than one occasion, hospitality of Elizabeth Abrams, Gabi Arredondo, Pedro Castillo, David Crane, Dana Frank, Jennifer González, Kirsten Silva Gruesz, Danand Adriana Guevara, Beth Hass, Amelie Hastie, Aída Hurtado, Norma Klahn, Kim Lau, David Marriott, Olga Nájera-Ramírez, Renya Ramírez, Felicity Schaeffer-Grabiel, Shelley Stamp, Dana Takagi, Julie Tannenbaum, Alice Yang, Judy Yung, and Pat Zavella. My colleagues in the Department of American Studies, particularly Michael Cowan and Charles Hedrick, helped me to realize this project by providing me with course relief and enthusiastic encouragement. Donna Davis, Kathy Durcan, Helen Hill, Julie Krueger, and Marti Stanton gave essential administrative support. Rosa-Linda Fregoso and Herman Gray have served as cheerleaders and taskmasters alike. I cherish their example and friendship.

I was lucky to receive a postdoctoral fellowship from the Ford Foundation in 2001–2002, which allowed me to conduct new research for this project and to revise my dissertation. I thank Rafael Pérez-Torres for serving as my faculty sponsor. I'm especially grateful for his patience, equanimity, and friendship. I'm also grateful to Luis Alvarez, José Aranda, Frank Barajas, Ernie Chávez, Ed Escobar, Elizabeth Escobedo, Matt García, Michelle Habell-Pallan, Carlos Haro, George Lipsitz, Anthony Macías, Curtis Márez, Eduardo Pagán, Ernie Rios, Horacio Roque Ramírez, Ricky Rodriguez, Sherrie Tucker, Deb Vargas, Danny Widener, and the participants in the 2002 Mexican American History Workshop at the University of Houston— Deena González and David Gutiérrez in particular—for their various invitations, nominations, and recommendations. Many of these friends, colleagues, and mentors have shared sources with me, read my work carefully, and provided me with indispensable feedback and valuable support.

This project has also benefited from the generosity of the Chicano Latino Research Center, Committee on Research, Humanities Division, and Institute for Humanities Research at the University of California, Santa Cruz. Support from these units enabled me to hire my research assistants, Ruby Rodríguez and Aimee Garza, and my editor, Sara Miles. I thank all of these women for their efficiency and acuity. Additionally, support from these units allowed me to travel to a number of libraries for research. Octavio Olvera in the Department of Special Collections at the Charles E. Young Research Library at the University of California, Los Angeles; Lillian Castillo-Speed and Marisol Zapater at the Ethnic Studies Library at UC Berkeley; and Sherna Berger Gluck, Shu-chuen Li, and Kristie French in the Department of Special Collections at the University Library at California State University, Long Beach, deserve special thanks for their tenacity and helpfulness.

This book would not be the same without the precious words and memories of Dee Chávez, Olga Cruz, María Elena Gamboa, Inés Hernández, Carolina Juárez, Lupe Leyvas, Hortensia López, Mary López, Connie Loza, Alice McGrath, Mary Lou Ochoa, Annie Rodríguez, and Laura Vargas. I thank each of these women for their candor and willingness to talk to me when I was a nosy, bumbling graduate student and newly minted assistant professor.

For their powerful visions and stimulating works of art, I thank Judith Baca, Barbara Carrasco, and Carmen Lomas Garza. I appreciate the support they've shown me by permitting me to reproduce their works here.

I'm indebted to Ken Wissoker, my editor at Duke University Press, for taking a keen interest in this project when it was still very nascent and seeing it through completion. I also thank his ever-reliable assistant, Courtney Berger, the production editor Pam Morrison, and the four anonymous readers at Duke University Press, whose reports were crucial in improving my manuscript. And I'm grateful to the anonymous readers at *Meridians* and *Frontiers*. They offered constructive criticism for chapters 2 and 3 respectively.

Finally, I thank my family. I'm especially grateful to my parents, Vince and Edna Ramírez, for the sacrifices they made for my education and for emphasizing the value and pleasure of learning. I thank my children, Carmen and Omar, for their endless inspiration and reminding me every day that there is life beyond work. And I thank my husband, Eric Porter. An attentive listener and exacting reader, he's served as a sounding board for half-baked ideas and is all too familiar with this book's numerous, not always flattering permutations. He's guided me through our peculiar profession and, all the while, cooked our meals, changed diapers, tended the garden, washed dishes, and fixed things that break around the house. I thank him for sharing his life with me and, in doing so, enriching mine.

As I move between discussions of the World War II period, the Chicano movement, and the post-9/11 era, I try to use terms appropriate to each period. For example, when discussing the early 1940s, I generally refer to people of Mexican descent in the United States as Mexican Americans, rather than as Chicanas or Chicanos, politically charged labels that gained currency with the Chicano movement. I use "Hispanic," "Latina," and "Latino" as umbrella terms when referring to people, including Mexicans, Chicanas, and Chicanos, with roots (however distant) in the Spanish-speaking world or Latin America. Likewise, as I discuss the pachuca as historical actor (women who called themselves pachucas or who took part in the Mexican American zoot subculture) and the discursive pachuca (the pachuca of public discourse), I often denote the latter by referring to it as a "figure" or—taking my cue from raúlsalinas—as *la pachuca*. Even though I maintain that agency is always mediated and, thus, it is often difficult for scholars who study the past to distinguish the historical actor from the icon or representation, I make this thorny distinction for clarity.

Finally, while I use "pachuca" somewhat gingerly throughout this book, I also use it very liberally. As I show in the following chapters, "pachuca" is a multifaceted label, one that was more often than not pejorative. I believe that for this reason, the Mexican American women I interviewed as part of this study were reluctant to call themselves pachucas, even though some wore zoot suits, "rats," and dark lipstick, spoke pachuco slang, enjoyed listening and dancing to jazz, and associated with other zoot-clad Mexican American youths during the early 1940s. I do not mean any disrespect when I refer to these women as pachucas. Instead, I wish to reclaim and complicate this label via their recollections and stories and my own readings of the iconic pachuca. By doing so, I hope to articulate "pachuca's" multiple and contradictory meanings and the breadth and complexity of Mexican American history, identities, and communities.

A GENEALOGY OF *VENDIDAS*

> Miss Morgan said she observed her three assailants, all wear-
> ing dark skirts and the long identifying coats of the zooters,
> near the tunnel entrance and heard one say: "Let's get her!"

On June 11, 1943, in the midst of the Zoot Suit Riots, the *Los Angeles Times* reported that three "female zoot suit gangster-ettes" attacked Miss Betty Morgan, a lone white woman, near the Third Street tunnel in downtown Los Angeles. Morgan recounted that her assailants tackled her, slashed her face and arms with a knife or razor, then disappeared into the night. The victim was treated at a nearby hospital.[1]

The Zoot Suit Riots, which took place in Los Angeles from roughly June 3 to June 13, 1943, are probably best known for their clashes between white servicemen and young Mexican American men, some of whom wore zoot suits. But who were the elusive "zoot girls" who allegedly set upon Betty Morgan and why did they do so?[2] Where were they from and where did they go after they fled the scene of the crime? And why are they absent in most accounts of the Zoot Suit Riots? In addressing these questions, *The Woman in the Zoot Suit* reinserts women—namely, pachucas—into narra-tives of the World War II–era, Mexican American zoot subculture, especially those about the Zoot Suit Riots and Sleepy Lagoon inci-dent and trial. Additionally, this book seeks to understand pachu-cas' absence from these narratives.

The Zoot Suit: Origins, Context, and Significance

The zoot suit emerged at a flashpoint in U.S. history. The instabil-ity of race, class, and gender categories; fear of nonnormative sexu-alities, especially unchecked female sexuality and homosexuality; and concern over the widening rift between adults and adolescents came to a head in the figures of the pachuca and pachuco during World War II. As the war brought Americans of different races and ethnicities into close proximity with one another in unprecedented ways on the street, battlefield, dance floor, and factory floor, citizenship and national identity were reevaluated and recontested.[3] For the first time, some (but not all) racial and ethnic minorities, such as Mexican Americans, were hailed as Americans as they were called upon to join the war effort. At the same time, people of color, fed up with being "half American," seized the exigencies of war to demand for themselves the rights and privileges of full citizenship.[4] For example, the "Double-V" campaign, mounted by the African American newspaper the *Pittsburgh Courier* in 1942, called for two simultaneous victories: the defeat of fascism abroad and an end to racial discrimination on the home front. Meanwhile, numerous people of color—for instance, members of the highly decorated 442nd Regimental Combat Team and 100th Infantry Battalion, both of which were composed of Japanese Americans—demonstrated their loyalty to the United States by joining a still-segregated military and giving life and limb in combat.

In addition to reaffirming racial and ethnic minorities' claims to U.S. citizenship, the Second World War mandated a shift in gender roles and relations as increasing numbers of women entered the labor force and took on jobs previously held by men. Between 1940 and 1944, roughly five million women, many of whom were wives and mothers, left their homes to work.[5] Those who found work in the defense industry were dubbed "Rosie the Riveter." Meanwhile, numerous men left their families to join the military or to seek employment in centers of war industry. Migration, housing shortages, and a lack of childcare threatened to tear families apart, while marriage, birth, and divorce rates surged.[6]

World War II also impacted relations between parents and children and the young and old. Juvenile authorities, academics, police officers, and civic leaders fretted over what they deemed "new patterns of adolescent behavior" and a spike in juvenile delinquency.[7] At this moment, the zoot suit emerged as a hallmark of generational difference. Indeed, a contemporary social scientist linked the ensemble to what he called "a spontaneous Youth Movement."[8] In particular, the look was popular among working-class jazz and jitterbug aficionados of various races and ethnicities in cities across the United States. Many of these young men and women found the zoot suit both stylish and practical. As one observer noted, the heavy shoes "anchor[ed] the boy to the dance floor as he [spun] his partner around."[9]

Mexican Americans born in the United States during the first decades of the twentieth century tended to differ sharply from their immigrant parents, many of whom had crossed the border in an effort to flee the social, political, and economic turbulence of the Mexican Revolution and to work in a rapidly industrializing Southwest and Midwest. Many of these youngsters were the first in their families to be born and/or reared in an urban setting, to speak English, and to attend school for an extended period of time. At the same time, they were reminded on a daily basis of their status as second-class citizens by de jure and de facto racial segregation throughout California and the Southwest. What's more, many came of age in the midst of the widespread poverty and nativist (specifically, anti-Mexican) sentiment of the Great Depression. The forced deportations of Mexicans and Mexican Americans during this period underscored the precariousness of their place in the United States.[10]

For several contemporary observers on both sides of the U.S.–Mexico border, pachucas and pachucos constituted a "lost generation."[11] They had been rejected by the United States but also appeared to have renounced all things Mexican, including their own parents. Consequently, they were pitied or ridiculed as cultural orphans, as *pochas* and *pochos* (Americanized Mexicans). According to the cultural critic Octavio Paz, the pachuco had "lost his whole inheritance: language, religion, customs, beliefs."[12] In other words, he was a cultural bastard. Even the word *pachuco* was of "uncertain derivation," he chided.[13]

Paz came to his less than flattering conclusions about pachucos after observing them while he lived in Los Angeles in the years immediately following World War II. By 1928, Los Angeles, the focus of this study, had the highest population of Mexicans and Mexican Americans of any city in the United States.[14] At first, the majority lived near the old plaza north of downtown, but as the city expanded, increasing numbers settled to the south and east. Despite restrictive housing convenants, many Mexican immigrants and their American-born children lived in neighborhoods, such as Watts and Boyle Heights, among people of various races, ethnicities, languages, and religions, including Eastern European Jews, Asian Americans, and African Americans. As the city, county, and region emerged as a hub for manufacturing and military installations during World War II, many

Mexican American and Mexican immigrant residents of Los Angeles also found themselves living among new arrivals from other states, including servicemen.

According to the historian Anthony Macías, the zoot suit surfaced in this polycultural crucible. Although it may not have been invented in Los Angeles (its exact origin is unclear, but the African American jazz vocalist Cab Calloway wore it during his performances in Harlem as early as the late 1930s), the ensemble became a sign of Los Angeles's "cross-cultural swing scene," even as it traveled well beyond the United States.[15] In brief, it symbolized a racially and ethnically diverse youth culture that was far from utopian or democratic, but that nonetheless represented an affront to convention—particularly Jim Crow.[16]

For many young Angelenos, the zoot suit was, in the words of one contemporary observer, a "declaration of independence."[17] However, for many adults, especially those who worked in law enforcement, it was the uniform of the impudent adolescent and juvenile delinquent. In Los Angeles, the ensemble surfaced as the city and county saw rapid population growth and a host of related problems, including housing shortages and an increase in automobile traffic, air pollution, and violent crime, especially among juveniles. C. B. Horrall, chief of the short-staffed Los Angeles Police Department, attributed the rise in juvenile delinquency to the wartime disruption of families. In response, the LAPD imposed a nine o'clock curfew on teenagers.[18]

The Sleepy Lagoon incident, much of which occurred well after nine at night, thrust the zoot-clad, Mexican American adolescent qua juvenile delinquent into the national and international media spotlight. This event took place in southeast Los Angeles on the night of August 1 and in the early morning hours of August 2, 1942, and involved at least two fights: the first at a swimming hole known as Sleepy Lagoon and the second at the nearby home of the Delgadillo family, where the bloody and battered body of twenty-two-year-old José Díaz was eventually found. Díaz had suffered a massive blow to the head and died without regaining consciousness. Ultimately, twenty-two young men, twenty-one of whom were of Mexican descent, were tried and convicted of conspiracy to murder. As Los Angeles newspapers closely followed *People v. Zammora,* the so-called gang slaying trial, second-generation, working-class Mexican American adolescents, especially pachucas and pachucos, became objects of scrutiny and concern for civic leaders, law enforcement, academics, journalists, and cultural commentators in general.[19] Indeed, the historian Elizabeth Escobedo points out that prior to August 1942, "the term 'pachuca' had not yet entered the lexicon of judicial discourse" in Los Angeles.[20] Only in the wake of the Sleepy Lagoon incident did "juvenile authorities beg[i]n to use . . . 'pachuco-type' and 'pachuca' to describe a number of young women of Mexican descent."[21]

Among Mexicans and Mexican Americans, the words *pachuca* and *pachuco* predated the Sleepy Lagoon incident. The historian Eduardo Obregón Pagán has examined possible etymologies of *pachuco* and concludes that it "appears to have derived from Tirili slang for El Paso."[22] Tirilis were a subgroup of Mexicans and Mexican Americans who allegedly "traffick[ed] in prostitution and drugs" in and around El Paso and "were reputed to live a wild life of fighting, drinking, drugs, and sex, not unlike . . . *la vida loca* known in barrios today."[23] Pagán looks to them as forerunners of World War II–era pachucos, noting that they were sometimes called "pachucos" and that "popular usage of the term likely spread [from El Paso] to Los Angeles along the railways as Tirilis expanded their areas of operation," or as they simply joined the stream of Mexicans and Mexican Americans who migrated westward in search of employment and a better life in the early decades of the twentieth century.[24]

By 1942, the zoot suit had become a defining feature of *la vida loca*—the Mexican American youth gang subculture—in Los Angeles, with members of East L.A.'s Hoyo Maravilla gang, for example, donning "the entire expensive uniform."[25] Still, not all Mexican American youths who wore zoot suits were gang members or criminals and not all Mexican American gang members wore zoot suits. Among members of White Fence, one of the oldest and most notorious gangs in East Los Angeles, "the pachuco style never caught on."[26] Moreover, not all Mexican American zooters considered themselves pachucas or pachucos. In interviews I conducted with Mexican American women who came of age in Los Angeles in the late 1930s, 1940s, and 1950s, the period in which the zoot suit was most popular among young Mexican Americans, some of my interviewees defined "zooters" and "zoot-suiters" as youths who wore zoot suits but who were not necessarily affiliated with gangs.[27] They distinguished them from "pachucas" and "pachucos," whom they defined as gang members. At the same time, many insisted that not all pachucas and pachucos were gang members and used "pachuca" and "pachuco" synonymously with "zoo-ter" and "zoot-suiter." As one interviewee put it, being a pachuca "was a look. Period."[28] In other words, she believed pachucas wore their hair, clothes, and makeup in a distinctive fashion and nothing more. These observations underscore the fluidity of "pachuca," "pachuco," "zooter," and "zoot-suiter" and reveal that they were contested terms that often took on multiple, competing, and often contradictory meanings, many of which I explore in the following chapters.

"Las Malinches"

The significance of "pachuca" was further complicated in "Origenes de 'Pachucos' y 'Malinches'" (Origins of "Pachucos" and "Malinches"), one of many articles to appear in the Los Angeles–based, Spanish-language newspaper *La Opinión* in the weeks following the Sleepy Lagoon incident. Throughout, pachucas were called *"malinches"* and were thus equated with the most ignominious traitor in Mexican and Chicano culture: La Malinche.[29]

The story of La Malinche (also known as Malintzin Tenepal, Malinalli, and Doña Marina) is one of betrayal. Legend has it that she was born into a noble family in the early sixteenth century in Coatzacoalcos, Veracruz. After her father died, her mother remarried and gave birth to a son. To ensure that he, rather than his older sister, received the family inheritance, Malintzin's mother feigned her daughter's death and sold her into slavery. Eventually, Malintzin, whose native tongue was Nahuatl, found herself living among the Tabascans, from whom she learned Mayan. In 1519, the Tabascan chiefs presented her to Hernán Cortés as a spoil of war. The multilingual slave served as the notorious conquistador's translator, travel guide, and concubine and is thus blamed for aiding the Spaniards in conquering Mexico. What's more, she is regarded as the literal and symbolic mother of modern Mexico's racial and cultural hybrids, *mestizas* and *mestizos*. In 1522, Malintzin bore Cortés's son and shortly thereafter was married to another Spaniard, with whom she had a daughter. In addition, she converted to Catholicism and was baptized Doña Marina. As the historian Rita Cano Alcalá points out, La Malinche has come to epitomize "woman's inherent unreliability, through her religious conversion, cultural assimilation, political collaboration, and most important, her sexual liaison with the enemy."[30] As both slave and traitor, she is *la vendida par excellence*: literally, she is the one sold; metaphorically, she is the sell-out.[31]

More so than *la pachuca,* La Malinche, as mythical figure and historical actor, has loomed large in Chicana feminist discourse since the early
1970s, when Chicana writers began to "expropriat[e] [her] from the texts
of others"—most notably, Paz's infamous 1961 essay "The Sons of La Malinche"—and to "fill . . . her with [their own] intentions, significances, and
desires."[32] Like the Virgin of Guadalupe, Mexico's patron saint, La Malinche functions as an archetype in Mexican nationalist discourse; both
figures represent maternity. Yet, where Guadalupe is "the Virgin Mother"
and "the mother of orphans" (that is, of universal man in general and
Mexico's Indians in particular), La Malinche is "the *Chingada* [the fucked
one], the violated Mother," and the mother of bastards—in other words, of
conquered Mexico.[33] According to Paz, "Her passivity is abject: she does
not resist violence, but is an inert heap of bones, blood and dust. . . . She
is nothingness."[34] In contrast, for a number of Chicana writers, Malintzin/
Malinalli/Marina/Malinche is historical actor, symbol of Mexican/Chi-
cano (post-)colonial misogyny, mother, sister, daughter, goddess, savior,
speaking subject, and feminist prototype. In sum, she has become, to bor-
row from the title of Norma Alarcón's landmark essay, "a paradigmatic
figure of Chicana feminism."[35]

The Chicano Movement, Chicana Feminism, and *la Familia de la Raza*

The link between feminism and La Malinche was made apparent during
the Chicano movement. Also known as *el movimiento* (the movement) and
la Causa (the Cause), the Chicano movement was a flourishing of political,
artistic, and intellectual activity among people of Mexican descent in the
United States in the 1960s, 1970s, and 1980s. As the historian George
Lipsitz points out, it was rich in "complexities and contradictions," for it
was "both nationalist *and* internationalist, class conscious *and* culturalist,
reformist *and* revolutionary."[36] Its precise birth date is difficult if not impossible to pin down. However, the National Farm Workers Association
strike, which began on May 3, 1965, in McFarland, California, is widely
regarded as an impetus, even though many Mexican Americans actively
worked for social change long before the 1960s (and continue to do so
today).[37]

Still, the movement was not limited to a single cause or specific region
and found expression and meaning not only in the organization of farm
workers but also in an explosion in the arts; in political activism; in the

claim that people of Mexican descent were the rightful inheritors of the U.S. Southwest; in mobilization against the Vietnam War; in the struggle for and implementation of Chicano studies at universities, colleges, and high schools; in the establishment of Chicano student organizations; in a celebration of *mestizaje* and Chicanas' and Chicanos' indigenous past; and in Chicana feminism. In brief, it stemmed from and contributed to the turbulent social and political zeitgeist in and beyond the United States from the 1960s through the early 1980s. Many of the Chicanas and Chicanos who shaped and were shaped by *la Causa* were influenced by contemporary social movements—in particular, black power, the American Indian movement, independence struggles in the Third World, student activism, and second-wave and third-world feminisms.[38]

Nonetheless, some Chicanos and Chicanas saw feminism as a dangerous distraction from what they deemed the most pressing concerns of the movement: race and class inequalities. They dismissed feminism as, in the words of Ana Nieto-Gómez, "an Anglo-oriented movement supporting the economically oppressive structure" and branded Chicanas who openly self-identified as feminists *malinches* and *vendidas*.[39] In her essay "La Femenista" (1974), Nieto-Gómez, a self-professed Chicana feminist, distinguished "*femenistas*" from "loyalists," those Chicanas who did "not recognize sexism as a legitimate issue in the Chicano movement."[40] Where the conservative loyalist wanted the institutions of marriage and motherhood "to remain the same," the more radical *femenista* "spoke about changing [the Chicana's] role in the *familia*."[41] As a result, "*Feministas* were viewed by the 'Loyalists' as anti-family, anti-cultural, anti-man and therefore . . . anti-Chicano movement."[42]

Nieto-Gómez's astute observations concerning the perceived threat of Chicana feminism to the Chicano (the male and masculine subject of Chicano cultural nationalism), the biological Chicano family and, by extension, Chicano culture and the Chicano movement point to the relationship of family to nation. During the Chicano movement, Chicano group identity was often conceived of and represented as *la familia de raza* (the family of the race), a concept I analyze in chapter 4. Even though the heteropatriarchal, nuclear family was and remains prevalent in Chicano cultural production, it is not unique to it. As a number of scholars across disciplines have shown, this family has functioned as a model, metaphor, and metonym for the larger collective in countless nationalist struggles, statist and otherwise.[43] To better understand its role as trope in a Mexican American context, I draw from ongoing conversations in Chicana and Chicano studies, especially among feminist and queer theorists.[44] These scholars have eloquently shown that as Chicanos envisioned themselves *la familia de la raza*, the heteropatriarchal, nuclear *familia* came to occupy a prominent and sacrosanct place in much movement-era cultural production, including speeches, scholarship, and visual art.

The configuration of nation—statist and cultural alike—as family is a key concern of *The Woman in the Zoot Suit*. As I link the World War II period and Chicano movement of the second half of the twentieth century, I compare the roles pachucas played on the wartime home front, a term that collapses the nation and space of domesticity, to their place within (and outside) *la familia de la raza*. I argue that *la pachuca* played a significant part in the articulation of U.S. nationalism and Chicano cultural nationalism during the Second World War and Chicano movement as constitutive other. Her position as a highly sexualized, alien threat during World War II, which I discuss at length in chapters 2 and 3, and her exclusion from *la familia de la raza*, which I examine in chapters 3 and 4, helped to define the United States and Chicano cultural nation respectively, as well as normative gender and sexuality, in terms of what they purported not to be. *La pachuca* was rendered an outsider on the inside by wartime U.S. nationalism and an absent presence by Chicano cultural nationalism.

El Pachuco and the Subject of Chicano Cultural Nationalism

Like the heteropatriarchal, nuclear *familia*, the figure of the pachuco plays a significant role in much movement-era cultural production. *El pachuco* shows up on cars, in tattoos, in advertisements, and in cartoons. For example, in "The Adventures of Kiki and El Cruiser," a cartoon series that ran in *Lowrider* magazine in the late 1970s, el Cruiser, an old pachuco, is "a cosmic vato [dude] who travels back and forth through time like the early vatos los Mayas."[45] An omniscient and sagacious mentor, he instructs Kiki, a "little homeboy," in Chicano history by transporting him in a magical "'38 ranflita" (car) to the mid-1930s, "the time of zoot suits and los pachucos." Upon landing at the corner of Boyle and First Streets in the heart of East Los Angeles, el Cruiser shows his protégé a complete zoot suit (naming the various parts of the ensemble in pachuco slang) and teaches him how to pick up "rucas," "wisas," and "hi-nas" ("chicks").[46]

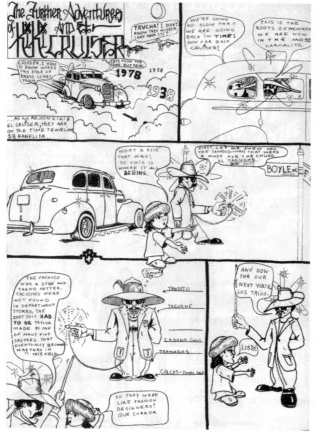

8. Detail from "The Adventures of Kiki and El Cruiser." *Lowrider* magazine, copyright 1978–79. REPRINTED BY PERMISSION OF MCMULLEN ARGUS PUBLISHING, INC., COPYRIGHT 1978, 1979, 2007.

In addition to appearing in artifacts of low, popular, or mass culture like *Lowrider* magazine, *el pachuco* has been the subject of scholarly works, such as Octavio Romano-V.'s essay "The Historical and Intellectual Presence of Mexican Americans" (1969) and Pagán's monograph *Murder at the Sleepy Lagoon: Zoot Suits, Race, and Riot in Wartime L.A.* (2003); in theater, such as El Teatro Campesino's *acto Los Vendidos* (first performed in 1967) and Luis Valdez's play *Zoot Suit* (which premiered in Los Angeles in 1978 and was released as a feature-length film in 1981); in poetry, most notably by José Montoya and raúlsalinas; in fiction, such as Tomás Rivera's short story "On the Road to Texas: Pete Fonseca" (1972) and Thomas Sanchez's novel *Zoot Suit Murders* (1978); and in works of visual art, like Ignacio

9. Edward James Olmos as El Pachuco in *Zoot Suit.*
COPYRIGHT JAY THOMPSON, ALICE GREENFIELD MCGRATH PAPERS, DEPARTMENT OF SPECIAL COLLECTIONS, CHARLES E. YOUNG RESEARCH LIBRARY, UNIVERSITY OF CALIFORNIA, LOS ANGELES.

Gómez's lithograph *Zoot Suit* (1979; the poster for Valdez's play).[47] For a glimpse of *el pachuco*'s prevalence in movement-era visual art, one need only turn to *Chicano Art: Resistance and Affirmation,* the catalog for the "interpretative exhibition of the Chicano art movement, 1965–1985." Both the exhibition and catalog feature a section titled "Urban Images," which includes eight images of pachucos from the 1940s and 1950s (out of a total of twenty-seven works). In contrast, only three works feature pachucas, two of which portray them alongside *el pachuco.*

At best, pachucas have been treated as ancillary in much Chicano cultural production, movement-era and otherwise. At worst, they have been overlooked altogether. To better understand their absence, I have found feminist critiques of Chicano cultural nationalism—namely, its androcentrism—illuminating.[48] Cultural nationalism emerged as a defining concept of *la Causa* beginning in the 1960s and was embraced by many Chicana and Chicano activists, artists, and scholars. As an intellectual, political, and social doctrine, it emphasized "ethnic unity" and upheld "culture as a force of liberation against American domination."[49] It has allowed Chicanas and Chicanos to critique the United States and, at times, has functioned as a competing and insurgent nationalism. As they condemned their status as second-class citizens, beginning in the 1960s self-professed Chicanas and Chicanos rejected the label "Mexican American" because of what they deemed its assimilationist connotations. With pride, they adopted "Chicana" and "Chicano," erstwhile pejoratives that had long been used to denigrate the poor, the Indian, and the *mestiza* and *mestizo* in Mexico and Mexican America. Alarcón has noted that the appropriation of these labels challenged the binational dyad Mexico/United States "through the inclusion of the excluded in the very interiority of culture, knowledge, and the political economy."[50] In imagining themselves a third nation, Chicanas and Chicanos looked to Aztlán, the mythical origin of the Aztecs (what some deemed the occupied American Southwest) as their homeland, rather than to Mexico or to what many were increasingly convinced was a greedy, white supremacist, and war-mongering United States.

Even though Chicana feminism and Chicano cultural nationalism are by no means mutually exclusive categories, Chicana feminists' relationship to cultural nationalism has often been vexed. Still, some, such as Nieto-Gómez, struggled to bridge feminism and cultural nationalism.[51] However, this proved challenging, for, as the anthropologist Patricia Zavella argues, "the fervor of nationalist ideology" silenced Chicana feminists as it "precluded [their] attempts to denounce sexism within the Movement or to point out Chicanas' subordination within Chicano families."[52] In addition to being silenced, Chicanas were rendered invisible by Chicano cultural nationalism. The literary and cultural critic Angie Chabram-Dernersesian has pointed out that the privileged subject of Chicano cultural nationalism was male: "el pachuco, el vato loco, el cholo, the Aztec, the militant Chicano, the existential Chicano, the political Chicano, the precocious Chicano, the Jungian Chicano-o-o-o."[53] Her emphasis on the *o* in Chican*o* is noteworthy because it points to the fact that even the ostensibly neutral and universal, albeit grammatically masculine, labels Chican*o* and Chican*os* erase Chican*as*. As they interpellate both Chican*os and* Chican*as*, these signifiers "subsume the Chicana into a universal ethnic subject that speaks with the masculine instead of the feminine and embodies itself in a Chicano male."[54] In other words, the conflation of the ideal Chicano subject with the male Chicano body erases Chicanas.

The embodiment of this ideal is apparent in Luis Valdez's play and film *Zoot Suit*. Valdez has described El Pachuco, its narrator-protagonist, as "a symbol of our identity, our total identity."[55] Building upon Chabram-Dernersesian's critique of Chicano cultural nationalism, the film critic Rosa-Linda Fregoso problematizes this character as a male and masculine identificatory locus. With his showy *tacuche* (complete with broad-brimmed hat and long watch chain), cool strut, and smooth tongue, El Pachuco embodies, in his own words, "the secret fantasy of every bato [homeboy, guy]."[56] However, as Fregoso argues, there is a discrepancy between the film's male and masculine subject of desire and those who are not *batos*—namely, Chicanas.

Chicano Historiography, from World War II to the Chicano Movement

Zoot Suit, which I discuss throughout this book, was one of many movement-era texts to transform the figure of the pachuco into an affirming icon. Many writers and artists, among them Valdez, reinscribed this figure with new meaning as they challenged a priori narratives that had pathologized pachucos as "bastards" or "queers."[57] In doing so, some recast *el pachuco* as a "symbol of early Chicano resistance" and harbinger of the Chicano movement.[58] His privileged place in the timeline of oppositional Chicano history is evident in "The Adventures of Kiki and El Cruiser," in which he is linked to an illustrious pre-Columbian past, and in his association with both the Sleepy Lagoon incident and Zoot Suit Riots.

For a number of scholars in Chicano studies, these events, and World War II more generally, represent a moment of origin and/or turning point in Mexican American history.[59] For example, according to the literary critic Luis Leal, the Zoot Suit Riots ushered in a new stage in Chicano cultural production—notably a "new type of literature . . . animated by a rebellious spirit."[60] He asserts that the riots "began an open confrontation" between Chicanos and the white American majority "that was to be intensified during the post-war years by the presence of thousands of returning Mexican-American veterans."[61]

The Mexican American GI figures prominently in Chicano historiography. Due in great part to their experiences during the war (both on the home front and abroad), many Mexican Americans began to look to the United States, rather than to Mexico, as their and their children's home. After fighting fascism overseas, veterans returned to the United States to demand full citizenship for themselves and other Mexican Americans. In Los Angeles as well as other Southwestern cities, the postwar years saw calls for integration, especially in public education and politics. For instance, in 1945, Mexican American parents successfully sued the Westminster School District in Southern California for placing their children in segregated classrooms. They gained an additional victory the following year and helped to pave the way for *Brown v. Board of Education* in 1954 when Governor Earl Warren repealed de jure segregation in California's public schools. Then, in 1949, Edward R. Roybal, a World War II veteran from East Los Angeles, was elected to the Los Angeles city council. As he was the first Mexican American to serve in city hall since 1881, his victory carried profound political significance, much like Antonio Villaraigosa's successful mayoral campaign fifty-six years later.[62] Meanwhile, numerous Mexican American veterans made inroads into the middle class by taking advantage of the GI Bill of Rights, which enabled them to pursue a college degree or vocational education and provided them with home and business loans.

In Chicano cultural production, including historiography, the figures of the pachuco and GI function as group archetypes in that they have played a significant role in shaping discourse on World War II and the second half of the twentieth century. Where the pachuco represents "the revolutionary Chicano" and self-conscious, stylized social marginalization, the World War II veteran stands for reformism and integration.[63] Indeed, the archetypal GI has served as a metonym for what some scholars call the "GI Generation": Mexican Americans born between 1915 and 1926 "who would eventually fight, work, and organize during World War II."[64] Furthermore, the GI is in many ways emblematic of what the historian Mario T. García has labeled the "Mexican-American Generation": the generation of Mexican Americans shaped by "the shared historical experiences of the Great Depression and World War II."[65] He maintains that reform, including integration, rather than revolution characterized this generation.

In comparison, for the "Chicano Generation," the generation of the Chicano movement, "reforms were not enough."[66] Nor was integration necessarily seen as a common or desirable goal. While the previous generation was identified with a "politics of supplication," the Chicano Generation has been defined by a "politics of confrontation."[67] This generation defied authority by publicly opposing the Vietnam War, exploitive agribusiness, police brutality, an exclusionary public education system, and insulting advertisements—for example, Frito-Lay's infamous "Frito Bandito." As they condemned the Frito Bandito, a cartoon character that stole corn chips, Chicanas and Chicanos engaged with the dominant culture in a war over meaning and demanded the right to self-representation. They did the same as they embraced *el pachuco*, a "subject . . . previously devalorized by U.S. dominant culture" and spurned by the previous generation, from racist Anglo academics to members of the Mexican American middle class.[68]

As the figure of the GI was transformed into that of activist and/or reformer, *el pachuco* endured in much Chicano cultural production as a rebel. In fact, even though its popularity waned and it changed somewhat (for example, snug leather jackets replaced oversized coats), the zoot look persisted among some Mexican Americans through the 1950s. It or at least its remnants were also evident in American popular and youth culture of the 1950s—for example, in Orson Welles's film noir classic *Touch of Evil* (1958) and in the figure of the "bad boy," as represented by Marlon Brando, James Dean, and a pompadoured Elvis Presley. Later, 1950s-era *pachuquismo* inspired various important movement-era literary and artistic works such as José Montoya's elegiac poem "El Louie" (1970), and Judith F. Baca's multimedia triptych *Las Tres Marías* (1976), which I discuss in chapters 4 and 5 respectively.[69] Yet, despite the importance of the 1950s in twentieth-century Mexican American history, this study brackets its subject, the pachuca, with the World War II period and Chicano movement. In addition to functioning as "bookends" in much Chicano cultural production and sharing a concern with nationalisms, both periods witnessed profound shifts in gender roles and relations, especially in the workplace, and overt challenges to normative masculinities.

This is a book about women, but it pays close attention to men and masculinities, especially to *el pachuco*'s transformation from "gamin dandy" to "Minuteman of *machismo*" and from confused *pocho* to cultural authority in art and literature of the Chicano movement.[70] To better understand these turns and their relationships to one other, I draw from Pierrette Hondagneu-Sotelo's and Michael A. Messner's observations regarding the relationship of race and class to masculinity. These sociologists read the "exaggerated embodiments and verbalizations of masculinity" enacted and displayed by "marginalized and subordinated men," such as working-class men and men of color, as "a desire to express power over others within a context of relative powerlessness."[71] In contrast, the masculinity of men who enjoy "considerable power and privilege over women and other men" is often deemed more egalitarian.[72] Similarly, the literary and film critic Judith Halberstam argues that masculinity is naturalized when performed by white middle-class men. It "becomes legible . . . where and when it leaves the white male middle-class body" and is taken up by the working-class man, man of color, or butch lesbian.[73]

With their flashy ensembles, which flew in the face of wartime rationing regulations and sober middle-class aesthetics, pachucos of the early 1940s appeared to repudiate American patriotism and conventional—specifically, heteronormative and bourgeois—masculinities, Anglo-American and Mexican alike. For this reason, a later generation upheld *el pachuco* as the avatar of an oppositional, rather than assimilationist, Chicano cultural identity and as a harbinger of the Chicano movement. For example, Tino Villanueva admired the stylish manner in which the pachuco "saunter[s]," "sway[s,]" and "leans the wrong way / in assertion" in his poem "Pachuco Remembered" (1972).[74] In lauding *el pachuco* as an icon and hero, cultural workers stressed that the zoot suit was more than a mere sartorial fad. Instead, they argued, it functioned as a sign of difference and defiance. Yet what happened when pachucas articulated difference and defiance? When they sauntered, swayed, and leaned the wrong way in assertion? When they appropriated the signifiers of coolness and fashioned themselves hipsters? In short, what happened when pachucas enacted and embodied resistance?

Just as "real" or normative masculinity has been claimed as the purview of white, middle-class men, resistance, including style as resistance, has been regarded as the province of Chicanos. As Chabram-Dernersesian contends, "if Chicanas wished to . . . figure within the record of Mexican practices of resistance in the U.S." during the Chicano movement, "then they had to embody themselves as males."[75] At the same time, they were expected to "adopt traditional family relations" due to the cultural nationalist obsession with the heteropatriarchal *familia de la raza.*[76] In chapter 4 I argue that *el pachuco* could be and was incorporated into *la familia de la raza* as father, son, and brother because he complemented and articulated many of the values, goals, and ideals of Chicano cultural nationalism: he came to symbolize fidelity to a distinct, affirming, and oppositional Chicano cultural identity and he served as an anodyne for an injured—in other words, emasculated—Chicano masculinity.

Perfidia

Although they have received far less attention than their male contemporaries and are erased by the androcentric label "GI Generation," female Mexican American defense workers and enlistees have helped to shape discourse on the World War II period in Chicana studies. They, too, are regarded by a handful of scholars as precursors of the social movements of the second half of the twentieth century. Escobedo, for example, traces what she calls Mexican American women's postwar "political voice" to "Rosita the Riveter," the Mexican American, female defense worker.[77] Because Rosita's experiences in the workplace provided her with "new job skills" and "a sense of self-worth,"[78] she has been identified as "pre-feminist" and has been credited with "plant[ing] the seeds for the sociopolitical and economic changes that would . . . launch . . . Chicanas into . . . the era of the social protest movement."[79] Similarly, the historian Lorena Oropeza asserts that the Second World War prompted numerous Mexican American servicewomen to experience "a burgeoning recognition of themselves as Americans."[80]

While I am not interested in upholding *la pachuca* as a precursor of the Chicano movement or prototype of Chicana feminism, I am concerned about her place in Mexican American history and cultural production. I am especially fascinated by pachucas' absence in narratives about origin and opposition, as well as by what happens when they are reinserted into them. What can these narratives tell us about pachucas and what pachucas can tell us about them?

Take, for example, accounts that describe *People v. Zammora* as "a landmark of progress for the Spanish-speaking peoples of the Southwest" and "the beginning of the Chicano movement."[81] Until recently, only a handful of writers or artists acknowledged the roles that women, especially Mexican American women, played in the Sleepy Lagoon incident and trial.[82] Few noted that some of the girls and young women who took part in these events—many of whom were branded pachucas—remained incarcerated and wards of the state long after their male companions were exonerated and released from prison.[83] This simple fact throws into question whole-sale celebrations of the successful appeal in *People v. Zammora*. For whom exactly was it a victory? What sort of social movement did it instigate and for whom? And why were the Mexican American girls and women who took part in this supposedly seminal event overlooked by a later generation of writers, artists, and activists?

Mexican American girls and young women, especially those branded pachucas, began to receive more than their fair share of attention from authorities both within and outside the home beginning in the early 1940s. With the Sleepy Lagoon incident, pachucas' attire, hair, and makeup, their use of unconventional slang, their putatively innate propensity for violence and crime, their suspected association with gangs, and their alleged sexual promiscuity were regarded by law enforcement, the dominant press, academics, and, in some instances, their own parents as indicators of their rejection of a socially sanctioned—namely, middle-class, Mexican-immigrant—femininity. And by appearing to betray gender norms during wartime, pachucas, many of whom were the bilingual and bicultural children of immigrants, seemed to betray the nation as well. Thus, in addition to describing them as morally and sexually loose, Angeleno newspapers demonized them as un- or even anti-American.

Meanwhile, for some Mexican immigrant parents, their zoot-clad children born in the United States were not Mexican enough. They lamented the "terrible freedom" the United States offered their daughters, some of whom painted their faces in "una manera escandalosa" (a scandalous manner) and donned skirts that were so short they exposed their knees.[84] Worse still, Mexican American girls and young women in Los Angeles increasingly ventured from their homes unchaperoned for leisure and work, with World War II providing them with new reasons and renewed justification for doing so.[85] As Escobedo argues, these girls and young women dealt a blow to "the flagging authority of the Mexican family to police female sexuality and to maintain traditional Mexican culture in the United States."[86] Further, they drew the attention and, more often than not, ire of law enforcement, juvenile authorities, and academics. Indeed, at times, "Americanization" was equated with shallow materialism and delinquency. As one contemporary observer remarked, "in becoming 'American'"—that is, in pursuing "nice clothes and a good time"—some Mexican American girls slipped into delinquency.[87]

and American womanhood? If the Chicano cultural nation has been configured as a heteropatriarchal family, then what role, if any, does or can she play in it? And if homophobia refers not only to the fear and hatred of homosexuals but to the "fear of going home . . . of not being taken in . . . of being abandoned by the mother, the culture, la Raza," as the feminist theorist Gloria Anzaldúa maintains, then where is *la pachuca*'s—in particular, the lesbian pachuca's—home and who is her family?[97] In other words, who has betrayed whom?

Locating *The Woman in the Zoot Suit*

One of my objectives in this book is to expose the junction of nation, race, class, gender, and sexuality and the ways these categories and points of identification affect and come into being via citizenship. Here, "citizenship" has multiple meanings. It refers to "formal and official" citizenship, to the articulation of rights, entitlements, territoriality, and the nationstate; to gradations of citizenship—for example, first-class and second-class citizenship or "alien citizenship"; and to nonjuridical membership in a collectivity.[98] According to the anthropologist Renato Rosaldo, these "more colloquial or vernacular" collectivities may be constituted in and by "the workplace, churches, schools, and friendship and family networks."[99] To his list I add the insurgent, illegitimate, or unofficial nation—specifically, the groups conceived by Chicano cultural nationalism.

As my broad definition of citizenship implies, "nation" and "nationalism" are also polysemous terms.[100] This book studies the United States as not only a politically organized grouping but a racial imaginary as well. In addition, it explores the "invisible nation" envisioned by Chicano cultural nationalists during the 1960s, 1970s, and 1980s.[101] Concerned with land, colonialism, and *mestizaje* (among other things), movement-era cultural nationalism or *Chicanismo* was by no means homogeneous or monolithic. As the literary critic Rafael Pérez-Torres points out, its many strands and fissures derived from multiple sources, among them,

> the nationalist movements—American Indian and Black—current in the political climate of the late 1960s; the Third World struggles for national sovereignty in the 1950s; the "nationless" status of Chicanos who, after fighting in World War II, returned to a country where they were still considered foreigners in the 1940s; the institutionalization,

following the Mexican Revolution, of Mexican national culture in the 1920s and 1930s; the usurpation of Mexican territorial rights in 1848; the continuous migrations of Mexicanos before, during, and after the U.S.-Mexican War; the struggle for Mexican independence from Spain begun in 1810.[102]

Put another way, Chicano cultural nationalism is a product of a combination of social and political forces, including nationalism, colonialism, and racism, that gave "rise to collective identity, community, and a sense of 'peoplehood.' "[103] In short, it posits that the de jure and de facto exclusion of Mexicans and Mexican Americans from the American polity has resulted in the existence of a "nation" within a nation. For cultural nationalists, the former is most evident in a discrete, subordinated, and vibrant Chicano culture.[104] And like all other nationalisms, Chicano cultural nationalism has fabricated and is fabricated by myths, symbols, traditions, and narratives.

The Woman in the Zoot Suit examines pachucas' role in the articulation (that is, enunciation and linkage) of national myths, symbols, traditions, and narratives during the Second World War and the Chicano movement. It foregrounds Chicanas' dis-identificatory relationship to nation and citizenship and their efforts to demand what Rosaldo describes as "full membership in a group" via and for *la pachuca*.[105] At the same time, this book attends to the ways that "state power and other forms of regulation," such as Chicano cultural nationalism, "define the different modalities of belonging."[106] In other words, it asks: How did pachucas as historical actors and *la pachuca* as sign help to define "America" and "American" during World War II, and how did the state and its apparatuses use pachucas and *la pachuca* to delineate citizenship? How did pachucas and *la pachuca* help to define "Chicano" and "Chicana" during the Chicano movement, and how did Chicano cultural nationalism determine who was or was not Chicano or Chicana via *el pachuco* and *la pachuca*?

To address these questions, I approach the figures of the pachuca and pachuco as "group archetypes," as recurring signs in cultural production that signify or reflect a larger group identity.[107] Furthermore, I treat them as "image icons." As Marita Sturken and Lisa Cartwright remind us, "an icon is an image that refers to something outside of its individual components, something (or someone) that has great symbolic meaning for many people."[108] As an archetype or icon, the World War II–era pachuco came to symbolize Chicano cultural identity, resistance, and style for a later generation of Chicano cultural workers. Meanwhile, his female contemporary, *la pachuca,* assumed a very different sort of iconic status as a *malinchista* or female traitor.

The Woman in the Zoot Suit brings together feminist, queer, and postcolonial theory to argue that pachucas' erasure in Chicano narratives of origin and opposition is connected to *malinchismo*—that is, to a highly gendered (namely female/feminine) treachery. To illuminate *la pachuca's* infidelity, I draw from Alarcón's meditations on the Mexican figure of La Malinche, as well as from theories of performativity (the repetition and disruption of symbolic categories).[109] I argue that, in the context of World War II and the Chicano movement, the pachuca, as *malinche,* gangsterette, *pocha,* alien, whore, and lesbian, failed to reproduce the ideal subjects of normative gender and sexuality and U.S. and Chicano nationalisms—hence her absence in much movement-era cultural production.

This interdisciplinary study draws from the questions and methods of history and literary criticism and seeks to contribute to conversations in American studies, ethnic studies (especially Chicano and Latina studies), and cultural studies, in particular, the study of visual culture (the manifestation of culture in visual form).[110] The conceptual mechanisms by which it approaches and understands its subject include representation ("the use of language and images to create meaning about the world around us") and visuality ("the quality or state of being visual").[111] With their distinctive clothing, hairstyles, and makeup, pachucas participated in a spectacular—that is, visible and public—subculture.[112] Their visuality and conspicuous occupation of public space are underscored in the epigraph with which I open this chapter: the *Los Angeles Times* reported that Betty Morgan "observed" her attackers on a city street. Yet she and, by extension, the newspaper's readers not only saw but interpreted them—in particular, their attire. Their "dark skirts" and "long identifying coats" were more than mere articles of clothing; they carried complex and profound meanings in the context of the Zoot Suit Riots and, later, the Chicano movement. It is to the zoot suit and its meanings that I now turn.

Chapter 1

DOMESTICATING THE PACHUCA

> It was the secret fantasy of every bato
> in or out of the Chicanada
> to put on a Zoot Suit and play the Myth
> más chucote que la chingada.
> LUIS VALDEZ, *ZOOT SUIT*[1]

> There was a time when we used to put our little zoot suits on.
> DEE CHÁVEZ[2]

The lines from Luis Valdez's *Zoot Suit* quoted in the epigraph above are spoken by the narrator, El Pachuco, who opens the play by slashing the drop curtain, a giant facsimile of the front page of the *Los Angeles Herald-Express*. Dated June 3, 1943, the newspaper's headline blares, "ZOOT-SUITER HORDES INVADE LOS ANGELES. US NAVY AND MARINES ARE CALLED IN."[3] From behind the oversized front page, El Pachuco emerges from the gash. Dressed in a complete zoot suit and with the torn newspaper in the background, he struts downstage—*más chucote que la chingada* (more pachuco-ish/ bad-ass than anyone else)—and begins his monologue.

The second epigraph comes via Delia "Dee" Chávez, a retired parole officer, avid golfer, wife, mother, and former *zooterina*. Dee was born in 1923 in El Paso to Mexican immigrant parents, the fifth of nine children, and raised in East Los Angeles. As a teenager, she, like many other young women and men of her generation, enjoyed listening and dancing to jazz. On weekends, she put on her gabardine zoot suit, which consisted of a long, "finger-tip" coat and full skirt that stopped at the knees, and used "rats" to pile her dark hair into a high bouffant. Then she and her friends headed to the Paramount Ballroom on Brooklyn Avenue, where, she told me, they danced the night away.

These epigraphs provide us with glimpses of the Mexican American zoot subculture, from the early 1940s to the Chicano movement. While Dee associated the zoot suit with jazz, dancing, and youthful exuberance and insouciance (as indicated, perhaps, by her use of the word "little"), for Valdez and many other writers, artists, and activists of the Chicano generation the zoot suit carried much deeper meaning: it signified a rich, oppositional, and distinctly Chicano identity.

Despite their differences, both epigraphs represent discursive interventions. From the start, Valdez's play foregrounds the pachuco's voice as it challenges "dominant regimes of representation," as depicted, for example, by William Randolph Hearst's *Herald-Express*.[4] By ripping apart the newspaper's front page, El Pachuco dismisses an official account of the Zoot Suit Riots, insisting that the pachuco's "will to be . . . elud[ed] all documentation."[5] In this act of refusal, *Zoot Suit* wrests the tale of the Zoot Suit Riots, the Sleepy Lagoon incident and trial, and wartime Mexican American zoot subculture from the mainstream Angeleno press, law enforcement, and academia—institutions that colluded in pathologizing second-generation Mexican American youth beginning in the early 1940s—and retells it from the point of view of a homeboy, a young Chicano from L.A.'s 38th Street neighborhood.

Zoot Suit's fabulous opening serves as an apt symbol for Chicano cultural production in general. As a minority discourse, Chicano cultural production has often interrupted and, in many instances, refuted master narratives that exclude or disparage people of Mexican descent in the United States. Chicana and Chicano cultural workers have challenged and reshaped what the political theorist Wendy Brown describes as "the constant implication of power among us—its generation, distribution, circulation, and effects"—in other words, politics—by constructing and contesting "a world of meanings, practices, and institutions" via visual art, literature, drama, music, dance, and scholarship (to list just a few cultural forms).[6] For example, Américo Paredes's "*With His Pistol in His Hand*" (1958), regarded by some as a foundational text of Chicano literature and literary studies, takes to task Walter Prescott Webb's unabashedly tendentious history *The Texas Rangers* (1935).[7] Similarly, Alurista's poem "Pachuco Paz" (1972) responds to Octavio Paz's essay "The Pachuco and Other Extremes" (1961), which belittles the pachuco as a lost, confused, and self-contemptuous *pocho* (Americanized Mexican) who "does not want to become a Mexican again" but "does not want to blend into the life of North America" either.[8] In contrast, "Pachuco Paz" opens with the affirmation that "we can all reach the point / of knowing ourselves / to be Mexicans in the north."[9] Playing on the word *paz,* its title simultaneously confronts and calls a truce with the esteemed Mexican writer and statesman.

Like Valdez and Alurista, numerous Chicano and Chicana cultural workers have actively rejected dominant discourse on the Mexican American zooter. Although I acknowledge the value and significance of many of their works, one of my objectives in this book is to point out that some have relied heavily upon and reproduced gender and sexual norms as they have redefined *el pachuco.* In short, *el pachuco*'s makeover from a helpless victim, ridiculous fool, clueless *pocho,* or diabolical menace to an icon of machismo, style, resistance, and cultural authority has not taken place in a cultural or social vacuum. Rather, it has occurred within a system of unequal power relations: a heteropatriarchy that privileges men and masculinity, circumscribes girls' and women's roles, demands heterosexuality, and punishes homosexuality.

In addition to recognizing what is gained by *el pachuco*'s transformation into an icon and hero, this study seeks that which is lost. All too often, valorizations of *el pachuco* have taken place at the expense of those who are not male or appropriately masculine, such as pachucas. Within the bulk of movement-era Chicano cultural production, pachucas have received far less attention than their male counterparts, in great part because of the threat they pose to normative gender and sexuality. More recently, however, some scholars have begun to include women, including pachucas, in their discussions of the zoot subculture, the Zoot Suit Riots, the Sleepy Lagoon incident and trial, and the World War II period, a moment that is generally regarded as a watershed for Mexican Americans. A handful have even placed them at the center of their analyses and, in doing so, they have offered discursive interventions of their own.[10]

This book seeks to add to this exciting body of scholarship, not only by foregrounding the roles Mexican American girls and women played in these important wartime events but also by examining the meanings these girls and women have ascribed to them, as well as to the zoot subculture and the figures of the pachuco and pachuca. Using archival sources and oral history, this chapter "domesticates" pachucas. That is, it reinserts them into narratives of Mexican American cultural identity, community, and history. To do so, it retells the tales of the Sleepy Lagoon incident and the Zoot Suit Riots, but this time with a focus on Mexican American women. It uncovers the ways in which these events prompted Mexican American women to redefine terms like "American," "Mexican American woman," and "pachuca," paying close attention to the ways they engaged the Angeleno press to do so. For evidence of their discursive interventions, I turn first to contemporary newspapers, then I draw upon interviews I conducted with eleven Mexican American women who were born between 1918 and 1937.[11] These women, among them Dee Chávez, came of age in East Los Angeles during the 1930s, 1940s, and 1950s, at the height of the zoot fad among Mexican American youths. Their observations represent a valuable contribution to discourse on the zoot subculture, for they reveal that not only *batos* (dudes) fantasized about or reveled in wearing zoot suits. *Las rucas de la Chicanada* (Chicana chicks) took pleasure and found meaning in doing so as well.

In this chapter, I focus on interviews with two women in particular, Dee Chávez and Mary López, because they underscore the gendered dimensions of citizenship—with "citizenship" referring not only to "one's legal relationship to a specific state" but, more broadly, "to an individual's membership in a collectivity."[12] I treat Dee and Mary, both of whom wore the zoot look as young women in the early 1940s, as citizens of individual families, "*la Chicanada*" (Chicana/o community), and the United States of America. In other words, they are sisters, daughters, wives, mothers, Chicanas, and Americans. As my interviews with them show, these women were also consumers, workers, patriots, and critics of the nation-state and the institutions that produce and bolster it, such as the dominant press. By highlighting their myriad and contradictory positions, I hope to complicate *la pachuca* and to expose the breadth of pachuca identities.

A Return to Sleepy Lagoon

Within Chicano studies, World War II is generally regarded as a turning point for Mexican Americans. Two events that greatly define this moment are the Sleepy Lagoon incident of 1942 and Zoot Suit Riots of 1943. The former has been described in masculinist terms as "a boyish fight over a pretty girl" and a brawl involving "homeboys."[13] Yet as a handful of scholars have recently shown, both young men and young women took part in what would turn out to be a very significant event in Mexican American history.

On the evening of August 1, 1942, a group of male and female youths, some of whom lived in the vicinity of nearby 38th Street, were attacked by another group of youths, identified in court records as "the Downey Boys," at Sleepy Lagoon, a reservoir near the intersection of Atlantic and Slauson Boulevards in southeastern Los Angeles.[14] Smarting from the beating, the young men and women returned to the 38th Street neighborhood and, after calling upon more friends—male and female alike—some returned to Sleepy Lagoon, presumably seeking revenge.[15] By then, the Downey Boys had departed. The youths noticed that there was a party at nearby Williams Ranch and headed there. A fight broke out immediately following their arrival. One participant recalled that "he heard women screaming and yelling . . . he could see girls pulling hair."[16] Another claimed that one of the uninvited guests attacked her sister: "he knocked her out and she fainted, and then after that there was just—everybody started fighting."[17] Indeed, both middle-aged men and teenage girls took part in what court records describe as a "general 'free for all' " at the home of the Delgadillo family at Williams Ranch in the early hours of August 2, 1942.[18] In the chaos, sixteen-year-old Betty Nuñez Zeiss and eighteen-year-old Dora Barrios came upon a wounded man lying in the dirt outside the Delgadillos' house.[19] Twenty-two-year-old José Díaz had suffered a massive head injury and was taken to a nearby hospital, where he died without regaining consciousness.[20]

Descriptions of the Sleepy Lagoon incident as a homosocial affair involving "homeboys" exclusively are inaccurate and eclipse the participation of girls and women. Court records show that they participated in the brawls at Sleepy Lagoon and Williams Ranch. Two teenage girls had the misfortune of discovering José Díaz's battered body. Three, Dora Barrios, Lorena Encinas, and Frances Silva, were held as suspects in what was dubbed "the Sleepy Lagoon murder case."[21] And numerous girls were picked up in the dragnet raids that took place in and around East Los Angeles on August 10 and 11, 1942.[22] Ultimately, ten ranging in age from thirteen to twenty-one years were held as witnesses in the case. Several were forced to testify in court against their neighbors, friends, and boyfriends who found themselves defendants in *People v. Zammora*, and at least five were then sentenced to the Ventura School for Girls, a California Youth Authority

10. Mexican American girls and young women associated with the Sleepy Lagoon incident (clockwise from top left: Frances Silva, Josefina "Josephine" Gonzáles, Juanita "Jenny" Gonzáles, Dora Barrios, and Lorena Encinas). *LOS ANGELES DAILY NEWS* NEGATIVES, COLLECTION 1387, DEPARTMENT OF SPECIAL COLLECTIONS, CHARLES E. YOUNG RESEARCH LIBRARY, UNIVERSITY OF CALIFORNIA, LOS ANGELES.

11. Police lineup of young women suspected of involvement in the Sleepy Lagoon incident, August 1942. *HERALD EXAMINER* COLLECTION, LOS ANGELES PUBLIC LIBRARY.

correctional facility "infamous at the time for its draconian disciplinary measures."[23] According to Alice Greenfield McGrath, executive secretary of the Sleepy Lagoon Defense Committee (SLDC), the girls and young women were never tried or convicted but were "sent up to the Ventura School for Girls, just on the grounds of having consorted with bad company."[24] Some remained wards of the state even after their male companions won their appeal and were released from prison in October 1944. For example, fifteen-year-old Juanita Gonzales entered the Ventura School in 1942 and was released and paroled the following year but remained a ward of the state until her twenty-first birthday in 1948—four years after the young men who stood trial in *People v. Zammora* were released from prison.[25]

While the Sleepy Lagoon case catapulted a handful of Mexican American girls and women into the public eye as juvenile delinquents, it also mobilized many others as activists. Josefina Fierro de Bright was already a seasoned organizer when she helped to form the SLDC with LaRue McCormick of the International Labor Defense.[26] In 1938, at the age of eighteen, she, along with Luisa Moreno, a labor leader, played a key role in establishing El Congreso del Pueblo de Habla Española, one of the first civil rights organizations for Latinas and Latinos in the United States. With Fierro de Bright presiding as executive secretary, El Congreso addressed a host of issues important to Mexican immigrants and Mexican Americans, including police brutality and juvenile delinquency. The pressures of war forced it to fold by mid-1942, but according to Mario T. García, the SLDC grew out of "the remnants of El Congreso" and Fierro de Bright bridged the two organizations.[27] Many of the parents of the defendants in *People v. Zammora* turned to her for aid in all likelihood because of the prominent role she had played in El Congreso. In addition to visiting the defendants in jail and attending their entire trial, she tapped her connections in the entertainment industry as she fundraised on behalf of the SLDC. (Her husband, John Bright, was a screenwriter and cofounder of the Screen Writers Guild of America.) With roots in what was then known as Los Angeles' "Mexican colony" and ties to Hollywood's Popular Front, Fierro de Bright served as an important link between the defendants' families and their supporters beyond the 38th Street neighborhood.

Lupe Leyvas played a similar role. After her older brother Henry was convicted for murder in *People v. Zammora,* she became a spokesperson for the SLDC. With Fierro de Bright's encouragement and guidance, the

12. Lupe Leyvas (with J. Edward Bromberg and Dooley Wilson) at a fundraiser for the Sleepy Lagoon Defense Committee at the Mocambo nightclub in Hollywood, December 1943. *LOS ANGELES DAILY NEWS* NEGATIVES, COLLECTION 1387, DEPARTMENT OF SPECIAL COLLECTIONS, CHARLES E. YOUNG RESEARCH LIBRARY, UNIVERSITY OF CALIFORNIA, LOS ANGELES.

13. Lupe Leyvas (second on left in front row) with youths from the 38th Street neighborhood, early 1940s. *Lowrider* magazine, copyright 1978–79. REPRINTED BY PERMISSION OF MCMULLEN ARGUS PUBLISHING, INC., COPYRIGHT 1978, 1979, 2007.

fifteen-year-old girl from the 38th Street neighborhood went from being, in the words of one observer, "a reluctant speaker" to "a very effective" and "helpful" orator who "made a big impression" at fundraisers and public meetings.[28] Yet, even before her involvement in the SLDC, Lupe was familiar with acting as a spokesperson of sorts. Bilingual and bicultural, she often served as her immigrant parents' translator and proxy. "I didn't learn household chores," she informed me in an interview. Instead, she learned "where the light company was and the gas and how to write a check or how to do a money order."[29] She recalled that she never failed to accompany her mother and the other defendants' mothers to court, where she took notes and translated on their behalf.

At the courthouse, McCormick approached the teenage girl and requested that she call a meeting of the defendants' mothers. The guilty verdict had just been announced, Lupe recollected, and the mothers were distraught and at a loss as to what to do next. At the meeting, which was held at the home of Margaret Telles, whose own son Robert was one of the defendants, McCormick and Fierro de Bright informed them about the appeal process and also instructed them to organize fundraisers, such as dances, to help pay for legal fees. Lupe remembered that these dances were a multigenerational effort: the mothers prepared and sold food, young men volunteered as security guards, and everyone paid admission at the door. In short, "we all went to the dance."[30] Meanwhile, Telles sold copies of Guy Endore's 1944 pamphlet *The Sleepy Lagoon Mystery* to help raise money. Like Lupe, she was bilingual and served as a spokesperson for the SLDC.[31]

As the historian Frank Barajas astutely notes, Margaret Telles and Lupe Leyvas "effectively breached the gendered cultural restrictions that confined women to the domestic sphere. Perhaps the transgression of such limiting roles, particularly for women of Mexican origin, was mitigated by the fact that they worked tirelessly and openly on behalf of male family members during a wartime period that required women in general to participate in the public sphere more than before."[32] While promoting awareness and raising money for the appeal, Lupe traveled well beyond her home and the 38th Street neighborhood. Her mother entrusted Fierro de Bright to "keep an eye on her" as she accompanied her to her speaking engagements in far-flung places like Hollywood, Santa Monica, and Beverly Hills.[33] With more than a hint of pleasure, Lupe recalled visiting the home of Rita Hayworth, a supporter of the SLDC. There, the actress gave her one of her own formal gowns and a pair of sandals. Lupe, whom Alice McGrath has described as "a beauty," wore the green and yellow ensemble to a fundraiser at the Beverly Hills Hotel.[34] Lupe also recounted attending a meeting at an especially luxurious home in Santa Monica, where she and several companions from the 38th Street neighborhood were taken aback by not only the host's swimming pool but an invitation to swim in it. All too familiar with being barred from public pools and having to swim in Sleepy Lagoon—described by one contemporary observer as a mere "gravel pit"—the youths were incredulous.[35] "We couldn't believe it," Lupe marveled. "There was no sign that said . . . 'No Mexicans Allowed.' Oh, we had the time of our lives!"[36] In addition to exposing Lupe to a world beyond the barrio, Fierro de Bright coached her in public speaking. "I was told I had to speak," Lupe noted, for Fierro de Bright maintained that it was important for supporters to "see someone from the . . . neighborhood."[37] The teenage girl stood before crowds of strangers and celebrities, including Anthony Quinn, Orson Welles, and Joseph Cotton, and implored them to make a financial contribution to the SLDC. Lupe proudly recalled, "We raised a lot of money."[38]

Although Josefina Fierro de Bright and Lupe Leyvas may have been the most visible Mexican American women involved on a regular basis in the SLDC, others worked doggedly behind the scenes on behalf of the organization and the young men who stood trial. For example, María Lerma served as the SLDC's first bilingual secretary.[39] Meanwhile, members of Madres del Soldado Hispano-Americano and the United Cannery, Agricultural, Packing, and Allied Workers of America (UCAPAWA), a labor union in which Latinas played a uniquely salient role, solicited signatures and donations from across Southern California on behalf of the organization.[40] Back in the 38th Street neighborhood, sixteen-year-old Dora Baca acted as vice chair of the Youth Committee for the Defense of Mexican American Youth, an organization that simultaneously raised money for the young men and supported the war effort by collecting scrap iron. Its address was the home of Margaret Telles, site of the initial meeting of the SLDC's representatives and defendants' mothers.[41] All the while, the mothers rallied on behalf of their sons. As one of the incarcerated youths noted in a letter written on April 11, 1943, to SLDC executive secretary Alice Greenfield, "I know that all the mothers are doing what they can for us."[42]

Finally, on October 4, 1944, the hopes, prayers, and efforts of the young men and their supporters were realized when the District Court of Appeal overturned the convictions and dismissed *People v. Zammora* for lack of evidence. Amid "hysterical screams and shrieks, laughter and cries of jubilation," the youths convicted and imprisoned for the death of José Díaz were freed and reunited with their families and friends at the Hall of Justice in downtown Los Angeles on October 23.[43] Because of the successful appeal, *People v. Zammora* has been described as "a vindication of the civil rights of our minority peoples," "a landmark of progress," and a "victory for Mexicans."[44] The case has been the subject of films, scholarly treatises, at least one academic conference, and a Broadway musical. However, it represented a partial victory. While "the boys," as the defendants/appellants were fondly known to the SLDC, were released from prison, several of the girls and young women who accompanied them to Williams Ranch on August 2, 1942, were denied due process, incarcerated, and monitored by the state for years to come. Although she contacted the California Youth Authority about them and visited them at the Ventura School for Girls, McGrath has described these girls and young women as "a missing group."[45] In a cruel twist of irony, they received much unwanted attention from the police, press, and district attorney in the days and weeks following Díaz's untimely death but appeared to have been all but forgotten by the time their male companions were released from prison two years later.

Indeed, these girls and young women literally never had their day in the court. On the one hand, the state deemed them menacing enough to put them behind bars. (In an interview in 1987, McGrath remarked that she was "appalled" by conditions at the Ventura School for Girls. "They were a hundred years behind the times, even in terms of ordinary penal practice in the forties," she recalled.)[46] Yet, on the other hand, the state did not treat the girls and young women as full citizens, as individuals deserving of punishment as well as protection—in the form of due process, a fair trial, a legitimate conviction, and an appeal. McGrath bemoaned the fact that the SLDC could do little for them and noted that they were excluded from the appeal because they had never been tried or convicted in the first place. "It was terrible, what was being done to the girls was criminal," she lamented, "but beyond our capability to act at that time." She explained that the SLDC was powerless in great part because the girls' parents had permitted the state to incarcerate them at the Ventura School: "Once the consent is given—and it isn't informed consent, it's a really contrived, manipulated event. But once the parent has given consent, it is very hard to do anything about it."[47] As a consequence, she recalled, "there was a lot of bitterness among the girls because they felt that they had been ill-treated and no consideration given them."[48]

Sex and the City

Like the girls and young women involved in the Sleepy Lagoon incident and case, Mexican American women have received little consideration in many discussions of the Zoot Suit Riots, one of several civil disturbances to occur in the United States during the summer of 1943.[49] The Zoot Suit Riots took place primarily in downtown, the southwestern edge of current-day Chinatown, Chavez Ravine (a barrio north of downtown, located where Dodger Stadium now stands), East Los Angeles, and Watts from roughly June 3 to June 13, 1943. They were marked by clashes between white servicemen and men of color, especially pachucos. Rampaging servicemen, at times accompanied by civilians, actively hunted zooters. When they apprehended them, they beat and "unpantsed" (disrobed) them and destroyed their zoot suits. Some also cut their victims' hair. Mauricio Mazón's perceptive assertion that the servicemen symbolically castrated zooters underscores the salience of gender—namely, masculinity—during the Zoot Suit Riots.[50] However, this event was by no means about men and masculinity exclusively.

If mentioned in discussions of the Zoot Suit Riots, women, white and Mexican American alike, are often described as sexual pawns in a conflict between white servicemen and Mexican American men.[51] In the weeks and months prior to the riots, servicemen complained to their superiors that pachucos had harassed their girlfriends and female family members.[52] Then, on June 2, 1943, one day before the riots broke, Los Angeles newspapers reported that a gang of pachucos abducted two young married women in downtown and raped them in a "zoot suit orgy" in nearby Elysian Park.[53] This story was followed by reports that zoot-clad Mexican American men had "insulted," "molested," "attacked," or "raped" white women—in particular, sailors' wives and girlfriends—and thereby instigated the riots.[54] In the midst of the civil disturbance, the Los Angeles Examiner quoted one angry sailor who declared, "We're going to do what the police haven't been able to. . . . We're going to make the streets of Los Angeles safe for sailors, for sailors' girls, and for the general public"; while the *Herald-Express* published a letter to the editor from "Mary G." of San Fernando, who complained, "We, the mothers, sisters, wives and sweethearts of the men in the armed forces, are not safe in our own country."[55] In contrast, Chester B. Himes refuted assertions that Mexican men had "accost[ed], insult[ed], or molest[ed] white women" in a July 1943 story he wrote for *The Crisis,* the newsletter of the National Association for the Advancement of Colored People. Likewise, Horace R. Cayton of the *Pittsburgh Courier* attributed the riots to white servicemen, who he claimed envied Mexican American male zooters and desired the "pretty brown creatures" with whom they consorted.[56]

In general, the dominant (that is, white and Anglophone) press attributed the Zoot Suit Riots to pachucos who preyed upon white women, while *The Crisis* and *Pittsburgh Courier,* both African American publications, blamed lecherous white servicemen who arrogantly believed it was their prerogative to "have an affair with any dark-skinned woman anywhere on earth."[57] At least one national magazine identified the "loose . . . girls of the Los Angeles Mexican quarter" as the culprits. According to this story, these opportunistic young women were quick to take advantage of the unsuspecting "sailor with a pocketful of money."[58] Combined, all of these accounts indicate that "sex was an important factor" in the Zoot Suit Riots, as one contemporary observer put it; at the very least it was perceived as such.[59]

In fact, since the nineteenth century, relations between Anglos and Mexicans have often been framed in terms of a sexual competition between men. For instance, the celebrated *Californio* bandits Tiburcio Vásquez and Joaquín Murrieta were allegedly driven to vigilantism in the 1840s and 1850s after white American settlers encroached upon their land and women.[60] Without a doubt, rape was and continues to be used as a means of terror and subjugation, especially in clashes between colonizer and colonized. And while I do not dismiss assertions that Mexican American women in Los Angeles were targets of sexual violence prior to and during the Zoot Suit Riots, I wish to point out that wartime accounts that reduce them to passive, interchangeable pawns in a conflict between discrete and warring groups of men fail to reveal the complex ways in which they were affected by this event, their responses to it, or the meanings they ascribed to it. Moreover, these androcentric narratives position Mexican American women as inherently disloyal—in other words, as heirs to what Rosa-Linda Fregoso has called "the legacy of La Malinche."[61]

The Violated Mother

Pachucas were clearly designated heirs to the legacy of La Malinche in an article published in the Mexican American newspaper *La Opinión* on August 26, 1942. In the days and weeks following the Sleepy Lagoon incident, Angeleno newspapers, including *La Opinión*, ran stories that purported to uncover the origins and secrets of pachuco and pachuca gangs. In this putative exposé, the Spanish-language daily, like its English-language counterparts, described in detail pachucos' and pachucas' strange attire and translated several seemingly unintelligible slang words, including "pachuco," into standard Spanish. But instead of referring to pachucos' female counterparts and companions as "pachucas," the story's author, Carlos Amezcua, called them *"malinches."* He claimed to be ignorant of the source of this moniker but proposed that it arose from the common folk as a disparaging nickname to denote the feminine element of a modern social plague ("un apodo despectivo del vulgo, para señalar el elemento femenino de esta moderna plaga social").[62]

In fact, words like "pachuco" and "zoot" were probably strange and new to numerous English- and Spanish-speakers in Los Angeles in August 1942, but to many Mexicans and Mexican Americans the term *malinche* was far from unfamiliar; nor was its origin a mystery. Since the sixteenth century, *malinche* has referred to the Christian Indian woman who, according to history and legend, aided the Spaniards in conquering the Aztecs. Throughout Mexico and much of Mexican America, La Malinche is regarded as a traitor and the violated mother of the modern Mexican people. She is known as *La Chingada* (the fucked one), where the conquistador Hernán Cortés is referred to as *El Chingón* (the big fucker).

By designating them *"malinches,"* La Opinión implied that pachucas were sexually available, as evidenced by their "degrading" (*"denigrantes"*) gang names, such as the "Cherry Gang" and "Bow-Legs."[63] And like their sixteenth-century namesake, pachucas were treacherous. By wearing relatively short skirts and excessive makeup and, in some instances, forming gangs, brandishing weapons, taking to the street, and accompanying pachucos on their raids, they appeared to betray middle-class definitions of feminine beauty and decorum. Worse still, they betrayed all Mexicans and Mexican Americans by defaming them in their adopted country. With indignation, regret, and shame, *La Opinión*'s exposé closed with the revelation that the gangs of pachucos and "*malinches*" consisted of youths of Mexican descent ("las pandillas de 'pachucos' y 'malinches' están formadas de jóvenes de ascendencia mexicana").[64]

In Mexican and Chicano Spanish, the feminine noun *malinche* (or *malinchista*) is synonymous with *vendida* (sell-out or traitor)—one who "has transgressed the boundaries of perceived group interests and values."[65] As both pawn and traitor, La Malinche is "literally the one sold" and "metaphorically the sell-out." The historian Rita Canó Alcalá notes that she has come to "epitomize . . . woman's inherent unreliability, through her religious conversion, cultural assimilation, political collaboration, and most important, her sexual liaison with the enemy."[66] This "inherent unreliability" or infidelity is predicated upon the perceived transferability—or, to use Norma Alarcón's word, "pawnability"—of women.[67] Building upon Claude Lévi-Strauss's argument that the exchange of women constitutes a fundamental principle of kinship and, thus, social organization, the anthropologist Gayle Rubin has emphasized that women "are transacted as slaves, serfs, and prostitutes, but also simply as women." Indeed, we are to be passed from fathers to husbands to sons and are to serve as "conduit[s] of . . . relationship[s]" forming the basis of patriarchal social order, "rather than . . . partner[s] to them."[68] *La Opinión* pointed to the trafficking of "*las malinches*" by describing pachucos as "explotadores de mujeres."[69] If the men with whom they associated were pimps, then pachucas were prostitutes: women who were bought and sold—in other words, *vendidas*.

The trafficking of Mexican American women is also apparent in much post–World War II discourse on the Zoot Suit Riots, from scholarly works to the 1992 film *American Me,* which opens with a scene in which a pachuca is raped by a gang of white servicemen while her male partner, a pachuco, is rendered impotent as he is beaten and stripped.[70] Most historians have presented the riots as a racist event and have ignored the fact that they were also sexist. Few have pointed out that, in addition to being "slandered and harassed by servicemen," Mexican American women in Los Angeles in the early 1940s faced sexism from Mexican American men who "did not want to share [them] with the 'gringo.'"[71] Accounts that locate Mexican American women as the rope in a tug-of-war between white and Mexican American men reveal a concern with woman's alleged inherent unreliability and transferability. What is more, they stress the ways in which the riots (and the events leading up to them) threatened to dissolve the boundary between public and private and the social (namely, race, class, and gender) hierarchies it purported to maintain.

A Tale of Two *Sitios*

On the home front, World War II transformed many U.S. cities into contact zones, spaces "in which peoples geographically and historically separated come into contact with each other and establish ongoing relations, usually involving conditions of coercion, radical inequality, and intractable conflict."[72] Pagán points out that as thousands of servicemen passed through Los Angeles, many found themselves stationed in neighborhoods with high concentrations of Mexicans and Mexican Americans. He argues that pachucos, already marginalized in a segregated city, appeared to resent and challenge what they perceived as "the intrusion of white military men into their social spaces." At the same time, these youths "refus[ed] to accept the racialized norms of segregated America."[73] With their flashy ensembles, distinct slang, extra cash (generated by a booming war economy), and rebellious attitude, pachucos and pachucas participated in a spectacular subculture and threatened the social order by visibly occupying public spaces, including the street and sites of leisure, like movie houses, dance halls, and soda fountains. One contemporary observer asserted that white servicemen resented "Mexican lads in zoot suits" precisely because they watched them "walking up and down the streets" of Los Angeles with their girlfriends.[74] According to the angry sailor quoted in the *Los Angeles Examiner* during the Zoot Suit Riots, these streets needed to be reclaimed "for sailors, for sailors' girls, and for the general public." The violence inflicted upon Mexican Americans during the riots indicates that they were not considered part of "the general public" and thus were not welcome in the public sphere. Allegations that pachucos had raped white women—specifically, sailors' wives—reveal that they were also deemed a threat to the white American home and, by extension, the home front, as symbolized by the body of the white woman or sailor's wife.[75]

Likewise, the public sphere, symbolized in great part by the street, has been defined in terms of not only race but gender and sexuality as well. Historically, the street has been seen as the domain of men, in particular white men, who generally enjoy more freedom of mobility than men of color. As Chester Himes remarked, "Mexican and Negro boys . . . cannot go out in Hollywood and pick up white girls," but "adventuresome" white servicemen intruded upon the "Mexican districts" in an effort "to pick up [Mexican girls] or take them away from their boy friends. . . . We hate to think of what might have happened to a darker-skinned Mexican in a white bar in a white district trying to pick up, or having already picked up, a white girl."[76] His remarks point to the collapse of space, race, gender, and sexuality, in particular, men's access to women.

Just as white men policed "white districts" and the white women who occupied them, Mexican American men controlled—or were supposed to control—the barrio, the Mexican American home, and Mexican American girls and women, including pachucas. Yet according to Beatrice Griffith, a social worker who worked with Mexican American youths in Los Angeles County during the 1940s, pachucas possessed a "dark beauty" that was "attractive to all males, light or dark."[77] Himes conceded that pachucos "might have . . . set upon" servicemen who pursued "their" women, and that these women "might have flirted" with their white suitors.[78] By the same token, Horace Cayton noted that Mexican boys prevented "Mexican girls [from] running around with white fellows" by "ostraciz[ing]" or "slap[ping] them [the girls] around a bit."[79] He concluded with the observation that Mexicans had a "closed society" and that "there [were] enough social controls to make it difficult for the white boys to take out these pretty little Mexican girls."[80]

These contemporary comments point not only to Mexican Americans' incursions into the public sphere during World War II but to the intrusion of white servicemen into the barrio and Mexican American household. As they entered neighborhoods like Chavez Ravine and Boyle Heights, these servicemen threatened Mexican American patriarchal "social controls," specifically, the home, family, and female body, all of which are frequently associated with the private sphere. One former pachuco stressed "the outright disrespect the sailors showed our families when they would try to crash our parties." He recalled, "One time three sailors just walked into our backyard while we were celebrating a [baptism], and one of the sailors put his hand under my mother's skirt trying to feel her up."[81] In fact, during the riots, the press reported that servicemen invaded Mexican American homes in search of prey.[82] In Beatrice Griffith's short story "In the Flow of Time" (1947), which draws from newspaper articles about the riots, a mob of sailors beats an elderly Mexican man on his front porch "'cause they said maybe he was the father of a zootsuiter."[83] Next, they burst into a house, where they are confronted by an outraged Mexican American mother who chastises them from her kitchen. While she and her children run for cover, they ransack her house.

By invading the Mexican American home, white servicemen threatened more than a mere lodging. Like the legions of social workers and missionaries who entered Mexican American homes during the early decades of the twentieth century in an effort to transform Mexican immigrants and their children into docile, English-speaking, Protestant Americans, they attacked a symbol, bastion, and reproducer of Mexican culture in the United States: the house and home.[84] The Mexican or Mexican American mother in particular embodied this putatively discrete culture. In contemporary newspaper accounts, this violated mother functioned as a gauge for the level of civic and social chaos generated by the Zoot Suit Riots: the East Los Angeles–based *Eastside Journal* reported that a police officer struck a woman who was holding an infant in her arms after she tried to stop him from arresting and carting away her zoot-clad, teenage son; *La Opinión* warned that rampaging servicemen attacked not only young Mexican American men but Mexican American women and children as well; and the city's dominant English-language newspapers announced that "a young mother with a baby in her arms was arrested" as they splashed photographs of twenty-two-year-old Amelia Venegas, a so-called lady zoot suiter and pachuco woman, across their front pages.[85]

All of these accounts point to the racialization, gendering, and heterosexualization of public and private, to the permeability of the boundary separating these ostensibly separate spheres, and to the chaos that ensues when that boundary disappears—when Mexican Americans enter oncesegregated spaces, when Anglos and Mexicans interact with one another (in particular, when they have bodily contact with each other), when white servicemen intrude upon the barrio and backyard gathering, and when Mexican American mothers and their children take to the street during a moment of civil unrest. These narratives demonstrate a concern with not only Mexican American men's—namely, pachucos'—newfound mobility and visibility in the wartime urban landscape but Mexican American women's as well. Moreover, these accounts point to Mexican American men's deteriorating "social controls" (that is, their eroding ability to control "their" women) and to shifting gender relations both outside and within the World War II–era Mexican American home in Los Angeles.

"Our Side of the Story"

Even though they provide us with a glimpse of what may have been the immediate reactions of some Mexican American women to the Zoot Suit Riots, none of the texts I discuss above emphasizes the complex and nuanced ways these women interpreted the events that unfolded around them in Los Angeles in June of 1943. For this, I first turn to statements by (or at the very least attributed to) Mexican American women published in the wake of the Zoot Suit Riots. Like *Zoot Suit*, which draws from newspaper stories and *People v. Zammora* (the Sleepy Lagoon trial transcript), these utterances, while brief and far from unmediated, represent a discursive intervention. They reveal how some Mexican American women inserted themselves into the public sphere (as represented by the press) and attempted to construct and contest a world of meanings and practices by interrupting and relativizing dominant discourse on the riots.

Several cultural workers, including Carey McWilliams and Luis Valdez, have offered persuasive arguments that the Los Angeles English-language newspapers were biased in their reporting of the Zoot Suit Riots. Indeed, when Josefina Fierro de Bright, representing what remained of El Congreso, met with Vice President Henry Wallace in June 1943 to appeal to the Roosevelt administration to end the riots, she presented him with letters of protest and "copies of Los Angeles newspapers as proof of the hysteria created by the press."[86] Still, there were moments when some newspapers were not as sensationalist or explicitly anti-Mexican as (and perhaps a bit more repentant than) others.

For example, as the *Examiner* and *Times* published photographs of an "irate mother" tearing apart her son's zoot suit, the *Daily News* featured on its front page a letter to the editor from another frustrated and concerned Mexican American mother.[87] However, where the *Examiner* and the *Times*'s mother blamed pachucos for leading her teenage son astray, the *Daily News*'s anonymous letter writer condemned American schools for fomenting "hatred," "racial discrimination," and consequently low self-esteem among Mexican American youth. She even suggested that schools were responsible for rendering "so-called 'pachucos' . . . Hitler's agents." Invoking and rejecting the Nazis' concern with blood—as well as the infamous

1942 Ayres report, which argued that by virtue of their "Aztec blood," Mexican Americans were intrinsically more violent than and, therefore, biologically inferior to white Americans—she charged, "In schools there are all nationalities, but only Mexicans are called by their ancestors' blood. There are Irish, Jews, English, French, Swedes, etc., but as long as they are born in this country they are Americans. Why not those of Mexican descent?" Additionally, the author of the letter claimed the United States as her home and full citizenship for herself and her four children. "My children and I are of Mexican descent, born and raised in this country. We are 100 percent Americans," she declared, adding that two of her sons served in the U.S. military. She closed her letter by assuming a representative role: "If you care to publish this you are welcome to do so. Many Mexican mothers feel just like I do but are afraid to express their opinions. Thank you."[88]

A statement by a group of Mexican American women published in the *Eastside Journal* echoed the letter in the *Daily News*. Like the letter writer, the group took on a metonymic function: according to the East Los Angeles newspaper, it represented "thousands of girls . . . in Los Angeles County whose characters ha[d] been defamed by the inferences in the daily newspapers." Beneath the headline "Mexican American Girls Meet in Protest" and a photograph of the group, the *Eastside Journal* reported that the young women had banded together to "protest . . . articles printed in Los Angeles daily newspapers"—in particular, those that "inferred that the girls' moral characters were questionable."[89] According to the SLDC chairman Carey McWilliams, the young women wished to respond to an especially libelous story that had portrayed so-called *cholitas* and *pachucas* as "cheap prostitutes, infected with venereal disease and addicted to the use of marihuana," but "the metropolitan press refused to publish" their letter.[90] As the group's spokeswoman declared, "We have not been able to have our side of the story told." According to the caption beneath their photograph, Al Waxman, publisher of the *Eastside Journal*, "promised the girls that his newspaper would serve as a vehicle for their message." "We are happy to present them to the public," he announced. To refute their defamation, the newspaper noted that none "of the girls . . . ha[d] ever been in trouble with the law and not one of them ha[d] a record with authorities," while their spokeswoman stressed that they were former honor students, defense workers, and "girls who have brothers, cousins, relatives and sweethearts in all branches of the American armed forces." Like the

Mexican-American Girls Meet In Protest

Meetings were held last week by a number of American girls of Mexican extraction in protest to the articles printed in Los Angeles daily newspapers. The girls asked Al Waxman, publisher of the Eastside Journal, to lodge a protest in their behalf with the city officials and newspaper publishers.

Articles in the larger Los Angeles papers inferred that the girls' moral characters were questionable. "It is true that they did not say that of every girl of Mexican extraction," said a spokesman for the group. "But the general public was led to believe that such was the fact. The girls in this meeting room consist of young ladies who graduated from high school as honor students, of girls who are now working in defense plants because we want to help win the war, and of girls who have brothers, cousins, relatives and sweethearts in all branches of the American armed forces. We have not been able to have our side of the story told."

Waxman, publisher of the Eastside Journal, promised the girls that his newspaper would serve as a vehicle for their message.

Not one of the girls in the above photograph has ever been in trouble with the law and not one of them has a record with the authorities. There are thousands of girls similar to these in Los Angeles County whose characters have been defamed by the inferences in the daily newspapers.

"It is a shame," said Waxman, "that these girls have been treated in this manner by the daily newspapers of this city. They deserve a better break and we are happy to present them to the public."

14. IMAGE COURTESY OF WAVE PUBLICATIONS GROUP.

Daily News's "100 percent American" letter writer, the "American girls of Mexican extraction" used the exigencies of war (for example, defense work or a relative or boyfriend in the military) to claim for themselves an American identity. Furthermore, they called themselves and were presented as "young ladies" (a term I examine more fully in the following chapter), the antithesis of sick, dope-smoking whores.[91]

The *Daily News*'s letter to the editor and the statement by the group of youths in the *Eastside Journal* offer glimpses of the ways Mexican American women responded to the Zoot Suit Riots and engaged and challenged some of the most powerful producers of meaning at the time: their city's most widely read newspapers. They show that while the press was instrumental in generating anti-Mexican sentiment in Los Angeles, it also provided Mexican American women with a forum for countering this hysteria. Furthermore, these utterances in the *Daily News* and *Eastside Journal* demonstrate that the violence of the riots afflicted not only the young men on the streets who were subjected to physical beatings but Mexican American women as well, many of whom did not consider themselves to be and clearly distanced themselves from pachucas. Indeed, this violence was both material and epistemic; it occurred in the street and on a newspaper page and was evident on individual bodies and in the words that purported to equate those bodies with filth, disease, and sexual promiscuity.

Moreover, the violence of the riots occurred in the silencing of countless other Mexican Americans whose utterances were never published. Like the eighteen youths whose statement and photograph appeared in the *Eastside Journal,* another group of young Mexican American women wrote and sent a letter to Los Angeles newspapers to dispute a "slanderous story." Yet where Al Waxman referred to the women whose photo and statement he published as "young ladies," Carey McWilliams described these other women as "real pachucas."[92] To prove their patriotism, they offered to donate blood to the American Red Cross, but the organization rejected it on the grounds that they were Mexican.[93] In addition, they claimed that they were virgins and even "insisted that they . . . be examined, as a group, by an officially appointed board of physicians."[94] However, unlike the *Daily News*'s "Mexican mother" and the *Eastside Journal*'s "Mexican American girls," the "real pachucas'" side of the story was never presented to the public by a Los Angeles newspaper.

Familiarizing *la Pachuca*

Via their published statements, Mexican American women in Los Angeles claimed full citizenship for Mexican Americans and feminine respectability for Mexican American women in the wake of the Zoot Suit Riots. In doing so, they attempted to redefine a number of signifiers, namely, "Mexican American," "American," and "lady." The group of pachucas McWilliams recalled also attempted to give new meaning to "pachuca."

Nonetheless, the photograph of the eighteen "Mexican American girls" and the caption beneath it in the *Eastside Journal* represent a repudiation of the figure of the pachuca. In this photograph, none of the young women wears the zoot look. With the exception of one woman sporting a pair of pants, all wear conservative, feminine attire, complete with high heels and bows. Still, the figure of the pachuca looms large here and represents an absent presence and constitutive other. By stressing that the "young ladies" were high school graduates and former honor students, that none had "ever been in trouble with the law" or "ha[d] a record with the authorities," and that all were patriotic Americans, the *Eastside Journal* in effect invoked the disreputable, delinquent, and disloyal pachuca only to reject her.

Interviews that I conducted with Mexican American women who were living in Los Angeles during the 1930s and 1940s reveal that many of my interviewees had a complicated relationship to the figure of the pachuca, not unlike several of the participants in Sherna Berger Gluck's landmark oral history collection *Rosie the Riveter Revisited*.[95] Like some of my interviewees, a handful of Gluck's expressed unease regarding the pachucas and pachucos they encountered in Los Angeles during the war years. In some of Gluck's interviews, which were conducted in the early 1980s, pachucas are described as "grotesque" and "lower class" "bad girls," while their male counterparts are called "pathetic," "dumb," and "ugly." One interviewee concluded that they were "just losers" who "brought a bad name to a lot of people who really didn't deserve it."[96]

Roughly twenty years later, some of the Mexican American women I interviewed expressed similar frustration, contempt, and even shame. For instance, María Elena "Helen" Gamboa, a retired office worker, mother, and grandmother who was born in 1919, described the pachucas and pachucos with whom she grew up in East Los Angeles as "a ridiculous mess." "I used to hate them," she remarked.[97] And while Enedina "Annie" Rodríguez did not criticize the pachucos who loitered outside the store near her family's home on Harvard Street in East Los Angeles, she admitted, "I was afraid of them myself." To many Mexican Americans, pachucos and pachucas represented danger and vice. More than one interviewee described pachucas as "bad girls" and claimed that they tucked knives into their "rats." Because they "could hide stuff"—namely, "cigarettes [and] knives"—in their hair, Annie recalled that "rats," along with short skirts and pulled-up socks (all hallmarks of the pachuca look), were banned at Stevenson Middle School in East Los Angeles in the early 1940s.[98]

At the same time, many of my interviewees empathized with pachucas and pachucos. They recognized the racial discrimination they faced, especially from teachers, law enforcement, and the mainstream press, and many were convinced that racist white servicemen, not Mexican Americans, were to blame for the Zoot Suit Riots. For example, Dee Chávez remembered, "I, we had the impression that [sailors] were out looking for trouble." The self-described "avid newspaper reader" found the press's coverage of the riots "rather biased": "It [the riot] was always blamed on the Mexicans, you know, looking for trouble."[99]

Some women even expressed admiration for pachucas and pachucos, especially for their sartorial style. Consuelo "Connie" Loza, a homemaker, mother, and grandmother born in 1923, thought the pachucas she saw at dance halls in downtown Los Angeles during World World II looked "real cool" in their contraband black stockings.[100] Despite fearing them, Annie Rodríguez found pachucos "nice looking" in their "draped pants."[101] And Mary López described pachucas and pachucos as "sharp" and "cool." With excitement, the great-grandmother and former factory worker at Diamond Walnut recalled how she "used to admire the boys" who hung out at the soda fountain at the corner of Seventh and Mateo Streets near downtown Los Angeles during the late 1930s and early 1940s. "Oh, their pants were gorgeous! They had a crease . . . and they came real small down here [the ankle] . . . I used to love those . . . long chains . . . and then some of them had a hat."[102]

Some of my interviewees waxed nostalgic about wearing their own zoot suits and sweeping their hair up with "rats." Dee Chávez, for example, happily reminisced about wearing her zoot suit to the Paramount Ballroom in East Los Angeles and Nu-Pike amusement park in Long Beach as a student at Garfield High School in East Los Angeles in the early 1940s. She cherished her "very good-looking" gabardine ensemble, in great part because she "paid a lot of money for [it]" and never owned more than one.[103] Similarly, Mary López proudly recalled wearing short skirts that showcased her "very pretty legs" and explained how she and her friends "put 'rats' . . . spongy things . . . in [our hair] . . . to hold our hair up" before heading to the soda fountain on Mateo Street or a *tardeada* (afternoon dance) at the Zenda Ballroom in downtown Los Angeles, where they danced to the music of Glenn Miller and Frank Sinatra.[104] Unlike most of my other interviewees, both women readily admitted to wearing pachuca styles. "That was the mode of dress at that time," Dee observed.[105]

According to Griffith, "the majority . . . of girls who dressed in the Pachuco style (when it was 'hep' to do so)" were not gang members but merely "wanted to be considered . . . up to date and not old-fashioned."[106] For Mary, pachucas and pachucos were not necessarily gang members. "It [being a pachuca or pachuco] was a look, period," she stressed.[107] She and Dee adopted this look simply because they found it "very stylish" and neither belonged to a gang, although each knew members of the notorious Mateo Street and Clanton gangs respectively.[108] When I asked Dee, a retired parole officer for the California Department of Corrections, what made her group of friends different from a gang, she emphasized that gang members were "normal human beings," but that they "stuck together" more so than other youths.[109] Similarly, Mary recalled that pachucas "weren't bad people."[110] Nonetheless, she distinguished herself and her group of friends from them. When I asked her how pachucas were different, she, like Dee, described them as more tight-knit.

As a young single mother and relative newcomer to the Mateo Street neighborhood, Mary López never quite felt a part of the pachucas' circle. She was born in 1918 in the small mining town of Jerome, Arizona, and after dropping out of high school and leaving her first husband, she moved to Los Angeles with her mother, brother, and infant daughter in the late 1930s in search of employment and a better life. The family landed at the corner of Seventh and Mateo because relatives already lived there. In addition to working on an assembly line at Diamond Walnut, Mary recalled that she earned seventeen dollars a week working as a restaurant cashier from six o'clock in the morning until two in the afternoon, plus five dollars a week caring for another child. Responsibilities within and beyond the home kept her busy and prevented her from socializing with many other young men and women. Still, her mother allowed her to rendezvous with her cousins and friends at the nearby soda fountain and to attend afternoon dances, which was Mary's favorite pastime, by caring for her baby in her absence. And even though "there was no money at that time," Mary remembered that she always managed to wear lipstick and to "dress . . . very well." She credited her mother, a factory seamstress, for providing her with the latest fashions, clothes that "never looked like they were from home."[111]

As for style, Mary described pachucas as "more extreme. Their hair was more extreme and their clothes were more extreme." The self-professed fashion maven claimed that she could tell whether or not one was a pachuca based on the height of her hair alone: "When they had it real high, they were pachucas." Then, she added that "your mother also told you" if someone was a pachuca. Parodying her mother, she exclaimed, "¡Oh no, no, no, mi'jita! ¡Pareces pachuca!" (Oh no, my dear daughter! You look like a pachuca!)[112] In other words, her mother's disapproval signaled to her that someone was a pachuca and therefore to be avoided.

Dee was also keenly aware as a young woman that "people didn't like [zoot suits]." She and her friends "saw nothing negative about [them], but apparently everybody else did." Recalling the attention they received as they rode the Red Car to Long Beach, she remarked, "They would look at us like we were going to make trouble. They claimed we had knives in our hair, which was stupid. I . . . never knew anyone that had a knife in their hair. It was so dumb, you know. . . . You might cut yourself." When I asked Dee to whom "they" referred, she responded, "The Anglos mostly, I suppose."[113] Yet pachucas and pachucos troubled not only whites but Mexican Americans as well, especially the parents of what has come to be known as the Mexican American Generation, Mexican Americans who came of age during the Great Depression and World War II.

For many of these parents, pachucas embodied not only a dissident femininity but a threatening, distinctly American identity as well, one characterized by the increased physical and social mobility of young women and by cultural hybridity, as evidenced by increased interracial/ethnic relations, bilingualism, and pachuco slang, which I discuss at length in chapter 3.[114] Most of my interviewees' parents were from Mexico, nearly all from rural towns and villages. In contrast, East Los Angeles was a densely populated, polyglot, and racially and ethnically diverse community from the 1920s through World War II. Many of my interviewees described their parents as loving but also as "strict," "conservative," and "traditional." As they adjusted to life in a new city and new country as waitresses, machinists, bakers, cooks, factory workers, nannies, seamstresses, homemakers, and laundresses (to list just a handful of their occupations), many of these parents struggled to keep their American-born daughters from becoming pachucas or associating with pachucos, whom Annie Rodríguez described as "the boys that were always in trouble." She speculated that her father, a shoemaker who arrived in the United States from Guanajuato around 1917, had had a run-in with some pachucos. Hence, "he didn't like them. He didn't like the way they spoke, how they dressed." The Mexican immigrant forbade his four American-born daughters from dating pachucos or adopting pachuca styles, such as wearing dark lipstick.[115] "Dark lipstick," Annie recalled, "for the longest time, you couldn't wear [it]. My father didn't like us to have any lipstick until . . . we got to high school . . . but . . . my [older] sisters . . . after my dad would say . . . a few times, 'No, no, don't do it' . . . my sisters would still go ahead and do it. You know, they would kind of sneak."[116]

While Annie Rodríguez recounted the restrictions her father imposed on her and her sisters, Dee Chávez and Mary López recalled that their mothers permitted them to dress in the latest fashions. (Indeed, in Mary's case, her mother, a professional seamstress, provided her with the latest fashions.) Interestingly, both Dee and Mary were raised in great part in households headed by women, and for this simple reason I draw more from their interviews than from others in this chapter. Dee's and Mary's experiences and recollections locate the pachuca and pachuca styles squarely in the home and thus redefine urban Mexican American womanhood and the Angeleno Mexican American family during the Second World War. They do so by situating the pachuca in a homosocial network of mothers, daughters, and sisters, one that reappears in movement-era Chicana feminist cultural production (the subject of chapter 4).

Despite pachucas' reputation for being disobedient and delinquent, neither Dee nor Mary considered herself rebellious as a teenager and, rather than claiming to have clashed with their mothers, both expressed great admiration for and tenderness toward them. Dee noted that her mother, a widow and immigrant from Chihuahua, "never looked at our [zoot] suits as anything detrimental." According to Dee, she "wasn't strict"; she had no need to be, for her nine children "were very respectful." In turn, their mother trusted that "we would not do anything bad."[117] Meanwhile, Mary praised her mother, a divorcée who hailed originally from New Mexico, as "a very fair, open-minded woman" who was "way ahead of her time." In Jerome, which Mary described as a small, "very narrow-minded town," her mother allowed her daughter to continue to associate with a young woman who became pregnant out of wedlock (when most other parents did not permit their daughters "to talk to girls when they got in trouble"). To support herself and her four children while they were living in Jerome, her mother ran a boardinghouse, where she manufactured contraband liquor on the side. Mary shuddered as she recalled the night the police raided the house, destroyed the distillery, and carried her mother off to jail. Although she described this experience as "terrible," she also noted that it allowed her to see how "very strong" her mother was.[118]

Even as young adults, both Mary and Dee continued to live in households headed by women. Mary left her first husband in Jerome around 1938. Until she remarried in the early 1940s, she lived with her mother, younger brother, and daughter in Los Angeles. Dee, meanwhile, was virtually a single mother. In 1942, at the age of nineteen, she and her sister, both of whom were pregnant and married to servicemen who were stationed overseas, moved in to what she called their "mother's home" at the corner of Blanchard and Fisher Streets in East Los Angeles. Dee described the early war years as "a hard period of life for me." She and her sister did not know if they would ever see their husbands again or if their children would know their fathers. All of her brothers were serving in the military. "My mother had five stars on her window," she recalled with pride. "All three of my brothers were gone and my husband and my brother-in-law." She and her sister, to whom she "was very close," turned to their mother "because we needed each other."[119]

Dee's and Mary's life histories show that pachucas were in fact a part of some Mexican American families and homes in wartime Los Angeles, at least in two in which there was a relative absence of patriarchal authority and an emphasis on relations between women. Because, as Fregoso has argued, "the pachuca is . . . the place that marks the limits of *la familia* and . . . introduces disorder into its essentially patriarchal project," she has been excluded from the (heteropatriarchal) family.[120] Annie's memory of her father's restrictions reveals the ways in which he attempted to control his family by barring pachucas (and pachucos) from his home. In contrast, Mary's and Dee's recollections of the support their mothers provided them and the freedom they granted them—including the freedom to go dancing and to wear "rats," lipstick, or a zoot suit—familiarize *la pachuca*; they insert her into the Mexican American home and family and, in doing so, they render her ordinary and mundane rather than unusual and exotic. Dee's description of her zoot suit as "little" in the epigraph with which I began this chapter further domesticates pachucas. It "tames" them by removing them from what Marie "Keta" Miranda has described as "the dangerous streets of the inner city," a setting in which the police, press, and academia have long located Mexican American youth.[121] Moreover, it disassociates the zoot suit from adolescent (male) rebellion and fantasy that movement-era works like *Zoot Suit* celebrated.

Conclusion: The Myth of *la Pachuca*

Although they wore pachuca styles, neither Dee Chávez nor Mary López considered herself a pachuca per se, in great part because neither belonged to what she deemed a formal gang. Nonetheless, their recollections of leisure, fashion, and family life complicate common perceptions and definitions of pachucas. They reveal that, while the zoot suit may have functioned as a symbol of racial, ethnic, class, and generational difference, some zoot-clad Mexican American girls, especially those with husbands and brothers in the military during World War II, were patriotic; that *zooterinas* actively took part in a consumer-wage economy; and that "rats," short skirts, and jitterbugging were not necessarily antithetical to being a loving and devoted daughter.

My interviewees' reluctance to self-identity with *la pachuca* affirms Escobedo's assertion that this figure represented "a controversial public persona [that] triggered decidedly mixed emotions and responses" among Mexican Americans during World War II.[122] On the one hand, pachucas were deemed violent, unpatriotic, and sexually promiscuous and were blamed for defaming Mexican Americans, especially young Mexican American women. On the other hand, they signified style, defiance, independence, generational difference, and youthful enthusiasm. Annie Rodríguez recalled somewhat wistfully that the pachucas in her neighborhood knew how to have a good time: "They used to party a lot . . . They used to have music . . . the music of the forties . . . and . . . [they] danced . . . every weekend."[123] According to Griffith, "hundreds of girls" adopted the pachuca look "in a spirit of adventure."[124] Yet there was a price to pay for adventure. As Vicki L. Ruiz notes in her oral history of young Mexican American women in the years between the two world wars,

> Many women wanted their parents to consider them dutiful daughters, but they also wanted degrees of freedom. While ethnographies provide scintillating tales of teenage rebellion, the voices of the interviewees do not. Their stories reflect the experiences of those adolescents who struggled with boundaries. How could one retain one's good name while experiencing the joys of youth? How could one be both a good daughter and an independent woman?[125]

I have found Escobedo's and Ruiz's insightful questions and observations helpful in better understanding my own interviews with Mexican American women. In these interviews, I detected the mixed emotions and responses that *la pachuca* stirred: many of the women with whom I spoke regarded her with a combination of fear, shame, condemnation, admiration, and respect. I believe some actively distanced themselves from *la pachuca* not only because she symbolized violence, disloyalty, and sexual promiscuity but because she also represented a threat to the heteropatriarchal family and thus was a social outcast. However, two of my interviewees readily admitted to and appeared to enjoy reminiscing about wearing "rats," short skirts, and finger-tip coats; one even did so using pachuco slang. Interestingly, when our conversations turned to *Zoot Suit*, which most of my interviewees had seen, nearly all lauded pachucas for what they saw as their fearlessness in the face of race, class, and gender discrimination.[126] One noted that pachucas were the only girls in her school who were brave enough to talk back to teachers, whom she described as openly hostile toward Mexican students.[127] Moreover, in discussions of *Zoot Suit*, even those who had been extremely critical of pachucas and pachucos expressed sympathy for and solidarity with them. For example, at the beginning of her interview, Helen Gamboa informed me that she was "disgusted" with pachucos and pachucas because "as far as I was concerned, they were giving all the Mexican people a bad name." She made an effort to distance herself from pachucas by claiming that she did not know that they even existed (then contradicting this statement by describing their hair and attire in minute detail). However, in her recollection of *Zoot Suit*, Helen referred to both herself and pachucas using the collective "we." She lauded both the play and film as "very well done" and illuminating because, as she put it, "I think it opened . . . people's eyes to how we Mexicans were treated."[128]

In addition to showing the power of a cultural artifact, *Zoot Suit*, to shape historical perspective and to expose the strengths and limitations of oral history, my interviews illustrate the value of retelling stories. My renarrativizations of the Sleepy Lagoon incident and trial and Zoot Suit Riots, along with my interviewees' recollections, reinsert what McGrath termed the "missing group" into Mexican American history. They show that Mexican American girls and women were more than just pawns in conflicts between men, that they have ascribed meanings to the world around them and thus have endeavored to reshape this world.

Finally, I hope that my interviews underscore the conflicting values assigned to the figures of the pachuca and pachuco between and within generations of Mexican Americans and Chicanas. For a later generation of Chicanas, pachucas, not unlike pachucos, were "mythic figures, outspoken and confrontational, fighting and smoking cigarettes on street corners and outside tienditas (barrio grocery stores) and thus carving their presence in the public sphere."[129] As both a myth and memory, *la pachuca*'s significance is shifting, often contradictory, and sometimes elusive.

Chapter 2

BLACK SKIRTS, DARK SLACKS, AND BROWN KNEES

Pachuca Style and Spectacle during World War II

"A Zoot Suit (for My Sunday Gal)" is about looking good. In this duet, the male vocalist announces that he wants "to look sharp enough to see my Sunday gal," while the female vocalist stresses that she wants to "look keen so my dream will say / 'Ain't I the lucky fellah' / So keen that he'll scream, 'Baby's in Technicolor!'" This 1942 swing hit, which was popularized by a number of singers and musicians including the Andrews Sisters, Dorothy Dandrige, and Benny Goodman, is not only about looking good; it is also simply about seeing and being seen. The female vocalist tells her "walkin' rainbow" that he wants a "reef sleeve with a right stripe / And a rare square, so the gals will stare / When they see you struttin' with your Sunday pal." Likewise, she aspires to be the object of attention and envy: she desires "a scat hat and a zag bag / And a slick kiss, so the other chicks / Will be jealous when I'm with my Sunday man."[1]

"A Zoot Suit (for My Sunday Gal)" is an important cultural artifact because it shows women participating alongside men in the wartime zoot subculture. Moreover, it paints a vivid picture of the zooter girl in her "brown gown with a zop top."[2] Other contemporary accounts provide equally detailed albeit more comprehensible descriptions of the female zooter (to most twenty-first-century readers at least). For example, in his essay "Gangs of Mexican American Youth" (1943), Emory Bogardus, a sociologist at the University of Southern California, observed that pachucas wore "a modified 'zoot suit,' with black skirts and hose, including the broad-shouldered and longer coat of the boy's costume."[3] And according to the social worker Beatrice Griffith, "The girls wore their own style of dress, consisting of a long finger-tip coat or letterman's sweater, draped slacks or a short, full skirt above or just to their brown knees, high bobby socks, and huaraches or 'Zombie' slippers. They usually made up heavily with mascara and lipstick, and the favorite hairstyle was a high pompadour with flowers and earrings."[4] At the time, a skirt that exposed the knees was considered short, if not indecent, and American women generally did not wear pants, especially outside the workplace.[5] These and other factors determined the meanings of the zoot look in wartime Los Angeles for the young Mexican American women who sported it and for those who observed them doing so.

In this chapter, I scrutinize the zoot suit as spectacle, with a focus on wartime pachuca style politics. By "style," I refer to a signifying practice, in this case, the display of the zoot subculture's codes via clothing, hair, and cosmetics. And by "style politics," I refer to an expression of difference via style. The British cultural theorist Angela McRobbie has lambasted early cultural studies scholars for defining style "as a male [and] never unambiguously masculine prerogative" and for equating " 'youth culture' " with "male youth cultural forms."[6] Within Chicano studies, few scholars have examined, much less acknowledged, pachuca style or the participation of Mexican American women in the zoot subculture. In contrast, el tacuche (the masculine zoot suit) and its wearer have received considerable attention. As Vicki L. Ruiz observes, "Among Chicano historians and writers, there appears a fascination with the sons of immigrants, especially as pachucos."[7] Yet, as the historian Dionne Espinoza warns, "Without an analysis of gender and women in youth culture, we miss seeing how cultural resistance is a gendered project in which women find spaces to embrace . . . democratizing possibilities."[8]

Like the previous chapter, this chapter offers an analysis of gender and women in youth culture. La pachuca is at its center. Yet, where chapter 1 explores the ways in which World War II–era Mexican American women attempted to appropriate privileged cultural categories from which they had been barred, such as "American," "lady," and "patriot," this chapter offers a close examination of their exclusion from these categories as it brings into relief the nexus of nation, race, class, gender, and heteronormativity. I argue that the zoot suit was construed as a sign of an aberrant femininity, competing masculinity, or homosexuality during the early 1940s. As a nonwhite, working-class, and queer signifier, it was perceived as un-American.

To make this argument, I look at the clothes, hairstyles, and makeup worn by many working-class Mexican American youths in Los Angeles during World War II. In other words, I study style politics. Although I define "politics" broadly, like many other students of popular culture I maintain that "style may be subversive, but it can never become a substitute for direct political campaigning."[9] As the cultural critic Kobena Mercer has argued, for African American zooters in the 1940s, "style was not a substitute for politics. But, in the absence of an organized direction of black political discourse and in a situation where blacks were excluded from official channels of 'democratic' representation, the logic of style manifested across cultural surfaces in everyday life reinforced the terms of shared experience—blackness—and thus a sense of collectivity among a subaltern social bloc."[10] Similarly, Robin D. G. Kelley maintains that "while the zoot suit was not meant as a direct political statement, the social context in which it was worn rendered it so."[11]

Following Mercer and Kelley, I treat the zoot suit as a "cultural surface in everyday life" and "political statement." What did this cultural surface and political statement mean in World War II–era Los Angeles? What shared experiences did it reinforce? And how did it express a sense of collectivity among Mexican American youths? In the previous chapter, I analyze the complicated meanings of the zoot suit for Mexican American women who wore it or came of age in Los Angeles at the peak of its popularity. I also study the ways these women engaged wartime public discourse on *la pachuca* (the iconic pachuca). In this chapter, I focus on this discourse as I examine representations of *la pachuca* in "official channels": Angeleno newspapers, academic treatises, and photographs from the early 1940s. I use these texts to illuminate the social and political milieu in which Mexican American youths wore "rats" and draped pants, a context defined in great part by fears concerning the instability of class, race, and gender categories, nonnormative sexualities, juvenile delinquency, and sedition. By comparing the figure of the pachuca, in particular the figure of the cross-dressed pachuca, to three contemporary archetypes—the "feminine patriot," Rosie the Riveter (the female war worker), and *el pachuco* (the iconic pachuco)—I argue that it came to embody these multiple fears.

To highlight pachucas' transgressions, I juxtapose the figures of the pachuca and pachuco. Although my focus is *la pachuca*, I discuss her along with her male counterpart in order to emphasize that the wartime Mexican American zoot subculture was not only a raced but a gendered project, one that was neither "truly separatist" nor homosocial.[12] Together, pachucas and pachucos cultivated a style that articulated a distinct working-class,

Mexican American identity shaped by the experience of the Second World War. However, rather than rejecting conventional (white, middle-class, widely acceptable) styles outright, these youths drew upon them and used them "in ways that alter[ed] or subvert[ed] their intended use-values."[13] As a contemporary observer noted, "Looking at the zoot suit, one is impressed by its *exaggeration* and *distortion*."[14] The masculine zoot suit exaggerated the conventional business suit, while pachucas' up-dos, pencil-thin eyebrows, and dark lips distorted a look popularized by some of Hollywood's leading ladies of the time, such as Veronica Lake and Carol Lombard. Inspired in part by movie-star glamour and enabled by the thriving wartime economy, young, working-class Mexican American women of the early 1940s laid claim to an American identity, one defined in great part by leisure, consumption, and the conspicuous occupation of public space. By doing so, they undermined exclusionary definitions of ladyhood and U.S. citizenship and, at the same time, forged a noticeable and unsettling collective identity. Studying this collective process of identification, along with "official" responses to it, is crucial to understanding the multivalent readings of pachuca style by the Mexican American women who created and observed it, this style's erasure in cultural production of the Chicano movement, and its eventual recuperation by Chicana feminists.

Leisure and Conspicuous Consumption

"A Zoot Suit (for My Sunday Gal)" attests that the zoot suit was emblematic of leisure and conspicuous consumption during World War II.[15] In their "drape shapes" and "hip slips," zooters could be seen dancing on Friday and Saturday, then "struttin'" (parading) on Sunday.[16] As the historian Nan Enstad points out, "Consumer culture can seem inherently opposed to serious political subjectivity."[17] However, the consumption of time and things carried profound, even subversive political significance during the early war years, a moment when Americans were called upon to forgo luxury and to make sacrifices for the greater good.

As newspapers, magazines, and newsreels featured stories about heroic servicemen overseas and patriotic workers at home, zooters in Los Angeles enjoyed themselves at the Zenda and Paramount Ballrooms, Pike amusement park, or simply at a street corner. In short, they were seen participating in leisure activities, including *inactivity*. In *Theory of the Leisure Class*, Thorstein Veblen reminds us that in leisure, "time is consumed nonproductively (1) from a sense of the unworthiness of productive work, and (2) as an evidence of pecuniary ability to afford a life of idleness."[18] In addition to appearing as if they deemed "productive work" unworthy—in other words, appearing lazy—zooters demonstrated that they had the ability "to afford a life of idleness." Like the rich, they gave the impression that they could "keep economic necessity," such as work, "at arm's length."[19]

At the same time, the zoot suit was far from inexpensive and, as the anthropologist Laura Lee Cummings points out, it could have been read as "a symbol of the work ethic and pride."[20] In fact, many zooters toiled long hours and saved their money in order to purchase the latest styles and to enjoy a few hours of fun. As I note in the previous chapter, Dee Chávez recalled that she could afford only one zoot suit, while Mary López recounted juggling multiple jobs both inside and outside the home and relishing the hours she passed at a *tardeada*. And in his autobiography, Malcolm X remembers that he carefully saved his earnings in order to purchase his first zoot suit. His second one, a sharkskin gray ensemble, cost "seventy or eighty dollars"—a remarkable sum of money for a hat, shirt, coat, pair of trousers, and pair of shoes for a working-class youth during the early 1940s.[21] However, rather than saving and scrimping, he bought his second zoot suit on credit.

As Kelley has noted, the zoot suit was instrumental in young Malcolm Little's self-transformation from country bumpkin to big-city hustler.[22] Malcolm X recollects that he was "countrified" when he left his home in rural Michigan. Upon his arrival in Boston, he quickly acquired "fashionable ghetto adornments," such as his zoot suits.[23] Across the country, Griffith noted that pachucas embellished the zoot look with makeup, jewelry, and flowers in their hair. For many young women and men who came of age in the early 1940s, the zoot suit and its accessories were signs of affluence. The booming wartime economy allowed a generation that had been forced to wear "welfare clothes" during the Great Depression to take pleasure in appearance and to "put its opulence in evidence."[24] Yet rather than copy middle-class styles, these working-class youths amplified them with their "rats," heavy makeup, shoulder pads, long coats, and thick-soled shoes. In doing so, they created a distinct style in which spectacle trumped verisimilitude.[25]

Indeed, a young, well-coiffed, lavishly dressed *Mexican* American was an especially subversive sight to behold in wartime Los Angeles, a city

15. Frank H. Tellez in his zoot suit. REPRINTED BY PERMISSION OF AP/WIDE WORLD PHOTOS.

whose most impoverished barrios lacked modern amenities like plumbing and paved streets. In June of 1943, while reporting the Zoot Suit Riots, the *New York Times* featured a photograph of twenty-two-year-old Frank H. Tellez in his zoot suit. The caption beneath the photo noted that Tellez's coat was "part of a $75 suit" and that his "trousers . . . [were] part of a $45 suit."[26] Meanwhile, the *Saint Paul Pioneer Press* quoted a pachuca who defiantly declared, "I paid $75 for my outfit and nobody is going to take it off me, either."[27]

By flaunting their disposable incomes, pachucas and pachucos underscored the instability of class and race categories. Via their expensive clothing, they demonstrated that Mexican Americans could and would climb the socioeconomic ladder. In fact, the Second World War saw increasing urbanization and proletarianization in the United States, especially among African Americans and Mexican Americans. To some working-class youths, especially recent transplants from rural areas to urban centers such as Malcolm Little and Mary López (who proudly recalled to me that her homemade clothes looked store-bought), the zoot suit functioned as a status symbol, a "method of advertisement" in Veblen's words, because its wearers were from the city, rather than *del rancho* (from the ranch).[28] However, to "people of taste"—namely, the middle and upper classes—the zoot suit was excessive.[29] What the "loud" zoot suit announced was that Mexican Americans—especially second-generation Mexican American adolescents—would not stay in their place—whether that place was social (for example, lower class or subservient) or physical. By riding in street-cars and loitering on sidewalks, pachucas and pachucos made themselves visible in their *buenas garras* ("cool threads," "glad rags"). As Eduardo Obregón Pagán argues, they claimed public space for themselves. They also laid claim to commodities that were considered unessential and even wasteful, especially when consumed by those who were supposed to be poor, humble, and invisible. In both cases, they "refus[ed] to accept the racialized norms of [a] segregated" and class-stratified America.[30]

Profligacy and Perfidy

Even though consumer culture functioned as a site of Americanization for many young Mexican Americans during World War II, certain purchases, like the zoot suit, were seen as evidence of their buyers' and users' un-Americanism.[31] In March 1942, the War Production Board (WPB) mandated a reduction in the use of fabric in the manufacture of women's and men's clothing and all apparel containing wool. Order L-85 "attempted to control yardage" and "introduced what was called the 'silhouette,'" a uniform dress design to be worn by all American women, while Order L-224 put restrictions on men's clothing and effectively banned the zoot suit.[32] Nonetheless, in their contraband stockings, long coats, broad-brimmed hats, and ballooning trousers, pachucas and pachucos continued to sport a flamboyant look that flew in the face of the WPB's requirements and the exigencies of the workplace.

Pachucas were characterized by not only their costly attire but their brazen attitude as well. As Griffith observed, "As important as the costume itself was the manner in which it was worn. A bravado and swagger accentuated the dark beauty of these girls, an impudence that was attractive to all males, light or dark."[33] While attractive to some, pachucas' "impudence"

16. A World War II–era poster discouraging workers from wearing loose clothes, which were deemed both impractical and unpatriotic. COURTESY NATIONAL ARCHIVES, PHOTO NO. NWDNS 44-PA-441C.

worried many others, like parents, teachers, police officers, and juvenile authorities. Their audacity and insolence were especially troubling at a moment when duty, conventionality, and respect for authority were supposed to overcome individual desires and individualism itself.

As a sign of personal extravagance and assertive individualism during a period of collective austerity and conformity, the zoot suit was rendered a sign of un-Americanism. While city officials considered banning it outright during the Zoot Suit Riots, the *Los Angeles Daily News* quoted a WPB spokesperson who warned, "Every boy who buys such a garment and every person who sells it is really doing an unpatriotic deed."[34] Furthermore, *el pachuco* was effectively equated with the draft-dodger: the *New York Times* announced that Frank H. Tellez was not fighting for his country because he had managed to obtain "a medical discharge from the army," and the *Los Angeles Daily News* reported that "scores of husky 18, 19 and 20-year-old zooters" had escaped military service because army officials did not wish to accept them "for fear they will 'be too much trouble.'"[35]

Pachucas and pachucos were even conflated with the Axis enemy during World War II. For example, in testimony before the Los Angeles County grand jury immediately following the Sleepy Lagoon incident, Captain Edward Duran Ayres of the Foreign Relations Bureau of the Los Angeles County Sheriff's Department argued that Mexicans appeared to be more akin to "Orientals" and thus to the Japanese enemy, than to Americans of European descent.[36] Similarly, Angeleno newspapers juxtaposed stories about pachuca and pachuco gangs with accounts alleging disloyalty among Japanese Americans and disgruntled American workers (particularly the United Mine Workers, whose strike in 1943 disregarded unions' wartime no-strike pledge).[37] Throughout the Zoot Suit Riots, rumors circulated that Nazi agents had infiltrated the barrio and were attempting to impress young, alienated, second-generation Mexican Americans in an effort to foment social unrest on the home front and to strain the United States' relationship with its Latin American allies.[38]

The conflation of the Axis enemy and pachuco was cemented in a cartoon published in the *Los Angeles Times* on June 12, 1943, one day after Allied forces captured the Mediterranean island of Pantelleria and in the midst of the Zoot Suit Riots. The cartoon, titled "His Pant-elleria," depicts a defeated Mussolini slumped on the ground. Beat-up and wearing only his underwear, he bears a striking resemblance to the defrocked pachuco. Meanwhile, a large hand, presumably belonging to Uncle Sam, looms above the Italian dictator and dangles a pair of pants that taper at the ankle.[39]

Both the Ayres report and "His Pant-elleria" cast Mexican Americans—especially pachucas and pachucos—as the enemy on the home front. As such, Mexican Americans were deemed undeserving of the rights and privileges of full citizenship or membership in a democracy. As the *Los Angeles Daily News* put it, the young, second-generation Mexican American in particular was "not ready yet to accept the responsibilities of democracy."[40] And in the days following the Sleepy Lagoon incident, a juvenile court judge who described Mexican American delinquents as a "disgrace to America" warned, "He who shames America in wartime is a traitor to

His Pant-elleria!

17. An editorial cartoon published in the *Los Angeles Times* on June 12, 1943, after the Allied victory on the Mediterranean island of Pantelleria. Defeated and disheveled, Mussolini bears a striking resemblance to the Zoot Suit Riots' "de-pantsed" zooter. REPRINTED BY PERMISSION OF THE *LOS ANGELES TIMES*.

the democracy that shelters him."[41] These comments indicate that the Mexican American zooter was unwelcome in the United States during the Second World War. However, as I show below, there was in fact a place for *la pachuca* and *el pachuco*. As internal enemy, they came to represent the nation's constitutive other.

Dressed to Kill

During the Second World War, *la pachuca* represented a specific threat on and to the home front because of the ways she diverged from feminine ideals as represented by the "feminine patriot" and Rosie the Riveter, prominent archetypes created to galvanize allegiance to the nation and Allied cause.[42] The feminine patriot symbolized "innocence, gentleness, idealism, continuity and safety"—in short, the besieged nation—and was usually depicted in American propaganda campaigns as a white, middle-class

18. The besieged nation as white wife and mother. COURTESY NATIONAL ARCHIVES, PHOTO NO. NWDNS 44-PA-97.

housewife and mother.[43] Newspapers, magazines, and posters encouraged these wives and mothers to contribute to the war effort by continuing to take care of their homes, their families, and their own appearance: they could preserve fruit in their kitchens, grow "Victory gardens" in their yards, mend old clothes, or simply look pretty.

The feminine patriot clearly was a "lady," a privileged category historically reserved for middle-class and wealthy white women. Although she may have dirtied her hands while toiling in her kitchen or garden, she was not unclean or coarse. Rather, as Enstad observes in her study of working-class women in the late nineteenth and early twentieth centuries, the lady was sexually pure and "delicate."[44] This ideal seems to have endured well into the twentieth century, as indicated by the "beauty" section of the *Los Angeles Examiner* on August 6, 1942, which instructed women who aspired to be ladies how to cultivate "feminine charm" and "ultimate daintiness."[45]

19. A pretty, perfectly coiffed WAC at work repairing a radio in a World War II recruitment poster. COURTESY NATIONAL ARCHIVES, PHOTO NO. NWDNS 44-PA-260C.

Unlike the feminine patriot who remained at home, Rosie the Riveter was far from dainty. In its famous "We Can Do It!" poster, the War Production Coordinating Committee showed her clenching her fist and rolling up her sleeve to expose a bicep. And in his cover illustration for the May 29, 1943, issue of the *Saturday Evening Post,* Norman Rockwell portrayed the archetypal female defense industry worker as androgynous, if not downright masculine. Meanwhile, popular novels, films, and cartoons reflected or prompted growing concern with the "amazon image" of women war workers.[46] One contemporary observer grumbled that it was difficult to distinguish female welders from their male counterparts and announced that "a new type of tough girl" had emerged: the "New Amazon," who word had it, could "outdrink, outswear, [and] outswagger the men."[47]

While numerous women entered the labor force by working in munitions factories and shipyards, others did so by joining the military. Like

Rosie the Riveter, many of these women did work that was not considered feminine. Some were mechanics, truck drivers, tank operators, and pilots. And like Rosie the Riveter, servicewomen were disparaged as "Amazons," as well as "queer damozels of the isle of Lesbos."[48] In 1944, the infuriated mother of a Women's Army Corps (WAC) recruit complained that the basic training camp to which her daughter had been sent was "full of homosexuals and sex maniacs."[49] Historians maintain that in fact many lesbians and butch (masculine) women were drawn to military service during World War II. Away from their families and friends for the first time in their lives and in a homosocial environment, some women came out as lesbians.[50] Even though they were often targets of hostility, there is evidence that military officials sometimes tolerated them within the ranks during the Second World War.[51] At the same time, government propagandists actively portrayed servicewomen as unambiguously feminine and harmless. Their femininity is foregrounded in recruitment posters depicting servicewomen performing an array of untraditional jobs, such as operating or repairing machines. With her sharp uniform, which included a tie, and perfectly coiffed hair, the idealized WAC was more than attractive: she was glamorous.

Even though images of women wearing coveralls or military uniforms were to inspire patriotism, the working woman was still required to "remain pretty and feminine for the boys," whether she was a civilian or member of the armed services.[52] In other words, she was still supposed to be a lady. American women were called upon to contribute to the war effort by sacrificing their allegedly innate femininity as they entered the labor force. At the same time, they were expected to do their part for the war by being pretty and ladylike, for most not only remained at home but also embodied the home front. Thus, although American media urged acceptance of women in jobs historically held by men, including jobs in the military, they also highlighted female laborers' femininity. The defense industry also actively feminized workers, including some Mexican American ones, by featuring them as "literal poster girls" in factory newsletters.[53]

Furthermore, women workers were positioned as maternal figures. As the historian Leila J. Rupp has argued, "the appeal to patriotism . . . made use of a concept of extended motherhood" as it "took on a personalized cast, urging women to work for their men."[54] Women were to enter the labor force as self-sacrificing, self-effacing, soldier-oriented patriots, rather

20. The feminine patriot's sacrifice. COURTESY NATIONAL ARCHIVES, PHOTO NO. NWDNS 44-PA-1032.

than as self-interested, ambitious, independent, career-minded individuals. As poster girls and/or surrogate mothers, they were called upon to do what they had always been expected to do within the confines of the domestic sphere: to care for the boys (their sons, husbands, boyfriends, and brothers). The war merely demanded that they do so outside the home and, in some instances, while wearing pants.

In her short skirt and heavy makeup, *la pachuca* appeared to be the antithesis of the practical and self-sacrificing mother: the whore. Like the feminine patriot who remained at home and the idealized woman war worker who tucked her curly locks into a chignon in the factory or shipyard, many pachucas appeared feminine, albeit excessively and dangerously so. Their attire, hairstyles, and use of cosmetics were not read as proof of conformity. Instead, they were seen as a declaration of insubordination. By exaggerating the accoutrements of ladyhood, pachucas appropriated more than simple commodities; they also claimed and thereby threatened a powerful (however attenuated) cultural category from which they had been excluded. As Enstad notes, "When working-class women dressed in elaborate styles, they staged a carnivalesque class inversion that undermined middle-class efforts to control the definition of 'lady.'"[55]

La pachuca embodied wartime fears of not only unbridled female sexuality but juvenile delinquency as well. This figure emerged in the United States at a moment when juvenile authorities, academics, police officers, and civic leaders worried about juvenile delinquency in general and "sex delinquency" in particular.[56] To combat "sex delinquency" such as prostitution, the Office of Community War Services' Social Protection Division sought to identify and correct the behavior of women who were suspected of engaging in sex outside of marriage. Additionally, Congress attempted to curb the proliferation of sexually transmitted diseases (STDs) among servicemen by prohibiting houses of prostitution near military bases with the May Act of 1941. Meanwhile, the Army and Navy offered sex education classes and issued prophylactics to servicemen.

Despite such efforts, the number of STDs continued to rise in the United States during the early war years, especially in the armed forces, a matter of concern for military brass, public health officials, and scholars. The sociologist Ernest W. Burgess attributed the dramatic increase in "venereal infection" among servicemen to the "prevalence . . . of . . . trailer camps" outside military bases, whose denizens often included Victory Girls.[57] Also known as "v-girls," "free girls," and "khacky-wackies," Victory Girls were young women who allegedly pursued sexual relations with servicemen to do their part for the Allied war effort. At the very least, they have been perceived and portrayed as overzealous albeit misdirected patriots. One historian, for example, avers that v-girls "would not think of having sexual relations with a civilian" and "refused money for their services"; rather, they "felt they were 'doing something for their country' when they had sex with soldiers."[58] And another claims that even though the v-girl "was next door to being a prostitute, there was about her at least a certain refreshing lack of cold professionalism."[59] In contrast, a Colliers story in March 1943 revealed that some v-girls had "no objection to the money in it."[60] The magazine reported that one sixteen-year-old girl charged servicemen a dollar for sex. At the end of one busy night, she had amassed thirty dollars.

Unlike v-girls, pachucas were not generally regarded as patriotic. Both, however, were deemed pernicious to society. When Los Angeles newspapers introduced "girl hoodlums" and "girl 'gangsterettes'" to their readers after the death of José Díaz in August 1942, they reported that these formidable young women fought, drank whiskey, smoked marijuana, talked back, cursed, and formed gangs.[61] Front-page headlines blared "Black Widow Girls in Boy Gangs" and "Girls Join in Youthful Gang Forays Here."[62] One newspaper quipped, "Particularly disturbing in one of the new outbreaks was the participation of several girls. It was hoped that the prevalent delinquency might be confined to the boys who stand accused."[63] Meanwhile, another newspaper announced that "girl gangs also exist in certain districts of Los Angeles city and county," and the Spanish-language daily *La Opinión* warned that female gangs with sexually suggestive names, such as the Black Widows, the Cherry Gang, and the Bowlegs, terrorized the city and county.[64]

Pachucas' sexuality became an object of concern and fascination for many contemporary observers. For example, Griffith described them as "'little tornadoes of sexual stimuli, swishing and flouncing down the streets.'"[65] Similarly, in his article "A Psychiatrist Looks at the Zoot Suit" (1944), Ralph S. Banay claimed that zooter girls "exaggerate[d] their . . . sexuality" on the dance floor.[66] He compared the jitterbug to a strip tease because it allowed bystanders to glimpse young female dancers' "v-shaped underwear."[67] Further, the psychiatrist contended that zooter girls were just as wild and promiscuous as their male counterparts, for "both sexes [were] reported to take part in drunken mass sexual releases."[68] All the while, the Angeleno press enticed readers with stories about pachuca gangs' "strange rites."[69] According to one newspaper, pachucas engaged in "free relationships" with pachucos but were unencumbered by "the stain of prostitution for the gang girl gives herself freely if she likes the boy. If she doesn't she knifes him or has other girls in her gang attack him."[70]

For many contemporary observers, pachucas' appearance was the tip of the iceberg: it was evidence, if not proof, of their abnormal sexuality. For instance, Banay asserted that female zooters emphasized "their . . . sexual characteristics in . . . very tight sweaters and Basque shirts with broad vertical stripes of many colors."[71] Newspapers in Los Angeles also described pachucas' hair, makeup, and clothing in vivid detail. *La Opinión*, for example, reported that "*las malinches*" wore very short black skirts ("falda negra muy corta"), that they painted their faces—in particular, their lips and eyes—in a scandalous manner ("una manera escadalosa"), and that they punctuated their racy ensembles with a bushy head of matted hair soaked in grease ("un greñero empabilado de grasa").[72] Meanwhile, the beauty section of the *Los Angeles Examiner* stressed the importance of "good grooming" and "daintiness" and encouraged American women to "let victory go to [their] head[s]" by rolling their curls into the letter "V."[73]

With their "rats," tight sweaters, and short skirts—"sometimes twelve inches above the knee," according to one newspaper—pachucas were not seen as neat or dainty.[74] Instead, they represented filth and excess. In fashion, excess has long been linked to tackiness, immorality, and sexual availability (think Anna Nicole Smith or Pamela Anderson).[75] In contrast, simplicity (à la Grace Kelly or Audrey Hepburn, for example) is frequently conflated with elegance and moral and sexual purity. Adjectives such as "elegant" and "tacky" are far from neutral and carry strong class connotations: the sober and subdued are often linked to the middle class, where intemperance is repeatedly associated with the working class. And working-class women, as the anthropologist Sherry B. Ortner argues, historically have been "cast as the bearer[s] of an exaggerated sexuality, against which middle-class respectability" has been defined.[76] Ironically, even though their makeup, clothes, and elaborate hairstyles may have been signs of disposable income and evidence of class mobility, pachucas were regarded as déclassé women vis-à-vis middle-class ladies. Indeed, *because* they made a show of their makeup, clothes, and hair, pachucas were deemed tacky and cheap—in other words, morally suspect and sexually available; as Enstad observes, "to be tasteful one did not become an object of display."[77]

Pachucas' self-perceptions and intentions notwithstanding, contemporary descriptions illustrate that young, zoot-clad, Mexican American women were construed as the embodiment of a hyperbolic and therefore dangerous and seditious sexuality during World War II.[78] At a moment when the proliferation of STDs was a matter of national security and "feminine charm" and "daintiness" were linked to women's patriotism, portrayals of pachucas as wild, dirty, and unkempt in the Angeleno press were tantamount to accusations of treason.[79] Indeed, in the midst of the Zoot Suit Riots, one newspaper warned that even though "zoot girls" were "'sharp-looking,'" "cute," "charming," and "always very sexy looking," they were "not particularly clean."[80] Meanwhile, "rumors of all varieties circulated over every bar and soda fountain," including one about "nine *pachuca* girls with knives in their hair [who] had been arrested and had confessed to a pact to seduce and murder sailors."[81] This rumor revealed that wartime fears of youth crime, wanton female sexuality, and treachery intersected in the figure of the pachuca.

As descriptions of their "brown knees" and "dark beauty" make explicit, pachucas' sexuality was not only coded working class but was racialized as well. References to the Black Widows, an alleged pachuca gang, and descriptions of pachucas' black coats, black skirts, and black trousers abounded in Los Angeles newspapers shortly after the Sleepy Lagoon incident and throughout the Zoot Suit Riots.[82] For some, *la pachuca*'s dark hair, skin, makeup, and clothing underscored her moral and physical impurity. Her darkness also made tangible her putative foreignness and produced and accentuated racial difference. As the sociologist E. Franklin Frazier noted in 1942, Mexican Americans were racially unclear: they "straddle[d] our differentiation between white and colored minorities."[83] As such, they represented a threatening, alien ambiguity during a period of heightened xenophobia and paranoia.

Clothes Make the Man

Like their clothes, hair, and makeup, pachucas' actions were closely monitored by authorities, including Los Angeles' dominant newspapers. Yet whereas zooter girls' appearance was criticized as monstrously feminine, their behavior was condemned as masculine. According to the wartime Angeleno press, they were "an integral part of . . . gang activities and nearly as immoral and vicious as the boys."[84] When the Zoot Suit Riots broke, newspapers reported that young women in zoot suits jumped and slashed a lone woman; taunted innocent high school girls; attempted a carjacking; and beat and robbed a soldier in a cafe in downtown Los Angeles.[85] Indeed, pachucas appeared to be even bolder and more intractable than their male counterparts. During the riots, they were accused of continuing to instigate brawls after male zooters had been arrested or hospitalized. For example, the *Herald-Express* warned that, even as the violence began to subside, "girl 'auxiliaries' to masculine mobs might . . . prolong the 'Battle of Gangland.'"[86] "Just when the boy gangs were about to shed their zoot suits wholesale and lie low before the civilian and military forces massing against them," the newspaper reported, the "female mobsters" vowed, "We won't quit. . . . It's them or us."[87]

As various scholars have shown, sometimes pachucas' masculine behavior included wearing *el tacuche*.[88] Cross-dressed women did not go unnoticed by the Angeleno press during the Zoot Suit Riots. One newspaper reported that a pachuca donned "the long zoot coat over a black skirt tucked into dark slacks." Others noted that pachucas did away with skirts altogether and wore "black blouses and slacks," "the peg-topped slacks and the long coats of their masculine counterparts," or "custom made slack suits—the exact replica of the boys' suits."[89]

What did it mean for a Mexican American woman to wear the masculine zoot suit during World War II, a period in which gender and sexual norms were simultaneously challenged and policed? Before answering this question, I want to reexamine the masculine zoot suit as worn by Mexican American *men* and the gender and sexual transgressions it represented. Although some contemporary observers described pachucos as excessively masculine, many derided them as too feminine, as, in the words of one Angeleno newspaper, "gamin dandies."[90] According to a story in *La Opinión*, pachucos wore their hair so long that they resembled Indians on the reservation ("peinados como los indios de las 'reservaciones'").[91] And in "A Psychiatrist Looks at the Zoot Suit," Banay complained that they cared more about their clothes and hair than about sports or their studies. Indeed, pachucos were pathologized as effeminate precisely because they, like women, participated in consumer culture, which historically has been gendered feminine.[92] Like women, they paid attention to their looks. And like women, they were looked at, as the title of Banay's article makes clear.

A photograph of two "unpantsed" zooters taken on a Los Angeles street during the Zoot Suit Riots captures *el pachuco* as object of spectacle. Here, a young Mexican American man, his chest and legs bare, sits on the sidewalk outside a theater. Another lies beside him on his back. The second youth still wears a shirt, pants, and shoes, but his clothing is disheveled. A crowd of curious and concerned onlookers, most of whom appear Mexican, and two police officers loom above the two young men. Some of the bystanders look down at them and others stare directly at the camera. In contrast, the boys avert their gaze. As if ashamed, the seated one looks to the ground and his companion turns his face away from the camera and, by extension, from us viewers. If, as the film critic Laura Mulvey argues in her landmark essay "Visual Pleasure and Narrative Cinema" (1975), men are actors who look and women are objects who are looked at, then the humiliated and exposed zooters in this photograph are feminized as spectacle. Their passivity and objectification are further underscored by their lack of control in this scene. While they may have welcomed attention when they

21. Zoot Suit Riots, June 20, 1943. REPRINTED BY PERMISSION OF AP/WIDE WORLD PHOTOS.

set out in their zoot suits, in this instance, they do not appear to be willing accomplices in their exhibition.

Because of images like this, several scholars have argued that servicemen symbolically castrated pachucos when they beat them, cut their relatively long hair, and "unpantsed" them during the Zoot Suit Riots.[93] For example, according to Mauricio Mazón, the riots enabled servicemen to reenact their own experiences in basic training, "a symbolically castrating experience, a death initiation rite."[94] During basic training, he writes, recruits "were hauled into depersonalized lines[,] swiftly given a haircut, 'unpantsed,' and put into the drab nondescript garb of the recruit's uniform."[95] Mazón offers a persuasive argument, one I want to build upon. However, I maintain that, in addition to feminizing pachucos, the rampaging servicemen simultaneously and paradoxically Americanized *and masculinized* what many perceived as the unpatriotic and effete pachuco.

With their flashy zoot suits, pompadours, and ducktails, pachucos were perceived as both un-American and unmanly. Even though the masculine zoot suit accentuated the male physique with its broad shoulders and cinched waist, it was still denigrated as feminine.[96] For instance, one contemporary observer likened the male zooter's knee-length coat to "a girl's skirt," while another compared "draped" pants to "sister's pre-war girdle." Yet a third noted that the male zooter's ensemble emphasized a "girlish waist."[97] For Banay, the male zooter's "silhouette [was] as much feminine as it [was] masculine." He maintained that the zoot suit was "evidence of an adolescent neurosis" and a "chaotic" and "ill-defined" sexuality. In comparing the pachuco to the white sailor, he observed that the former concealed his masculinity with long, curly hair, a long coat, and a pair of baggy pants that "completely hid . . . the genital characteristics." The latter, on the other hand, "emphasized if not delineated his masculine development" with "his short blouse and tight-fitting trousers." "There should be little wonderment that in Los Angeles the two extremes led to violent clash," the psychiatrist concluded.[98] Long after the Zoot Suit Riots, *el pachuco* would continue to be described as feminine and would be pathologized as "sexual[ly] pervers[e]" and "queer."[99]

For many Americans during World War II, not just Banay, the clean-cut white serviceman and *el pachuco* represented polar opposites. The former symbolized more than a gender norm; he represented the apotheosis of American masculinity. The latter was his antithesis. Indeed, *el pachuco* was deemed unmanly precisely because he was deemed un-American. According to his critics, he was a lazy and vain coward who spent his time shopping, primping, hanging out, goofing off, and causing trouble, rather than buying war bonds, fighting the enemy, or doing honest work. By cutting pachucos' hair and tearing off their zoot suits, the rioting servicemen destroyed signs of a competing and nonnormative masculinity, of homosexuality, and, by extension, of un-Americanism. They highlighted the connection between cultural assimilation and heteronormativity as they expedited and intensified these violent social processes on the streets of Los Angeles.

When worn by a Mexican American *woman* during World War II, *el tacuche* became all the more transgressive. Three photographs present us with images of women in the masculine zoot suit. In the first, three young women, alleged members of a girl gang, are led by a police officer to a car. They are dressed remarkably alike: each wears a white shirt (one with the sleeves rolled up), dark trousers, and sandals. All have long hair; the third has teased hers into an especially high bouffant. As they file into the car, only one of the young women looks directly at the camera. She is not smiling. Instead, she almost appears to be scowling. In the background, curious onlookers, some of whom appear distraught, watch the girls from

22. Suspected members of the Black Widows, a pachuca gang, being taken into police custody. *Los Angeles Times*, August 9, 1942. PHOTO BY JACK A. HEROD. COPYRIGHT *LOS ANGELES TIMES*. REPRINTED BY PERMISSION. SPECIAL THANKS TO TRISHA VAN HORSEN AND CARY SCHNEIDER OF LOS ANGELES TIMES REPRINTS.

a distance. Others look to the photo's far-right edge, where a second police officer appears to stand. Half his body is cropped off, but the baton he brandishes is visible.

In the second photograph, a young woman identified as Ramona Fonseca wears a finger-tip coat, a shirt with a wide collar, loose trousers, and a pair of huaraches. Where the three young women in the first photo are on a city street, Fonseca stands before a curtain in what appears to be a studio and, leaning on her left leg and extending her right, she assumes a pose similar to that of the archetypal pachuco. If, as Pierre Bourdieu contends in *Photography: A Middle-Brow Art*, "striking a pose means respecting oneself and demanding respect," then this young woman holds herself in high esteem and expects others to see her accordingly.[100] With painted lips and her dark hair lifted high above her head, she does not shy away from the camera. Instead, she looks directly at it and offers a sly smile.

Last, in the third photograph, published in a 1978 issue of *Lowrider* magazine, a woman wearing the masculine zoot suit, complete with a

23. A young Mexican American woman posing in a zoot suit, 1944. SHADES OF L.A. COLLECTION, LOS ANGELES PUBLIC LIBRARY.

1947. La Dora El Paul, La Lupe y "La Chubby" Q-Vo Raza

24. A Mexican American woman in *el tacuche*. *Lowrider* magazine, copyright 1978–79. REPRINTED BY PERMISSION OF MCMULLEN ARGUS PUBLISHING, INC., COPYRIGHT 1978, 1979, 2007.

double-breasted coat, a pair of "Punjab" pants, what appears to be a tie, and huaraches, stands outside a building with a man and two other women. The caption beneath this photo reads: "1942: La Dora, El Paul, La Lupe y La Chubby. Q-vo raza."[101] La Dora, the cross-dressed woman, holds her head high—almost cocked at an upward angle—and looks away from the camera. Like Fonseca, she offers a slight grin, perhaps even a smirk.

Despite their attire, none of the women in these photographs appears entirely masculine, especially by early-twenty-first-century standards. All have long hair and some seem to be wearing earrings and lipstick. However, if we bear in mind *el tacuche*'s meanings during the early 1940s, a moment in which women challenged traditional gender roles and the threat of the masculine woman (the "Amazon") loomed large in public discourse, then these women are not entirely feminine. All wear pants, and the alleged gang members are on what appears to be a dark city street, the putative domain of men and masculinity. Although there is evidence that some young Mexican American women found pants "very fashionable and chic" (à la Greta Garbo or Katharine Hepburn) during World War II, many of the older, Mexican immigrant women who joined them in the workplace were reluctant to give up the dresses they had worn "all their lives." One former defense worker recalled that these older women "never really adjusted to wearing what they considered to be men's clothing." In fact, "many of them were clearly embarrassed" by the uniforms they were required to wear at work.[102]

Even during the Second World War—indeed, not until much later in the twentieth century—pants were not entirely acceptable for either *doñas* (respected older women) or "young ladies" (respectable young women).[103] This is apparent in the photograph of the group of Mexican American girls published shortly after the Zoot Suit Riots by the *Eastside Journal*.[104] As I note in the previous chapter, the self-described "young ladies" gathered for this photograph to stress that they were patriotic and decent. All but one display the trappings of feminine decency: pretty dresses, ribbons, and high heels.

In contrast, the three alleged gang members, Fonseca, and La Dora wear the masculine zoot suit, a sign of *working-class* masculinity, disloyalty to the nation during wartime, sexual transgression, and criminality. Although the three alleged girl gangsters do not wear the complete *tacuche*, their suspected criminality is accentuated by the fact that they are being led into what is probably a squad car by police officers. Moreover, women who cross-dressed in public or who failed to wear at least three articles of women's clothing could be arrested for "male impersonation" during the 1940s and 1950s.[105] In short, in the dominant Anglo-American and Mexican American cultures of the period, the zoot suit signified illicit activity and street-smarts, neither of which was (or is) connected to normative and middle-class femininity, and both of which would come to be associated with butchness.

Although they may not have identified as butch—that is, as women who are "more comfortable with masculine gender codes, styles, or identities than with feminine ones"—I want to read the three alleged gang members, Fonseca, and La Dora as such.[106] The term "butch" may not have been used among Mexican Americans during the early 1940s, but this should not rule out its retrospective and self-conscious use as an analytic category.[107] I compare these women to butches to show that *la pachuca*, like the butch Chicana and Latina, is, in the ethnographer Karla E. Rosales's words, an "outcast" who "breaks all the gender rules and roles assigned to her as a woman."[108] Moreover, I study *la pachuca* as butch in order to make sense of her later recuperation by Chicana feminist artists and writers, some of whom would cast her as ambiguously feminine or explicitly masculine.

Unlike the "young ladies" featured in the *Eastside Journal,* the three alleged gang members, Fonseca, and La Dora are masculine. They are also masculine when compared to La Lupe and La Chubby, the two women who appear in the photograph with La Dora. Where Fonseca's and La Dora's ensembles conceal their bodies, La Lupe's and La Chubby's accentuate a voluptuous silhouette. La Chubby wears a dress cinched at the waist with a belt and a pair of high, open-toe sandals, while La Lupe displays the feminine zoot look: dark lipstick, a form-fitting V-neck sweater, a short pleated skirt, and *tacones* (heels).

At the same time, a twenty-first-century viewer may argue that the three young women, Fonseca, and La Dora are *not* butch because they are easily identifiable as women with their long, perfectly coiffed hair, makeup, and earrings. On the other hand, this viewer may describe them as butch precisely *because* they are identifiable as women. Distinguishing butches from cross-dressed women who passed as men, the historians Elizabeth Lapovsky Kennedy and Madeline Davis note, "The masculine image that butches projected [in the 1940s] was of necessity ambiguous—otherwise they would have been passing women, not butches."[109] In other words, the effect of butchness, for Kennedy's and Davis's interviewees at least, was predicated upon ambiguity, upon the presence or appearance of an identifiable female body clothed in masculine garments.[110]

One may argue that the three alleged gang members, Fonseca, and La Dora are butch because their attire signified a working-class identity. In *Vested Interests: Cross-Dressing and Cultural Anxiety,* the literary critic Marjorie Garber argues that terms like "crude" and "rough" may connote "lower-class behavior."[111] Since World War II at least, the "crude" or "rough" woman—in other words, the butch, the bulldyke, the bull dagger—has been associated with the lower or working classes, who, as I argue above, historically have been deemed oversexed in relation to the middle and upper classes.[112] Thus, by donning identifiably working-class, masculine garb, the three young women, Fonseca, and La Dora *become* butch. By wearing an outfit that signaled gender and sexual transgression, they betrayed gender norms and, in doing so, they betrayed the nation.

To sum up, in wartime Los Angeles, pachucas and pachucos represented an unsettling gender paradox: the former were simultaneously regarded as excessively and inadequately feminine, while the latter were masculinized, emasculated, or homoeroticized by their critics, Anglo-American, Mexican, and Mexican American alike. Together, pachucas and pachucos queered not only dominant American culture but respectable (that is, middle-class and heteronormative) Mexican American culture as well. The outfit they shared—a coat and a pair of trousers—destabilized race, class, and gender categories. Zoot suits on Mexican bodies provoked myriad unsettling questions, such as Who is an American? Who is middle class? Who is a lady? What is femininity and what is masculinity? Where, when, and why does the feminine or female morph into the masculine, and where, when, and why does the masculine or male turn into the feminine? Ultimately, Chicano cultural nationalists would "unqueer" the Mexican American zoot subculture and regender *el pachuco* as masculine. He would be celebrated as an exemplar of normativity and heroism in much cultural production of the Chicano movement. *La pachuca,* in contrast, would remain inappropriately feminine and inappropriate by virtue of being masculine.

Conclusion: (Un)Intelligible Bodies and the Fragments of History

While the mainstream press rendered the bodies of the feminine patriot and woman war worker intelligible by linking them to patriotism and femininity, *la pachuca*'s body was nearly unintelligible to American nationalism during World War II. The feminist critic Susan R. Bordo defines the "intelligible body" as "our scientific, philosophical, and aesthetic representations of the body—our cultural conceptions of the body, norms of beauty, models of health, and so forth. But the same representations may also be seen as forming a set of practical rules and regulations through which the living body is 'trained, shaped, obeys, responds,' becoming, in short, a socially adaptable and 'useful body.'"[113] Whether her zoot suit consisted of a short skirt or a pair of dark pants, la pachuca defied the "set of practical rules and regulations through which the living body is trained [and] shaped." As a working-class consumer, she destabilized class and race categories. As a Mexican American, she embodied a discrepancy between the racialized subject and the ideal national subject. And as a monstrously feminine or masculine woman, she troubled gender and sexual categories. In short, la pachuca was of no use to the war effort or American jingoism, except as constitutive other. Unlike Rosie the Riveter and the servicewoman, housewife, and mother featured in wartime American propaganda, and unlike the figure of the pachuco in much movement-era cultural production, she was not absorbed by nationalisms as a citizen.

La pachuca betrayed gender norms and in so doing she betrayed the nation, first during World War II and then during the Chicano movement. Her exclusion from the privileged cultural categories of "citizen," "lady," and "patriot" during the Second World War foreshadowed what was to become of her during the Chicano movement, which, revolutionary politics notwithstanding, all too often maintained gender norms and heteronormativity. Her big hair and high skirt, exaggerations of the accoutrements of ladyhood, and her appropriation of el tacuche, a signifier of a vexed and then sacrosanct masculinity, did not make her a faithful copy of World War II's ideal feminine patriot or of the Chicano movement's lionized pachuco. Rather, they emphasized her infidelity.

The images that I study in this chapter provide us with only part of la pachuca's story. As the historian Melani McAlister warns, "There is . . . a danger in using photographs for the writing of history. Photographs invite us to see them as transparent representations, as a kind of historical record. Yet, photographs are inevitably fragments."[114] Undeniably, the images I discuss here are fragments; they are glimpses of wartime pachucas and pachuca style. Aspects of this style, such as the tall, sometimes bleached hair, fine, arched eyebrows, and dark lips, endured for decades to come as they were passed on to the cholas and cha-chas of the late twentieth century. In fact, in recent years, hallmarks of pachuca style have been appropriated by white celebrities like Gwen Stefani and Madonna and have thus found their way back to Hollywood.[115] Yet despite the spectacle she made during World War II, *la pachuca* has often been overlooked by many.

Chapter 3

SAYING "NOTHIN'"

Pachucas and the Languages of Resistance

On the evening of June 9, 1943, twenty-two-year-old Amelia Venegas left her East Los Angeles home with her baby to buy milk at a nearby store. Shortly thereafter, she was arrested for disturbing the peace. Angeleno newspapers reported that the "lady zoot suiter" had attempted to smuggle a pair of brass knuckles to "zoot suit hoodlums" to assist them in the Zoot Suit Riots. In addition, she supposedly had urged a gang of pachucos to attack sheriff's deputies in her neighborhood. "I no like thees daputy sheriffs," the *Herald-Express* quoted her.[1]

Although newspaper photographs do not show her wearing a finger-tip coat or short, full skirt—identifying features of the pachuca look in wartime Los Angeles—Venegas was nonetheless called a "pachuco woman" and "sympathizer with the zoot suit fraternity."[2] As I show in the previous chapter, the zoot suit signified difference and defiance in the United States during World War II. Both the ensemble and, more often than not, its Mexican American wearer were deemed unpatriotic and un-American and were even directly linked to the Axis. In Venegas's case, the incorrect grammar and caricatured Mexican accent attributed to her emphasized that her transgression was twofold: she was not only un-American but unladylike as well.

The previous chapter, like many studies of pachuquismo, stress the symbolic economy of style: clothes, hair, and, to a lesser extent, makeup. This chapter seeks to add to this body of work by focusing on another important—albeit literally unspectacular—stylistic element of wartime pachuquismo: language and speech. Like their African American counterparts who spoke jive, many pachucas and pachucos spoke pachuco slang (also known as *caló*).[3] Additionally,

25. Amelia Venegas, so-called pachuco woman, 1943. *HERALD EXAMINER COLLECTION, LOS ANGELES PUBLIC LIBRARY.*

many used pochismos (lexical borrowings) and a working-class-inflected form of American English. During the Chicano movement of the 1960s, 1970s, and early 1980s, these linguistic varieties, like zoot suits, became signs of both difference and opposition for a number of Chicana and Chicano writers. They signified a refusal to conform to the status quo and a distinctly racialized, working-class, urban youth style. In short, many of the utterances of Mexican American zooters came to signify resistance, style, and style as resistance.

The concept of resistance has had an indelible impact on the study of popular culture in the United States as well as on Chicano studies and cultural and ethnic studies more broadly. Drawing from James C. Scott's metaphor of the "hidden transcript," Robin D. G. Kelley, for example, argues that the "veiled social and cultural worlds of oppressed people frequently surface in everyday forms of resistance—theft, footdragging, the destruction of property."[4] Within African American and Chicano studies, the zoot subculture of the World War II period is often looked to as an example of a "hidden transcript." As Kelley notes, "The language and culture of zoot suiters represented a subversive refusal to be subservient."[5]

This chapter explores the language and culture of zoot suiters. However, by focusing on women speakers of pachuco slang, I examine the relationship of resistance—what Kelley describes as the "subversive refusal to be subservient"—to gender and style, specifically coolness and hipness. "Coolness" refers to self-control; "hipness" to knowledge and sophistication. Both terms connote style and, as I argue below, social marginalization. This chapter examines the gendering of Chicano resistance and style and Chicano resistance as style. It asks what are the genders and sexualities of Chicano resistance and does Chicanas' resistance differ from that of Chicanos? In addressing these questions, I draw upon a wide array of sources, including a poem, short story, corrido (ballad), trial transcript, and play, in order to better understand the linguistic varieties of pachucos and pachucas in the 1940s—namely, caló, pochismos, and nonstandard American English—and the ways in which their utterances were recuperated by a later generation of Chicana and Chicano cultural workers. I argue that, where male speakers of pachuco slang have been upheld as icons of resistance and cultural affirmation, female Mexican American speakers have faced heavier consequences. Like Amelia Venegas, they have been mocked, punished, or silenced for failing to reproduce the ideal subjects of U.S. national identity (the loyal, white, Anglophone citizen), of an oppositional Chicano cultural identity (*el pachuco*), and of normative femininity (the "lady").

Because recovering Chicanas' past use of pachuco slang—what the late feminist sociolinguist D. Letticia Galindo termed a "taboo language" for women and girls—poses particular challenges, this chapter also emphasizes silence.[6] In exploring the meanings and uses of silence for those who called themselves and were called pachucas, I argue that Chicanas' silence can be and has been as oppositional, rich, and complex as their male counterparts' speech. My hope is that this chapter will provide us with a glimpse—or, more precisely, an echo—of the voices and silence of the pachucas of the 1940s and will contribute to both zoot studies and feminist scholarship on the linguistic varieties and practices of Chicana homegirls in the late twentieth and early twenty-first centuries.[7] Finally, I hope that my work not only complicates conventional notions of Chicano defiance and style as it exposes their masculinist and heterosexist underpinnings but also amplifies the less audible forms of Chicana resistance.

"Double Talk" and Duplicity

In addition to scrutinizing pachucos' and pachucas' hair and clothes, law enforcement, newspapers, and social scientists demonstrated a concern with pachuco slang beginning in the early 1940s. Described by scholars as both a "pidgin dialect" and "creole language," pachuco slang draws from Spanish, English, pochismos, and caló.[8] (Although caló is one component of pachuco slang, the two terms are often used interchangeably.) Contrary to claims that it is distinctly and exclusively Mexican American, caló is a product of the Old and New Worlds as it borrows from indigenous American languages, such as Nahuatl, and from zincaló, the idiom of the Spanish gypsies. For centuries, it has been associated with the underclass, with, in Mauricio Mazón's words, "the criminal, the poor, and the uneducated."[9] In particular, it has been associated with the Tirilis, a subgroup of Mexicans and Mexican Americans who reputedly trafficked in sex and drugs in and around El Paso–Juárez in the early part of the twentieth century.[10]

In general, social scientific studies of pachuco slang have emphasized criminality. For this reason, it has been labeled an argot, "a secret language or conventional slang peculiar to a group of thieves, tramps or vagabonds."[11] Yet, as Galindo cautions, "early research conducted by Anglo social scientists" tended to be more alarmist than "ethnosensitive," as evidenced, for example, by the title of Lurline Coltharp's study *The Tongue of the Tirilones: A Linguistic Study of a Criminal Argot* (1965).[12] Likewise, articles on pachucas and pachucos (and Mexican American youth in general) that appeared in the Angeleno press during the early 1940s highlighted sex, drugs, and violence. For instance, a *Los Angeles Times* story in July 1944 that purported to expose the sinister pachuco underworld reported, "Gang members speak a strange argot unintelligible to the uninitiated."[13] The newspaper translated several supposedly exemplary words from pachuco slang into English, such as *yisca* ("marihuana"), *la jefe* ("the leader of a local gang"), and *volte* ("jail").[14]

In fact, for many Mexican American youths of the 1940s, pachuco slang was "hep" and nothing more. Yet more than merely pointing to a generation gap, caló words, such as *chale* (no) and *orale* (right on, attention), accentuated what some contemporary observers perceived as more deep-set and troubling differences. A story in August 1942 in the Spanish-language newspaper *La Opinión*, for instance, dismissed pachuco slang as a combination of "pochismos y jerga" (pocho-isms and slang) and lamented that its speakers were neither truly Mexican nor full-fledged Americans.[15] A pochismo is a lexical borrowing or loan word that combines English and Spanish, such as *marketa* (instead of *mercado*) for market.[16] Similarly, a pocha or pocho is an Americanized Mexican or Mexicanized American. Just as pochismos have been dismissed as "a tragic sign of language decadence," the invective *pocha/o* originally signified cultural and linguistic degradation, retardation, and lack.[17] Many Mexicans have used the term to chastise and deride Mexican Americans, especially those who appeared to have "ruined their Spanish without ever quite learning English."[18] As one scholar averred, pochos "did not do a good enough job imitating the Yankee."[19]

Pochos and pochas not only did a poor job at imitating Yankees; they also failed to mimic Mexicans adequately. Neither this nor that, they appeared to be more cultural void than cultural hybrid. Their ability to speak English, Spanish, and pachuco slang, to code-switch, and to invent neologisms was not seen as a sign of a creative and rich bilingualism or multilingualism but as evidence of an utter lack of language. Paradoxically, on the eve of the Zoot Suit Riots, the *Los Angeles Times* published a story in which juvenile delinquency was attributed to "language variance in the home—where the parents speak no English and cling to past culture."[20] According to the logic of this assertion, second-generation Mexican American youths did not necessarily lack culture. Rather, they possessed too much of the wrong sort of culture (Mexicanness) and too little of the right kind (Americanness).

For many Mexicans and Americans, the language(s) of second-generation Mexican Americans were regarded as a mark of infidelity and lapse in what the literary critic Lisa Lowe calls "identical equivalence."[21] Unlike English or Spanish, pachuco slang supposedly indicated a failure to reproduce an authentic, clear-cut, or legitimate national identity. During World War II, it was deemed evidence of a refusal or inability to conform—to assimilate, in other words—and cast doubt on its speakers' allegiance to the United States, rather than signaling an alternative form of Americanness.

Indeed, since the earliest days of the republic, fluency in English has been regarded as a sine qua non of American identity.[22] During the riots, stories in the Angeleno press about an alleged Axis plot to stir up unrest on the home front underscored the commensurability of standard, unaccented English and authentic Americanness. As civic leaders publicly speculated that Axis agents had instigated the riots by infiltrating the city's barrios and prompting young Mexican Americans to attack white servicemen, newspapers reported that "an enemy agent"—identified as such because he spoke "broken English"—had been spotted in Watts.[23] In the midst of this paranoia and xenophobia, the so-called double talk of pachucos and pachucas did little to affirm their Americanness.[24]

"Dude Talk" and the Birth of Cool

Long before the (white) "bad boy" emerged in Cold War America (for example, Holden Caulfield, Elvis Presley, and James Dean), young American men of color—in particular, African Americans and Mexican Americans—came to represent youthful rebellion.[25] Although black jive, which the jazz vocalist Cab Calloway described as "Negro slang, the super-hip language of the times," and pachuco slang are far from identical, they have shared some similarities.[26] For example, both have helped to produce and to express dissident working-class masculinities in the United States. At times, these masculinities have defied socially sanctioned (specifically white and middle-class) masculinities as they have privileged street-smarts over formal education and have found expression by reversing the signifiers and referents of standard American English (for example, "bad" meaning "good").

For some social scientists, black jive and pachuco slang were more than just colloquial speech; they were evidence of a disturbing insubordination on the part of their speakers. In the wake of the 1943 Harlem riot, the psychologists Kenneth B. Clark and James Barker fretted that the African American zooter's "habitual, seemingly deliberate, disregard of . . . the simple rules of grammar in his everyday speech" indicated a "generalized defiance of the larger society."[27] Twenty years later, in the midst of the youth movement of the late 1960s, caló was linked to rage: it was described as "a 'snarl' language" that reflected "an uncompromising attitude of anger, sarcasm, cynicism, and undifferentiated rebellion."[28] Of particular concern to both generations of scholars was zooters' "excessive use of profanity in ordinary conversation."[29] In an essay on caló, George Alvarez insisted that the "expletives chinga and pinchi, which are analogous to the English word 'damn,'" could be found "in almost every caló utterance."[30] And recalling his days as a young hustler, Malcolm X claimed, "Every word I spoke was hip or profane."[31]

By the late 1960s, the pachuco was more than an avatar of youthful rebellion. Like Malcolm X, he became a symbol of racial and ethnic pride as movement-era Chicano cultural workers, among them the poet and artist José Montoya, embraced him as a symbol of cultural affirmation and resistance. Montoya's poem "El Louie," perhaps one of the most scrutinized Chicano literary works, recounts the life and times of Louie Rodríguez, a cool, charismatic, and doomed pachuco from the small town of Fowler in California's rural San Joaquin Valley.[32] Written in pachuco slang, the poem points to the beauty and elegance of the vernacular and vulgar (the common and rough). Although the narrator concedes that "Fowler no era nada como / Los, o'l E.P.T. [Fowler was nothing like / L.A. or El Paso] Fresno's / westside was as close as / we ever got to the big time," Louie exudes big-city flair nonetheless.[33] He wears tailor-made zoot suits and renames himself "Blackie," "Little Louie," and "Diamonds."[34] A local celebrity of sorts, he is famous throughout the small towns of central California, such as Selma and Gilroy, and his panache is on par with that of a movie star: "melodramatic music, like in the / mono [movies]," seems to accompany him as he swaggers into the Palomar dance hall, Nesei's pool parlor, or a parking lot fight.[35] And when he "sport[s] a dark topcoat" in San Jose, the metropolis, he "play[s] in his fantasy / the role of Bogart, Cagney / or Raft."[36] Tragically, "booze y la vida dura [and the hard life]" catch up with Louie and he dies alone in a rented room, in all likelihood of a heroin overdose.[37] The narrator laments his death as an "insult" and "cruel hoax" yet speculates that it was "perhaps like in a / Bogart movie"[38] and maintains that he had "class to the end."[39] Even in death, Louie manages to evoke Hollywood glamour.

Contrast the pachuco's portrayal in "El Louie," a cultural product of the Chicano and youth movements of the second half of the twentieth century, to his denigration in Mario Suárez's short story "Kid Zopilote" (1947). After Pepe García, the protagonist, spends a summer in Los Angeles and returns to his hometown, Tucson, he not only looks different (now that he wears a zoot suit and combs his hair in a ducktail) but "his language had changed quite a bit, too."[40] Having picked up pochismos in "Los Angeles,

Califo [California]," Pepe tells his mother, "Ma, I will returniar [return] in a little while" every time he leaves the house.[41] When he comes back, he reports, "Ma, I was watchiando [watching] a good movie, that is why I am a little bit late."[42] In the end, Pepe and Tucson's other pachucos are punished for their big-city airs when they are beaten by a group of respectable Mexican Americans, then thrown into jail, where their zoot suits are destroyed and their hair is cut. Upon their release, "they crept home along alleys, like shorn dogs with their tails between their legs, lest people should see them."[43]

While "Kid Zopilote" expresses disdain for the pachuco, "El Louie" redeems him as the apotheosis of Chicano style. Pepe García, an emasculated dandy, is embarrassed by his square appearance and shuns attention after his hair is shorn. Louie Rodríguez, in contrast, epitomizes macho style and flourishes in the limelight. Wearing "buenas garras [cool threads]," he cruises around town in a "48 Fleetline, two-tone."[44] And if Pepe is a ridiculous pocho, then Louie exemplifies seamless cultural hybridity: he dances both "el boogie" and "los mambos."[45] Furthermore, he does not want for "rucas [chicks]—como la Mary y / la Helen."[46] Pepe, meanwhile, has a hard time getting a girl to dance with him: "When he went to the Tira-Chancla Dance Hall very few of the girls consented to dance with him. When they did, it was out of compassion."[47] Adding injury to insult, Pepe is beaten by a group of squares and is further humiliated by the police. In contrast, Louie, a decorated Korean War veteran, demonstrates that he is a "soldado de / levita con huevos [a very ballsy soldier]" as he moves between the battlefield and street brawl.[48] With a "smile as deadly as his vaisas"—that is, with a smile as deadly as his hands—he embodies masculine power, both in the form of charm and violence.[49]

Since its initial publication in 1970, "El Louie" has been upheld as an exemplar of pachuco poetry and Chicano literature in general because of both its content and form.[50] As the literary critic Alfred Arteaga asserts, its language "matches its content: the verse is as thoroughly Chicano as is Louie's life."[51] Yet how "thoroughly Chicano"—or Chicana—is "El Louie" when it is written in pachuco slang, a linguistic variety that has been designated male and masculine? Like black jive, pachuco slang's origins are in activities and realms generally associated with men and masculinity, such as the criminal underworld, androcentric jazz subculture, and working class, which, in and of itself, is often configured as male and masculine.

Consequently, it has been widely regarded as a "male-dominated, intra-group form of communication."[52] As one of Galindo's informants put it, it is "dude talk."[53]

For some movement-era Chicanos, many of whom were baby boomers who prized youthful rebellion and defied authority by protesting the Vietnam War, boycotting agribusiness, and demanding Chicano studies in high schools, colleges, and universities, the pachucos of the previous generation were "vatos de huevos [ballsy guys]" and "vatos firmes [stoic or steadfast guys]"—two of "the most complimentary terms in the caló vocabulary," according to one scholar—because they articulated a distinct and dissident cultural identity in the face of denigration, assimilation, and erasure.[54] In other words, pachucos were hip and cool, terms that connote self-conscious social marginalization, resistance, and transgression.[55] The latter refers to an affected affectlessness, to emotional self-control and relaxation. The former originally meant wise or sophisticated and could signify worldliness in general and knowledge of the underworld in particular. While the concept of cool pointed to the masculine ideal of emotional detachment, "hip" was the antonym of "innocent," a characteristic ascribed to both children and the ideal (read virgin) bride.

Just as "real" (white, middle-class, Anglophone) Americanness has been linked to mimesis and assimilation, U.S. racial and ethnic minority identities have been and still are associated with authenticity and fidelity—in other words, with "keeping it real." The link between language and "realness" is evident in Malcolm X's *Autobiography* (1964). In a refreshing reading of this work, María Josefina Saldaña-Portillo argues that Malcolm X revels in his ability to speak jive, contrary to claims that he appeared to dismiss his hustling days as "a destructive detour on the road to self-consciousness and political enlightenment."[56] Indeed, he opens the chapter marking his transition from country bumpkin to urban hipster with a paragraph intended "to display a bit more of the slang that was used by everyone I respected as 'hip' in those days."[57] Furthermore, he reveals great pride in his command of the vernacular, for his fluency supposedly indicated that he was closer to and, therefore, the most appropriate leader of "the ghetto black people." He recounts translating jive for a putative black leader who, after being approached by a "Harlem hustler . . . look[ed] as if he'd just heard Sanskrit." In this recollection, Malcolm distinguishes the confused "downtown 'leader'" from the slick "Harlem hustler," both of whom serve as respective metonyms for "'middle class' Negro[es]" and "ghetto blacks."[58] For Malcolm, black jive, the language of poor, urban African Americans, functioned as a cultural identity marker, as a sign of authentic blackness; while standard American English, the language of middle-class blacks who lived and worked outside the ghetto (for example, "downtown"), smacked of selling out.

Malcolm's observations concerning the chasm between the real and the fake point to another set of binary oppositions: the hipster and the square, and, by extension, masculinity and femininity. A "fake" black man or "wannabe" white man, the figure of the Uncle Tom has been linked to "passivity, obedience, docility, accommodation, and submissiveness"—characteristics that are frequently associated with women and femininity.[59] As a Tom, the "downtown 'leader'" Malcolm encounters is helpless and dependent: he must rely on Malcolm to translate for him. In addition, he is a square, for he is not "hep to the jive" (he does not understand jive, nor is he worldly or aware). As Norman Mailer has posited, if one is not hip, then "one is Square."[60] Similarly, George Alvarez contends that in pachuco slang "there is no grey area between an escuadra [square] and a vato loco."[61] In other words, if one is not hip, then one is square, and if one is square, then one is not a vato loco, a highly gendered term comparable to today's "dawg" (as opposed to "bitch"), (male) "gangsta," and, in its most general sense, "dude" or "guy." Thus, if one is not hip, then one is not a guy, and, according to the logic of the sex/gender binary, if one is not a guy, then one is female or feminine.

Yet since the early 1940s at least, coolness—in particular, black and brown coolness—has not just been coded masculine; it is also often coded heterosexual. Its opposite, uncoolness, has been equated with social incompetence and physical impairment, with being "lame" and "a sissy."[62] Likewise, in the late 1960s, George Alvarez identified *puto* (homosexual) and *culero* (coward) as the "most derogatory" terms in caló.[63] Both invectives are homophobic and denote anal sex: *culero* derives from *culo*, which is the equivalent of "ass" in American English; while *puto* refers to a male homosexual and "speak[s] to the passive sexual role taken by . . . men . . . in the homosexual act."[64] The latter is related to the word *puta*, which means female prostitute. As the sociologist Tomás Almaguer observes, "It is significant that the cultural equation made between the feminine, anal-receptive homosexual man and the most culturally-stigmatized female in Mexican society (the whore) share a common semantic base."[65]

Instead of being celebrated as cool or hip, Chicana speakers of pachuco slang have been branded putas.[66] In addition, they have been dismissed as *cantineras* (barflies, drunks) and gang members' girlfriends.[67] In other words, they are ancillary. As John Leland points out in his history of hipness, women are generally not recognized as hipsters per se but as (male) hipsters' auxiliaries, "either the apron strings from which male hipness takes flight or the enticements it consumes along the road."[68] The hipster flees his reproving mother in order to enjoy whores and other good-time girls. Indeed, the film and literary critic Susan Fraiman argues that the figure of mother, like the minivans and suburbs with which it is often associated, is the antithesis of cool.[69] To maintain hipness, the hipster must forsake his mother, his wife, and his children. In short, he must distance himself from domesticity and socially sanctioned femininity.

Pachuco slang's ban from the Mexican American domestic sphere and its incommensurability with socially sanctioned femininity are apparent in *Hoyt Street* (1993), Mary Helen Ponce's autobiography. Ponce, who grew up in Southern California's San Fernando Valley during the 1940s and 1950s, recounts that when a friend inadvertently responded to her grandmother in caló, the girl was promptly sent to her room "to escape being slapped by her older brother, who allowed no disrespect for his grandma."[70] The concept of *respeto* (respect) within and toward the biological family also resonates in Galindo's study of Tejanas and pachuco slang (1992). A number of her interviewees claimed that they would not use pachuco slang in the presence of their fathers out of "respeto." And one reported that, while her brothers could speak pachuco slang among themselves, they were not allowed to speak it to their parents. "If the girls used it, we were reprimanded. Especially by my mother; she wouldn't tolerate it."[71]

According to Galindo, pachuco slang is a "'taboo language' for women and girls."[72] Many have been prohibited from speaking it and some have even actively distanced themselves from it lest they be labeled the sort of woman who deviates from the home, such as a puta or cantinera. For instance, in her study of the Tirilis, Coltharp maintained that many of the young women she encountered understood caló, but were "horrified" when she attempted to enlist their aid as translators.[73] She concluded that no law-abiding woman "would admit that she even understood one word of the language."[74]

As the language of the outlaw, rebel, and hipster, pachuco slang is masculine. Since the early 1940s, it has provided young, working-class,

Mexican American men with a means—literally, a vocabulary—"to prove their manhood and vent their frustrations."[75] In short, pachuco slang has allowed men to oppose the status quo. Like black jive, it has helped them to produce and shape a distinctly raced and classed masculinity and to challenge dominant (white and middle-class) definitions of manhood. Yet unlike black jive, much of which has been incorporated into standard American English, pachuco slang has remained relatively insular, thus making it all the more distinct and dissonant. Additionally, its connections to Spanish and caló render it more alien and therefore more threatening to a white and Anglophone American identity. In speaking it, young Mexican American men have become icons of un-Americanness, resistance, and style, from the chukos suaves of the 1940s, to the vatos locos of the postwar period and the dawgs of the early twenty-first century.

Yet what happened when young Mexican American women spoke pachuco slang during the 1940s? And what or whom did they resist by speaking it, along with nonstandard forms of English and Spanish, at a moment of not only increased social and cultural homogenization but changing expectations of women, especially outside the home? To address these questions, I juxtapose three cultural artifacts in the following sections: a corrido, *People v. Zammora* (the Sleepy Lagoon trial transcript), and Luis Valdez's play *Zoot Suit*. Together, these texts show that Chicanas who spoke pachuco slang challenged not only white Americanness and middle-class comportment but normative gender as well. They failed to imitate white, Anglophone Americans and respectable ladies alike but were still not homologous with their male counterparts, pachucos. And while *el pachuco* would come to embody an idealized Chicano masculinity and subjectivity during the Chicano movement, the so-called tough-tongued pachuca would be ignored or maligned.[76]

"El Bracero y La Pachuca"

The pachuco's transformation from effete social pariah (Pepe García, for example) to macho cultural hero and icon in movement-era Chicano cultural production (such as Louie Rodríguez) is probably most apparent in *Zoot Suit*. With the play's premier in 1978, interest in zoot suits and pachuco slang appeared to resurge among Chicanos. Throughout the late 1970s and early 1980s, *Lowrider* magazine featured advertisements for not only el tacuche but the *Dictionary of Pachuco Slang*, which guaranteed to make

27. Advertisement for the *Dictionary of Pachuco Slang.* *Lowrider* magazine, copyright 1978–79. REPRINTED BY PERMISSION OF MCMULLEN ARGUS PUBLISHING, INC., COPYRIGHT 1978, 1979, 2007.

26. Advertisement for zoot suits and accessories. *Lowrider* magazine, copyright 1978–79. REPRINTED BY PERMISSION OF MCMULLEN ARGUS PUBLISHING, INC., COPYRIGHT 1978, 1979, 2007.

its reader "the baddest vato en tu barrio [dude in your neighborhood]." Nostalgia for the 1940s was also evident in 1940s-themed fundraiser dances sponsored by the magazine. Advertisements called on attendees to wear zoot suits and promised an evening of not only disco but "boogie woogie" and "big bands" as well.[77]

Zoot Suit featured "boogie woogie–influenced Pachuco songs" by Lalo Guerrero, who, along with other Mexican American musicians of the 1940s and 1950s such as Don Tosti (né Edmundo Martínez Tostado) is responsible in great part for helping to preserve contemporary pachuco slang. Because of these musicians' efforts, pachuco slang of the 1940s and 1950s has been recorded not only in anthropological, sociolinguistic, or literary works but in popular music as well.[78] While many if not most songs in pachuco slang were sung by men, the corrido "El Bracero y La Pachuca" is extraordinary because it prominently features a female vocalist.[79]

"El Bracero y La Pachuca" was written by Miguel Salas and recorded in 1948 in Los Angeles by Dueto Taxco and Mariachi Los Caporales del Norte. Although it is not a product of the World War II period, I discuss it here because it features both pachuco slang and a female vocalist. Like "A Zoot Suit (for My Sunday Gal)," it is a duet sung by a man and woman. Its lyrics, however, are in a combination of Spanish and pachuco slang and recount the unlikely union of a mellifluous Mexican bracero and pachuco-slang-speaking pachuca who meet at a dance. Using proper Spanish, the bracero attempts to woo the pachuca with poetry. When she responds, both he and the listener learn that she is an uncouth pocha who does not understand or appreciate the beauty of her suitor's words. She tells him, "Ya tíreme bute chancla / traserito sin sabor, / ya me esta cayendo sura [Cut it out and let's dance / you're so square that / you're getting on my nerves]."[80] Then, in her solo, she matches the bracero's poem with one attributed to the "Tírilí" (reefer man):

> Nel ese, ya parale con sus palabras
> del alta que por derecho me aguitan ese,
> mejor pongase muy alalva con
> un pistazo de aquella, y un frajito
> del fuerte pa' despues poder borrar. Ja . . .
>
> Slow down man
> cut out that high-toned
> poetry jazz, you're really bringing me down.

You better have a drink and get with it,
and then smoke a joint to mellow out. Ha![81]

Whereas the bracero's poem speaks of "rosas encarnadas . . . con sus lindas aromas [red roses with their beautiful perfume]," the pachuca's is about boozing it up and smoking dope. And while the bracero implores the pachuca to love him "porque te quiero . . . porque te adoro [because I love you . . . because I adore you]," the pachuca demands that he cut the crap and simmer down. Apparently, he does as he is told, for in the final stanza, we learn that our hero and heroine dance the night away and are married the next morning.

As is often the case in romance, opposites attract; the bracero and pachuca are drawn to one another precisely because "eran muy diferentes [they were very different]." In addition to contrasting proper Spanish and pachuco slang, "El Bracero y La Pachuca" juxtaposes *lo mexicano y la pocha* (the Mexican and the pocha), the country and the city, and high and low cultures. Despite his association with agricultural labor, the bracero exemplifies high culture and politesse. Using especially flowery Spanish and hyperbolically correct diction, he addresses the pachuca as "mujer del alma mía [woman of my soul]" and "linda princesa encantada [beautiful enchanted princess]" as he recites poetry to her. In contrast, the pachuca speaks with the "whining nasal quality" and "sing-song" rhythm often attributed to pachuco slang, addresses the bracero as "ese [dude/man]," rejects his "palabras del alta [lofty speech]," and does not hide the fact that he bothers her.[82] If "toughness" in language is associated with "manliness" and "working-class culture" and "femaleness . . . with respectability, gentility, and high culture," then "El Bracero y La Pachuca," reverses gender stereotypes (even if it does offer a hackneyed tale of heterosexual romance).[83] The ballad's respectable and genteel bracero represents high culture with his proper, perfectly enunciated Spanish poetry. As such, he is feminine. Meanwhile, the slang-speaking pachuca is a coarse philistine and therefore a traitor: as a boorish woman who speaks pachuco slang, she assumes a masculine position and betrays gender norms.[84]

People v. Zammora

The betrayal of normative (white, middle-class) Americanness and femininity via speech is also evident in *People v. Zammora*, the Sleepy Lagoon trial transcript. It is especially apparent in testimony by Bertha Aguilar, a fourteen-year-old girl from the 38th Street neighborhood who was involved in the Sleepy Lagoon incident. After José Díaz's death, the police began to arrest suspects in what they determined was a murder case on August 3, 1943. The grand jury hearing commenced the following day, and the criminal trial opened on October 13. It ended three months later on January 15, 1943, with the conviction of the twenty-two defendants.

Along with several other girls and young women, whom court documents refer to as the defendants' "girl companions" (friends, neighbors, girlfriends), Aguilar was incarcerated at the Ventura School for Girls and was forced to testify before the Los Angeles County grand jury and in *People v. Zammora* in connection with Díaz's death.[85] Although we do not know whether they ever called themselves pachucas, these girls and young women were labeled such by the mainstream Angeleno press. And just as the prosecution drew attention to the defendants' zoot suits and long hair, putative hallmarks of juvenile delinquency, it also pointed to the coats, coiffures, and black dresses that their "girl companions" had donned the night of August 1, 1942.[86] Meanwhile, the district attorney and dominant Los Angeles newspapers repeatedly referred to the female and male youths as a "gang." Not surprisingly, by the time the defendants were convicted of conspiracy to murder in January 1943, *People v. Zammora* was known as the "'zoot suit' murder case."[87]

In court, Aguilar reported that, immediately after crashing the Delgadillos' party, she entered a fight when she saw that a group of approximately five women had attacked her friend Delia Parra. She stated that, initially, "I didn't do nothing. I didn't want to do nothing, but when I seen the girl, you know, put up the bottle to hit Delia, I ran towards her."[88] Consequently, Aguilar was struck in the leg with the bottle and was left with scars. During cross-examination, defense attorney Anna Zacsek asked to see the scars and both the defense and prosecution suggested that "the young lady step along the jury rail and hold that leg up so that the jury [might] see it."[89] Aguilar complied. When Deputy District Attorney John Barnes noted that the scars did not appear to be anything more than mere scratches, Aguilar retorted defensively, "Well, they sure were."[90]

Even though she was described as a "young lady," both the content of her words and her words themselves—combined with the manner in which her statements were recorded by the court—suggest that Aguilar was not quite a "lady." In the 1942 edition of *Etiquette: The Blue Book of Social Usage*,

Emily Post insisted that the "oft-heard expression, 'You know she is a lady as soon as she opens her mouth,' is not an exaggeration."[91] The arbiter of social manners and good taste instructed would-be ladies "how to cultivate an agreeable speech."[92] She implored them not to mumble but bemoaned the loud and shrill voice as "extremely bad form."[93] Additionally, Post advised her readers, especially those who wished to climb the social ladder, to avoid incorrect grammar (in particular, phrases such as "I seen it") and "the vernacular of today."[94] While she stressed that there was no place for "coarse or profane slang" in a lady's vocabulary, she deemed "certain words and phrases in common use," such as "swell," "O. K.," and "you betcha," acceptable, even though they interfered with "perfect diction."[95]

Regardless of how seriously its readers heeded its advice and admonitions, Post's *Etiquette* points to the intersection of language, gender, and class. It shows women—especially those with middle-class aspirations—how to reproduce or perform "ladyness," a particular kind of femininity, via language.[96] Decades later, the feminist sociolinguist Robin Tolmach Lakoff would examine the relationship of language to gender in her groundbreaking *Language and Women's Place*. According to Lakoff, women—specifically, white, middle-class, American women—speak and, more importantly, are supposed to speak "women's language," which is characterized by "hypercorrect grammar" and "superpolite forms."[97] Of course, not all women speak "women's language" and not all speakers of "women's language" are white middle-class women. Indeed, since its initial publication in 1975, Lakoff's study has received much warranted criticism—in particular, for positing the a priori existence of a universal, timeless, and homogeneous feminine identity projected or displayed by language. At the same time, *Language and Woman's Place*, like Post's *Etiquette*, points to a multiplicity of femininities, to different ways in which to enact femininity or womanness. It exposes the constructedness of gender, race, and class and shows the ways in which these social categories and relations come into being via language.

Throughout *People v. Zammora*, Anna Zacsek, the only female attorney in the courtroom (and, coincidentally, a former professional actress), clearly spoke Post's "agreeable speech" and Lakoff's "women's language."[98] By and large, she used correct grammar and was respectful, even when she took issue with Judge Charles Fricke or one of the prosecutors. Indeed, at times, she was cloyingly polite. For example, when Judge Fricke complained that fifteen-year-old witness Juanita Gonzáles was inaudible because she repeatedly turned her head away from the microphone while testifying in the witness stand, Zacsek instructed her, "Will you please be a good girl and take this microphone in your hand—you have talked on telephones, haven't you Juanita?"[99] In an effort to underscore her own feminine authority, the defense attorney assumed a maternal role in the courtroom and claimed that she was "just old enough to know how to handle children" such as the uncooperative Gonzáles.[100]

In contrast, most of the young, Spanish-surnamed female witnesses, including Gonzáles, used speech that was neither grammatically correct nor polite. Many sprinkled their sentences with double negatives and the contraction "ain't" and defied Emily Post with their improper use of the verb "seen." For example, when Deputy District Attorney Clyde C. Shoemaker asked Aguilar how many cars she saw at Williams Ranch the night of the fight, she replied, "I seen about two."[101] Furthermore, the court reporter indicated that Aguilar used improper or incorrect diction by recording her use of the words "nothing" and "going" as "nothin'" and "goin'." In this instance, Shoemaker asked her if she was with defendant Henry Leyvas on the night of August 1, 1942. Aguilar impatiently reminded him,

> I said I wasn't going to say nothin.' Don't ask me no more things. You can punish me—
> MR. SHOEMAKER: We ask you to answer that question, Bertha.
> A: I ain't goin' to answer it.[102]

Because there is no audio recording of her testimony, whether or not Aguilar actually stated "nothin'" and "goin'" is unclear. Regardless, to my knowledge this is the only instance in the entire trial transcript (which is thousands of pages in length) in which the court reporter truncated a speaker's words. By doing so, he rendered Aguilar's utterance a slang locution, an expression of improper or incorrect diction. In effect, he masculinized her words.[103] And just as a caricatured Mexican accent was attributed to Amelia Venegas by the *Los Angeles Herald-Express* during the Zoot Suit Riots, attention was drawn to Aguilar's "slight accent" in the courtroom.[104] By using incorrect grammar and allegedly substandard diction, she appeared both unladylike and un-American.

Although we do not know whether Aguilar had an accent or whether she really dropped the *g* in "nothing," her speech clearly was not polite or indirect, two characteristics of "women's language," according to Lakoff. The following exchange between her and Shoemaker further illustrates her candor and tenacity:

> Q [BY SHOEMAKER]: Now state whether or not at the time you testified before the Grand Jury, on August 4, which was three days after [the Sleepy Lagoon incident], that your memory was better on the subject than it is today. What is your answer, Bertha? Talk right into the microphone.
>
> A [BY AGUILAR]: I am not going to say nothing. I told you all I wasn't going to say nothing.
>
> Q: Will you answer that question?
>
> A: No.
>
> Q: The question is, whether your memory was better when you testified before the Grand Jury than it is today. Will you answer that? What is your answer? What is your answer, Bertha? Will you answer the question?
>
> A: You don't have to holler at people. I am right here.
>
> Q: I am not hollering at you.
>
> A: You sure are.
>
> Q: I am just talking in an ordinary tone of voice.
>
> THE COURT: Answer the question, Bertha. You are just wasting time. Will you answer the question?
>
> A: No, I won't.
>
> MR. SHOEMAKER: Will your Honor direct the witness to answer the question, please?
>
> THE COURT: Answer the question, Bertha. There is no reason why you cannot answer that question.
>
> (No response.)[105]

Instead of cultivating "agreeable speech" by using a "pleasing voice," "hypercorrect grammar," and "superpolite forms," Aguilar displayed and then boasted about injuries she claimed to have sustained in a fight. (As Galindo has noted, boasting, also known as *cábula* or *vacilada* in pachuco slang, "is generally confined to male speech behavior.")[106] Furthermore, the bold teenager repeatedly and adamantly refused to cooperate with authorities; ordered the deputy district attorney to refrain from asking her any more questions; indicated that she was willing to face punishment, rather than yield to his demands; reprimanded him for "hollering" at her; openly disagreed with him; and, finally, refused to speak. It should come as no surprise that she was held in contempt of court for refusing to answer the prosecution's questions.[107] However, the charge was rescinded after she offered the judge what was described as a "rare smile."[108] That is, she was rewarded after behaving as a lady should.

By saying "nothing" (or "nothin'") rather than "anything," Aguilar demonstrated a disregard for (or unawareness of) the rules of grammar. And by saying nothing (by refusing to speak), she flouted the authority of the state, as represented by the deputy district attorney and judge. As Eduardo Obregón Pagán observes, "Most of the girls [forced to testify against their male companions] refused to implicate the boys and subverted the trial proceedings or defied the court outright."[109] Aguilar further disobeyed and hamstrung the prosecution by playing the role of good subject and, at the suggestion of the state, claiming to have forgotten what happened the night she and her friends crashed the Delgadillos' party. Even after Shoemaker attempted to "refresh" her memory by citing her August 1942 grand jury testimony (taken just days after José Díaz's death), she insisted that she was unable to remember what happened. "I don't remember nothing," she stated. "When I went to Ventura they told me to forget everything."[110] Similarly, during cross-examination, Juanita Gonzáles reported that when she entered "Juvenile," she was instructed "to forget all this as quickly as possible."[111] The two teenage girls continued to stymie the prosecution by refusing to say anything lest they incriminate themselves. For instance, when Shoemaker asked Gonzáles on what grounds she refused to testify, she responded, "On the grounds you may charge me for the murder of Joe Diaz, like you done to the boys."[112] Aguilar offered a more curt reply when asked why she would not answer one of the prosecutor's questions: "I don't know, but I ain't going to answer it that's all."[113] Others refused to cooperate by not speaking clearly, thus breaking yet another of Post's rules of feminine speech. Eighteen-year-old Dora Baca, for example, claimed to suffer from a sore throat when both the prosecution and defense complained that she was inaudible on the witness stand.[114]

In "Life and Language in Court," Lakoff argues that, while "the giver of information" (the speaker) usually holds power in everyday speech, in court, "the giver of information" (the witness) does not control topics for discussion "or their interpretation and has no say over when the conversation begins and ends. The witness is generally a neophyte in the court-room; the lawyer, a polished professional . . . the attorneys are running the show."[115] Undeniably, Aguilar and the other teenage girls and young women who found themselves reluctant witnesses in *People v. Zammora* were neophytes in the courtroom vis-à-vis the judge, lawyers, court report-ers, bailiffs, and others. Yet, as Kelley reminds us, "One also finds the hidden transcript emerging 'onstage' in spaces controlled by the powerful, though almost always in disguised forms."[116] Despite her youth and inex-perience, Aguilar showed remarkable bravery and resolution in the witness stand. Within her words (and lack thereof) we find a "hidden transcript" in the form of defiance, evasion, and refusal. At times, her resistance is overt (for instance, when she reprimands Shoemaker for "hollering" at her). Yet, at others, it is less easily recognized—for example, when she claims to have forgotten the ill-fated events of August 1 and 2, 1942, and in instances when she refuses to speak at all, which the transcript notes as "No response," Aguilar's strategic use of silence reveals that the absence of words "has its own contours, its own texture."[117] It compels us to rethink resistance and to recognize the many contradictory and hidden forms it may take. Her refusal to speak shows us that, like the creative wordplay of young Mexican American men, silence, too, can express opposition, especially when it comes from someone whose speech is overdetermined by the fact that she has already been spoken for and about.

Indeed, Aguilar's life has been marked by silence. She passed away in 1999 and, beyond her family and close friends, very little is known about her.[118] According to a friend who grew up with her, she was "very strong and defiant." As a girl, she "was a pachuca who hung around the neigh-borhood," and as an adult, she associated with the Brown Berets.[119] Yet, unlike the male defendants in *People v. Zammora*—in particular, Henry Leyvas—Aguilar's participation in the Sleepy Lagoon incident and subse-quent trial was not celebrated or valorized in *Zoot Suit*.

Zoot Suit

When *Zoot Suit*, a play about the Sleepy Lagoon incident and Zoot Suit Ri-ots, opens, the audience is told that it is about to see a "construct of fact and fantasy."[120] In writing the play, Valdez deftly drew directly from contem-porary Angeleno newspapers and *People v. Zammora*. He also based many of the characters on real men and women—for example, Hank Reyna, the protagonist, is based on defendant Henry Leyvas; Hank's sweetheart, Della Barrios, is based on Henry Leyvas's girlfriend Dora Baca; and the loud, foul-mouthed pachuca Bertha Villarreal is in all likelihood based on Bertha Aguilar.

Bertha Villarreal is by no means a major character in *Zoot Suit*. However, she plays an important role, especially in relation to Della. Bertha first appears in scene 7, "The Saturday Night Dance," where she encounters her ex-boyfriend Hank dancing with Della. After Hank rejects her advances, she dismisses Della as his "new huisa [broad]" and "little fly chick." Hank then tells his ex-girlfriend to "beat it," to which she retorts, "Beat it yourself. Mira [Look]. You got no hold on me, cabrón [stupid]. Not anymore. I'm free as a bird."[121] In addition to using pachuco slang, incorrect grammar, and profanity, Bertha revels in violence. Anticipating bloodshed, she excitedly exclaims "ALL-RIGHT!" when a fight breaks out between Hank's younger brother and the leader of the rival Downey gang. As the Downey gang retreats, she shouts at them, "¡Chinga tu madre! [Fuck your mother!]" and insists that she "could have beat the shit out of those two rucas [chicks]."[122]

Although Valdez describes her as "cool and tough," Bertha is actually quite loud and animated.[123] As Rosa-Linda Fregoso observes, she shows lust, exhilaration, and anger and is ridiculed "as exaggerated and hypersexed."[124] In contrast, the character of El Pachuco, Hank's alter ego, always plays it cool. When Hank begins to worry about the fact that he is the prime suspect in the Sleepy Lagoon murder case, El Pachuco demands that he "hang tough" and "stop going soft."[125] Indeed, El Pachuco keeps cool even as he is stripped to a "small loincloth" and is beaten by a group of white servicemen during the Zoot Suit Riots. In Valdez's words, he exits this scene "slowly . . . with powerful calm."[126]

As a number of feminist scholars, including Fregoso, have shown, the female, Mexican American characters in *Zoot Suit* fall into two categories: "the virgin or the whore, the long-suffering mother or the 'cheap broad.'"[127] Della, Hank's loyal girlfriend, is the virgin; in the film, she is described as "very pretty," "very young," and "innocent."[128] Although her strict father does not approve of her relationship with Hank, she promises to marry the latter upon his return from the war. When her sweetheart ends up in jail rather than in the Navy and she is sent to the Ventura School for Girls, he is her "only hope."[129] All the while, Hank two-times her, even though he concedes that Della "did a year in Ventura" and "stood up for me when it counted."[130] Furthermore, unlike Bertha, Della mostly speaks grammatically correct English and does not wear a zoot suit. (Interestingly, only at the end of the play, after she has been released from the Ventura School, does she curse or insert some pachuco slang into her sentences.) In sum, she is not a pachuca. As Hank's mother observes, she does not look "like a puta . . . I mean, a pachuca."[131]

Bertha Villarreal, on the other hand, is both pachuca and puta. In the film, Della wears saddle shoes and modest dresses, including a jumper reminiscent of a Catholic school uniform; Bertha, meanwhile, shows leg and cleavage. Moreover, Hank's father describes her as "the one with the tattoo," a sign that she is a real or "hardcore" pachuca and quite possibly a gang member.[132] Yet even though she is Della's antithesis, the two young women have one thing in common: both are uncool. Bertha acts the fool at the Saturday night dance; Della loses her cool in the courtroom when she is forced to testify against Hank. During examination, she, like the real women forced to testify in *People v. Zammora*, shows defiance and refuses to answer some questions. Ultimately, however, she cracks under pressure; she fails to hang tough and goes soft.

Although *Zoot Suit* earned much critical praise, it was not well received by some of the real-life men and women who took part in and were affected by the Sleepy Lagoon incident and trial. As defense attorney George Shibley (portrayed by the character George Shearer) complained, the play "perpetuate[d] some seriously damaging distortions of the Sleepy Lagoon murder case."[133] In 1979, one year after *Zoot Suit* opened in Los Angeles, several of the former defendants filed a $2.5 million lawsuit against Valdez, charging "invasion of privacy and intentional and negligent infliction of emotional distress." "That event ruined my life," Gus Zamora (of *People v. Zammora*) lamented.[134] Decades later, he claimed that he was still haunted by the Sleepy Lagoon incident and its aftermath and insisted that the play had opened up old wounds.

One reason why it has been difficult for me to acquire information about Aguilar's life from her close friends and family (and why I do not identify those interviewees who did talk to me) is because some were "shocked" and "insulted" by her portrayal as Bertha Villarreal in *Zoot Suit* and are loath to talk to an academic writing about this play.[135] Whereas the Sleepy Lagoon trial transcript shows us that Bertha Aguilar was courageous, self-possessed, clever, and articulate, *Zoot Suit* reduces her to a boisterous buffoon and "cheap broad" via the character of Bertha Villarreal. Sadly, the play makes this extraordinary young woman intelligible by transforming her into a whore.

Because it posits Mexican American women as either virgins or whores, *Zoot Suit* restricts and even bars their agency. As Judith Butler has pointed out, agency and agents are not recognized as such when they fail to adhere to preconceived notions of agency and agent. She asks, "What kinds of agency are foreclosed through the positing of an epistemological subject precisely because the rules and practices that govern the invocation of that subject and regulated its agency in advance are ruled out as sites of analysis and critical intervention?"[136] In Valdez's play, men are complex and vibrant agents and heroes. They function as sites of analysis and offer critical interventions. Women, in contrast, are uninteresting stereotypes. Like much of the early, alarmist scholarship on women speakers of pachuco slang, *Zoot Suit* fails to appreciate Chicanas' complex relationship to coolness and hipness and misrecognizes the ways in which they have expressed resistance via both language and silence. Ultimately, it renders their artful and oppositional use and rejection of words a condemnation and mockery.

Conclusion: Taming a Wild Tongue

In chapter 5 of *Borderlands/La Frontera*, "How to Tame a Wild Tongue," Gloria Anzaldúa confronts the "linguistic terrorism" that Chicanos and Chicanas have endured.[137] In addition to being robbed of Spanish and being told that we do not speak it or English well enough, Chicanas in particular have had to overcome a "tradition of silence."[138] Anzaldúa enumerates some of the labels applied to women who talk too much or too loudly: *hocicona* (big mouth), *repelona* (whiner), *chismosa* (gossip). "In my culture they are all words that are derogatory if applied to women," she observes, adding, "I've never heard them applied to men."[139]

Bertha Aguilar's working-class and pocha tongue was tamed twice: first, by the state, which found her threatening enough to incarcerate her at the Ventura School for Girls; then by *Zoot Suit*, which transforms her into a recognizable, downright trite subject: the hocicona Bertha Villarreal. As Lakoff points out, the "young girl" who refuses to speak women's language "is exceedingly brave—in fact, reckless," for there are consequences for not "talk[ing] like a lady."[140] At the same time, she reminds us, those women who do speak women's language also pay a high price: they/we are deemed stupid, frivolous, and, I would add, easily manipulated ("pushovers"). In short, "a woman is damned if she does and damned if she doesn't."[141] Yet if Lakoff's universal female subject (the white, middle-class, American woman) faces a double-bind, then Chicanas face a triple one. Those who "keep it real" by speaking pachuco slang—who remain faithful to an oppositional cultural identity—betray gender norms. And those who adhere to normative definitions of female and feminine decency by speaking Lakoff's women's language betray the Chicano culture of oppositionality and are whitewashed. In either case, they/we are branded traitors.

Undeniably, *Zoot Suit*, which is still performed and screened across the United States, has proven itself an effective tool for generating discussion on the Sleepy Lagoon trial, Zoot Suit Riots, and Mexican American zoot subculture of the World War II period.[142] In my research, I have also found it to be valuable in my interviews with Mexican American women who came of age in Los Angeles during the 1930s and 1940s. Initially, many of these women were reluctant to talk to me about the zoot subculture of their youth and vehemently denied that they were or even knew pachucas (for reasons that I hope this book makes apparent). However, when our conversations turned to *Zoot Suit*, which nearly all of my interviewees had seen, some waxed nostalgic about wearing "drapes" and "ratting" their hair as teenagers. One even reminisced in pachuco slang. I find it sadly ironic that a brilliant cultural product exposing the capacity of art to shape historical perspective and the promises and pitfalls of oral history also warps the words of and, ultimately, silences its primary pachuca character.

While *Zoot Suit* continues to receive much well-deserved attention, it does not have the final say when it comes to Chicana speakers of pachuco slang. Literary works by a handful of Chicana feminist writers offer more complex and nuanced portrayals of women speakers of pachuco slang, including pachucas.[143] Within the multidisciplinary field of Chicano studies, these texts merit additional scrutiny, for they add to our conversations on pachuquismo and can assist us in recognizing and understanding the multiple, often contradictory languages of resistance.

Chapter 4

LA PACHUCA AND THE EXCESSES

OF FAMILY AND NATION

By the late 1960s, *el pachuco* had emerged as an icon of resistance in much Chicano cultural production. Prior to the
Chicano movement, this figure did not play an especially prominent role in literature, theater, scholarship, art, music, or film by
Mexican Americans. When *el pachuco* did appear, he tended to be
treated with disdain or pity. For example, in Mario Suárez's short
story "Kid Zopilote," which I discuss in the previous chapter, the
pachuco is a fool. And the pachucos who make a brief appearance
in José Antonio Villareal's novel *Pocho* (1959) are victims. They are
"defeated" and make a mere "show of resistance."[1] In contrast, ten
years after the publication of *Pocho, el pachuco* would be anointed
as a "resistance fighter" and "Minuteman of *machismo*."[2] In 1970,
the *Los Angeles Times* columnist Rubén Salazar called him a "rebel"
and "folk hero."[3] And, on the eve of the 1978 premiere of *Zoot Suit*,
Luis Valdez credited *el pachuco* with giving "impetus to the Chicano
Movement of the 1960s."[4]

Taken together, these works serve as a rich repository of *el pachuco*'s iconography and shifting significance. They expose a generational rift between pre-movement and movement-era writers and
artists and the ways cultural production creates, nurtures, sustains,
and transforms collective memory over time. Differences notwithstanding, *el pachuco* is an outsider in the works, pre-movement and
movement-era alike, mentioned above. In Suárez's and Villarreal's
texts, he lurks at the fringe of Mexican America and is a source of
embarrassment or an object of pity. And as Valdez and many of his
contemporaries centered *el pachuco* in narratives of Chicano history
and cultural identity, they still located him at the margins of the
United States and rendered him an emblem of anti-Americanness
or an alternative Americanness.

For instance, the original subtitle of *Zoot Suit*, "A New American Play," positions *el pachuco* and pachuquismo as distinctly American or, at the very least, as products of the United States.[5] At the same time, Valdez's play complicates Mexican Americans' relationship to Americanness as it accentuates pachucos' marginality during World War II via its account of wartime racism and xenophobia. All too eager to report to the U.S. Navy, Hank, the protagonist, is reminded by his alter ego El Pachuco, "This ain't your country. Look what's happening all around you. The Japs have sewed up the Pacific. Rommell is kicking ass in Egypt but the Mayor of L.A. has declared all out war on Chicanos. On You!"[6] Even though *el pachuco's* multiple positions—American, non-American, and anti-American—may appear incompatible, all articulate and are articulated via nationalism, for this figure has been recuperated as not only a sign of Americanness but an icon of Chicano cultural nationalism as well.

This chapter studies the figures of the pachuco and pachuca against the backdrop of Chicano cultural nationalism, an intellectual, political, and social program which holds that, due to histories of imperialism, racism, and segregation, people of Mexican descent in the United States have separate experiences, values, and traditions from the white, Anglophone majority and thereby constitute a nation in and of ourselves. To paraphrase Valdez's Pachuco, it maintains that "this ain't our country" and often emphasizes the need for cultural, political, and economic independence from a capitalist, Eurocentric, and imperialist United States. Cultural nationalism was a defining feature of the Chicano movement of the 1960s, 1970s, and early 1980s and continues to resonate in much Chicano cultural production today.

In this chapter, I examine representations of *la pachuca* and *el pachuco* in a variety of movement-era works, including poetry, visual art, and theater. I am animated by a number of questions, such as, What did the figures of the pachuco and pachuca signify at this particular moment in Mexican American history? How and why were their meanings similar or different? And why was the figure of the pachuco so prevalent in Chicano cultural production, where that of the pachuca has remained relatively invisible? Of particular concern is the cultural nationalist configuration of Chicano community as *la familia de la raza*. I argue that while *el pachuco* could be and was incorporated into cultural nationalist ideology as a father, son, or brother, *la pachuca* was excluded because of the ways she articulated a dissident femininity, female masculinity, and, in some instances, lesbian sexuality, consequently threatening the heteropatriarchal family. To illustrate la pachuca's distortion and defiance of heteronormative gender, I turn to several feminist movement-era literary and artistic texts in which she plays a prominent role. Paying close attention to the butch lesbian pachuca in particular, I highlight the ways this figure has challenged national identities and forged new, alternative communities. In doing so, I expose the ways in which la pachuca, especially the queer pachuca, disrupts and exceeds narrow definitions of the family, the nation, and the nation as family.

Inspired by a number of scholars in feminist and queer studies, I approach the family as a "locus of struggle"—that is, as a contested site of inclusion and exclusion and unequal power relations.[7] Even though I focus in great part on the heteronormative Mexican American/Chicano family, I define "family" broadly and do not limit my discussion to this particular configuration exclusively. Similarly, while much of my analysis revolves around and relies upon nationalisms (statist and insurgent alike), I also point to the ways in which a handful of feminist works—in particular, by Inés Hernández, Judith Baca, and Cherríe Moraga—have revised Mexican American history, redefined la familia de la raza, and imagined extra-, trans-, or postnationalist group identities via the figure of the pachuca. Like many other movement-era cultural artifacts, including Zoot Suit, these works "speak . . . back to power, subvert . . . its authority, and invert . . . its icons."[8] By doing so, they show the power of cultural production to envision and to articulate new communities and new subjects.

The Family of Man

During the Chicano movement, el pachuco's history was rewritten. While Octavio Paz had derided him as a bastard, Chicano cultural workers transformed him into a (or the) father or son of la Causa. For example, the anthropologist Octavio Romano-V. located el pachuco at the end of a heroic continuum that included the celebrated nineteenth-century Californio bandit Joaquín Murrieta and the Mexican revolutionary Pancho Villa.[9] Meanwhile, others pointed to him as "the true vanguard . . . of the present Chicano social revolution" and "the first Chicano freedom-fighter . . . of the Chicano movement."[10] Poets lauded el pachuco as a "precursor" of the contemporary social struggle who "was / there when they weren't allowed to eat in restaurants" and in "the time of the 'zoot suits.'"[11] Similarly, Valdez identified pachuquismo as "a direct antecedent of what has come to

28. A young César Chávez (third on right) sporting a zoot suit, 1941.
Lowrider magazine, copyright 1978–79. REPRINTED BY PERMISSION OF
MCMULLEN ARGUS PUBLISHING, INC., COPYRIGHT 1978, 1979, 2007.

be termed 'Chicano consciousness.'"[12] The playwright and director paid
homage to two pachucos in particular: his cousin Billy Miranda and his
cousin's good friend, a young man by the name of César Chávez. He remembered Miranda and Chávez as "tall," "proud," and "confident teenagers" and attributed his interest in Chicano history and sense of cultural
pride to the former.[13] Valdez even claimed to have learned the word "Chicano" from his late cousin, to whom he dedicated *Zoot Suit*.[14] Likewise,
Chávez has been credited with sparking the Chicano movement on May
3, 1965, with the National Farm Workers Association strike in McFarland,
California.[15]

As culmination and germinator of the Chicano movement, *el pachuco*
is heir to a tradition of resistance (extending back to Joaquín Murrieta and
Pancho Villa at least) and a, if not *the,* origin of this legacy. In either case,

he is part of an androcentric genealogy, one node in a network of *carnales* or brothers. A key tenet of Chicano cultural nationalism, *carnalismo* (brotherhood) has been linked to male gangs and pachucos, whom Valdez has described as "intensely loyal to each other."[16] In recasting *el pachuco* as a role model, movement-era writers and artists also redeemed the male youth gang as a model for group identity. As Rosa-Linda Fregoso observes, "The transgressive nature of Chicanos as 'gang members,' formally articulated as a pathological masculinity in dominant discourse, [was] rearticulated into the positive masculine attributes of brotherhood and Chicanismo."[17] This valorization of brotherhood permeated some of the more significant movement-era texts, such as the 1969 *Plan Espiritual de Aztlán* and *Zoot Suit*.[18]

For various cultural nationalists, the family—in particular the hetero-patriarchal family—served as an appropriate, if not ideal, model for Chicano group identity. As the cultural critic Richard T. Rodríguez has noted, images of *la familia* abounded in Chicano print and visual media, from mimeographed booklets to murals, throughout the 1970s.[19] Meanwhile, activists and scholars collapsed the community qua nation with the family. For example, in "Chicano Nationalism: The Key to Unity for La Raza," a speech originally delivered at California State University, Hayward, in 1969, Rodolfo "Corky" Gonzáles, the founder of Denver's Crusade for Justice, asserted that nationalism simultaneously constituted and emerged from the family unit: "Nationalism becomes *la familia*. Nationalism comes first out of the family."[20] Similarly, the sociologist Maxine Baca Zinn identified the concept of *la familia de la raza,* along with that of carnalismo, as "a guiding principle of the Chicano movement" in her influential essay "Political Familism: Sex-Role Equality in Chicano Families." In an effort to refute "common portrayals of our families as deviant, deficient, and the chief cause of Mexican subordination in the United States," she extolled the "Chicano kinship system . . . as a source of trust, refuge, and protection in a society that systematically exploits and oppresses Mexicans."[21] At the same time, she maintained that it also functioned as a site of patriarchal oppression.

Zinn was not alone in critically assessing the patriarchal Chicano family during the 1970s. Many of her contemporaries, such as Marta Cotera, Ana Nieto Gómez, and Barbara Carrasco (to name just a few), echoed her concerns.[22] For example, Carrasco's lithograph *Pregnant Woman in a Ball*

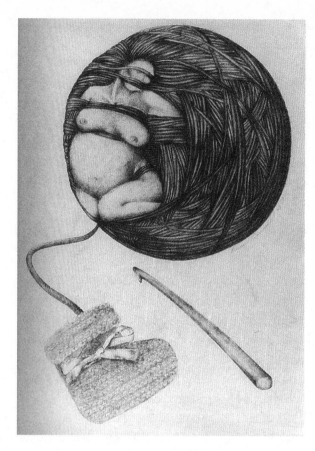

29. Barbara Carrasco, *Pregnant Woman in a Ball of Yarn.* Lithograph, 14 x 11 inches. COPYRIGHT 1978, BARBARA CARRASCO.

of Yarn (1978) offers a powerful critique of motherhood (and tempers the romantic portrayals of maternity offered by the cult of the Virgin of Guadalupe in particular). In the 1980s, feminist critics such as Cherríe Moraga, Gloria Anzaldúa, and Norma Alarcón confronted both the misogyny and homophobia of the heteropatriarchal Chicano family.[23] Feminist scholars continue to problematize the configuration of Chicano community as a fraternity or patriarchal, heteronormative family. As the historian Cynthia Orozco has pointed out, Chicano "family ideology" has limited women's roles by conceptualizing " 'Woman' . . . as a married adult with children."[24] This narrow conceptualization is apparent in a plethora of movement-era texts, such as Rodolfo Gonzáles's celebrated epic poem *I Am Joaquin/Yo Soy Joaquín* and Armando B. Rendón's didactic *Chicano Manifesto.*[25] In both of these works, Mexican women and Chicanas appear overwhelmingly as venerable suffering mothers and loyal wives. In effect, Chicano "family ideology" has ignored Chicanas who are not (or not exclusively) wives or mothers—"teenagers, single women, women without children, lesbians, and the elderly."[26] To this list we may also add pachucas.

Rebel with La Causa

Admittedly, el pachuco has not always been included in the ideal or normative (nuclear) Mexican American family. During the zoot panic of the early 1940s, pachucos and their gangs appeared to threaten its stability and integrity. In the midst of the Zoot Suit Riots, Los Angeles newspapers published a photograph of one Mrs. Vera Duarte Trujillo tearing apart her son's zoot suit trousers after the fifteen-year-old was "shot in a gang roundup." The "irate mother" and her husband, the boy's stepfather, "deplored his association with . . . older zoot suiters" and insisted that they tried to keep him at home, "but he kept slipping away."[27] In other words, they failed to compete with the parenting he received from the older zooters. However, the Trujillos were far from exceptional, according to the Los Angeles Times. On the eve of the outbreak of the riots, the paper reported that immigrant parents were unable to control their wild American-born children and consequently were responsible for a host of social ills, including juvenile delinquency (especially among girls), out-of-wedlock pregnancies and births, and the rising rate of sexually transmitted diseases.[28]

Likewise, el pachuco's heir or "latter day prototype"—the vato loco—was not always or easily absorbed into la familia de la raza during the Chicano movement.[29] His vexed relationship to and in the Chicano collective is evident in a Brown Beret recruitment advertisement that appeared in the newspaper La Causa in the 1960s and 1970s. As the historian Ernesto Chávez notes, this appeal "primarily targeted . . . gang members, the so-called 'vatos locos.'" An illustration depicted a potential recruit wearing cholo garb, slouching, and carrying a bottle of beer underneath a banner proclaiming "Bato Loco Yesterday." That picture was followed by another showing the same man in a Beret uniform, with his back erect, his right arm outstretched, and his fist clenched in the power symbol. A banner above proclaimed "Revolutionist Today, Be Brown, Be Proud, Join the Brown Berets."[30] Although this before-and-after illustration rejects the vato loco, it also hails him. Drunk and disheveled, he is recognized as a potential revolutionary, a sort of diamond-in-the-rough, prodigal son, or, to draw from the title of an old corrido, "hijo desobediente."

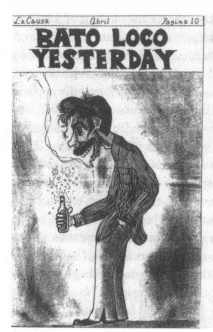

30. From *bato loco* to Brown Beret—the cholo becomes a revolutionary, as depicted in the Brown Beret newsletter *La Causa*.

"El Hijo Desobediente" (The Disobedient Son), which dates back to around 1910, has been translated from Spanish into pachuco slang and recounts a fight between two pachucos, one of whom defies his father and thereby appears doomed to a violent and early death.[31] In an effort to stop the fight between the two pachucos, the father orders his son to back off, but the son drives him away and threatens to stab him. In response, the father warns, "For that which you have just said / Your life will be gone / Before the sun sets."[32] Bad to the bitter end, the son then gives his father instructions for his own (the son's) burial, confirming the high price of filial disobedience. Yet despite his recalcitrance, the pachuco is a son nonetheless, as the ballad's title makes clear; he is simply an especially wayward one. Even in his unruliness, he is still admirable, for defiance of authority (including breaking the law) was reinterpreted by some as a "revolutionary act" during the heady days of the movement.[33] Along with the *pinto* (ex-convict) and Aztec warrior, the pachuco of the past and cholo of the present could be and were an integral, even revered, part of the Chicano imaginary, whether they were disobedient sons or proud, disciplined revolutionaries.[34]

Like her male counterpart, *la pachuca* was deemed a threat to the patriarchal family beginning in the early 1940s. Yet during the movement there was a place in the Chicano nation for (male) rebels and warriors. Chicanas were expected to participate in the so-called revolution by maintaining the status quo and extant intraracial gender relations rather than altering or overturning them. As the sociologist Alfredo Mirandé asserted in his essay "The Chicano Family" (1977), Chicanas constituted "the mainstay of the culture and its traditions." As such, they could "counter the encroachment of colonialism" by "perpetuat[ing] the language and values of Chicanos."[35] More so than their fathers, brothers, or sons, Chicanas, especially mothers, have long been regarded as the keepers of "the cultural homefires."[36] We have been charged with preserving and imparting to future generations cultural customs and values, from making tortillas by hand to practicing Catholicism and speaking Spanish. In her rich social history of Mexican American women in Los Angeles during World War II, Elizabeth Escobedo illustrates the ways in which wartime concerns regarding women's changing social roles (particularly greater participation in public life) and a marked demographic shift within the Mexican American population (in which those born in the United States outnumbered immigrants from Mexico) intersected in the figure of the second-generation pachuca. As pachuca daughters—many of whom had been branded pochas—"caked on makeup, teased their hair, and hiked [up their] skirts . . . for a night of jitterbugging in a downtown ballroom"—well beyond the relatively insular "Mexican colony" and the watchful eyes of their parents and *compadres* (extended kin)—some immigrant parents feared "an end to Mexican customs and traditions" and bemoaned what they saw as "the flagging authority of the Mexican family to police sexuality and retain ethnic culture."[37]

Meanwhile, the pachuca wife/mother was maligned and mocked in the mainstream Angeleno press during the Zoot Suit Riots. When twenty-two-year-old Amelia Venegas was arrested by sheriff's deputies at an East Los Angeles street corner on June 10, 1943, for disturbing the peace, her infant child was taken to jail with her, then passed along to a relative. In addition to appearing to be an incompetent mother, Venegas was portrayed as an unfaithful wife because she allegedly sympathized and attempted to collaborate with, in the words of one reporter, "the reat pleat boys [who] . . . attacked many sailors," even though her husband was himself a Navy enlistee. When asked about her spouse, she responded that he was "very far away."[38] In the absence of patriarchal authority, it seemed that chaos reigned and the nuclear family fell apart as pachuca mothers (and their babies) took to the streets.

With few exceptions, pachucas are not seen as daughters, mothers, wives, or sisters.[39] Instead, within much Chicano cultural production, they are often depicted as sex objects, especially in visual culture (for example, on cars and in tattoos).[40] Although *Zoot Suit* portrays *la pachuca* as sister and daughter (via the character of Lupe Reyna, Hank's younger sister), it still sexualizes her. Indeed, Lupe is acutely aware of her status as sex object. Dressed in a short skirt and finger-tip coat, she tries to sneak past her parents, Dolores and Enrique, as she heads to the Saturday night dance (in the film, she exits the house by crawling out a bedroom window). When Dolores spies her outside, she cries out, "¡Válgame Dios! Guadalupe, are you crazy? Why bother to wear anything?" Similarly, Enrique exclaims, "¡Ay, jijo! Where's the skirt?!" After invoking La Malinche, the most notorious whore in Mexican history, he orders Lupe to change her clothes and tells her, "I will not have my daughter looking like a. . . ." Interrupting her husband, Dolores adds, "Like a puta . . . I mean, a pachuca," conflating the whore with *la pachuca*.[41]

As a daughter and sister, Lupe is not permitted to be a pachuca and, by extension, a *puta* (whore). Fregoso argues that *la pachuca* has not been included in the patriarchal family—except, I would add, as the daughter's, sister's, or mother's constitutive other: the whore—because she "failed to do what the Chicano family demands of girls and women." That is, pachucas "rejected and challenged parental norms by refusing to stay inside the home. Their provocative language and dress style served to further refute la familia's authority." As I point out in previous chapters, not all pachucas were disobedient and disrespectful daughters, even though they wore short skirts and "rats" in their hair. Still, as Fregoso maintains, *la pachuca* as signifier marks "the limits of la familia" and "introduces disorder into its essentially patriarchal project."[42] This is evident in the commotion Lupe causes in *Zoot Suit*. When her parents demand that she change her clothes, she turns to Hank, who wears a zoot suit of his own, for support. Yet her older brother orders her to "do what they say." Lupe then points out that they grant him the freedom to "wear his drapes," and their father responds, "That's different. He's a man. Es hombre."[43] As this exchange reveals, there is still a place (and a comfortable one at that) for the pachuco within the Reyna household. As a man (and the oldest son to boot), Hank benefits from and so attempts to preserve the hierarchy of the heteropatriarchal family. His sister the pachuca, on the other hand, exceeds its limits. In the film, she literally occupies the space outside the family's house as she hides from her parents on the front porch while Hank and his father converse man-to-man over tequila at the kitchen table.[44]

As *Zoot Suit* illustrates, the figure of the pachuco often articulated and complemented the values and goals of Chicano cultural nationalism. In particular, it functioned as an icon of resistance against middle-class and white American norms and values (as represented by El Pachuco), as an emblem of *carnalismo* and *familia* and, by extension, as a symbol of homosocial community and heteropatriarchy (as represented by Hank Reyna). Hence this figure could be found in much movement-era cultural production. Yet what happened when *el pachuco*'s "masculine strengths," such as coolness, defiance, and sexual prowess, were articulated by, through, and with *la pachuca*?[45] Because she threatened *la familia de la raza* and the traditional gender roles that it has reproduced and upon which it has been predicated, this figure was conspicuously absent in much movement-era cultural production. As Fregoso observes, "Perhaps, the production of *pachuca-chola*-homegirl urban identities has not been celebrated by many of us precisely because her body defies, provokes, and challenges the traditional basis of our representation and formulation of the Chicano nation."[46] Yet some feminist cultural workers have not ignored *la pachuca*, her body, or her voice. Some have reinserted her into a Chicana imaginary and, by doing so, they have problematized and redefined this community and its subjects. Let us now turn to a variety of works—poetry, visual art, and drama—in which pachucas play more than a secondary role.

La Pachuca in Chicana Literature and Art, 1975–86

The texts I discuss at length in this section are by no means the only ones by Chicana feminists to focus on pachucas. I emphasize them in particular because of the relatively close period in which they were produced, an eleven-year span that I identify as part of the Chicano movement; because of what I see as their thematic commonalities; and because of the relatively limited attention they have received from other scholars. Other works that showcase or invoke *la pachuca* include Carmen Lomas Garza's gouache *Las Pachucas, Razor Blade 'do* (1989), which I discuss in the epilogue; Mary

Helen Ponce's novel *The Wedding* (1989); and Laura del Fuego's novel *Maravilla* (also published in 1989). While many of the poems in Evangelina Vigil's wonderful collection *Thirty an' Seen a Lot* (1982) and Olivia Castellano's poem "Estos Vatos with Their Intellectual Conversations" (1984) do not explicitly feature pachucas, they are written from a feminist perspective in pachuco slang.[47]

Each of these works is unique, but all problematize gender norms (some more obviously than others). As they position *la pachuca* as both feminine and masculine, they simultaneously reify and destabilize binary gender systems. For example, in *The Wedding*, Lucy Matacochis, a petite pachuca who diligently paints her fingernails "bright purple or hot magenta" every other day, earns a living by toiling in the hot, muddy agricultural fields of the San Fernando Valley in the 1950s. She "enjoy[s] nothing more than a good fight" and "intimidate[s] everyone, including her mother." Hence the pachucos of her community complain that, despite her feminine appearance, she "acts too tough fer a dame."[48]

Pachuca Poetry

Poetry played a prominent role during the Chicano movement, with poets such as Alurista, José Montoya, and raúlsalinas sharing their poems at conferences, festivals, marches, and rallies. Pachuco poetry—poems about pachuquismo usually written by pachucos or former pachucos—constituted an important part of movement-era cultural production.[49] Because of their content and form, I contend that Carmen Tafolla's "Los Corts (5 Voices)" and "and when I dream dreams," Inés Hernández's "Para Teresa," and Cherríe Moraga's "Later, She Met Joyce" constitute movement-era pachuca poetry.

Written originally between 1975 and 1979, "Los Corts (5 Voices)," "and when I dream dreams," and "Para Teresa" are probably three of the earliest Chicana literary works to feature the figure of the pachuca.[50] "Los Corts (5 Voices)" is divided into five sections, each representing the voice of a particular speaker: *la madre* (the mother), *el chamaquito* (the little boy), *la pachuquita* (the little pachuca), the dropout, and *la viejita* (the old woman). In a combination of Spanish, English, and pachuco slang, *la pachuquita*, who calls herself "La Dot," dismisses her classmate la Silvia as a "pinche puta" (damn whore) because Silvia has dared to encroach upon el Larry, "el más good-looking de to'a la class [the best looking boy in all the class]" and the object of Dot's affections. Dot vows to defend herself "con la navaja [with the knife]" against Silvia, who, word has it, has threatened to jump her at school. "You bet muchacha [girl]!" *la pachuquita* boldly exclaims, "Aquí 'toy—lista! [I'm here and ready]."[51]

Where *la pachuquita*'s nemesis is a fellow classmate in "Los Corts (5 Voices)," "and when I dream dreams" locates the pachuca against and in opposition to a white supremacist and punitive United States. This poem, written from the perspective of a highly educated Chicana and former pachuca reflecting on her youth, indicts the narrator's junior high school for criminalizing Mexican American students for speaking Spanish and crafting their own distinctive style and dissident femininity. "So we wandered the halls / cool chuca style [. . .] / never knowing we were (s'posed to be) / the toughest junior high in town," the narrator recalls.[52]

Like Tafolla's poems, Inés Hernández's "Para Teresa" is set at a school and it, too, is about a conflict between girls. Yet unlike "Los Corts (5 Voices)" and "and when I dream dreams," this autobiographical poem is not written from the point of view of a pachuca.[53] Rather, its narrator recounts an unpleasant run-in with a tough pachuca by the name of Teresa in the 1950s. Teresa "grew up fighting" and played a "game of deadly defiance / Arrogance, refusal to submit."[54] By the sixth grade, she flaunted her sexuality with her "dyed-black-but / reddening hair," "full petticoats, red lipstick / And sweaters with the sleeves / pushed up."[55] The narrator, in comparison, was an honor student and obedient daughter who was "Certainly never allowed to dye, to / tease, to paint myself."[56] When, during lunch hour, Teresa and her gang corner her in the girls' restroom and accuse her of being a teacher's pet, the narrator insists that she does "nothing for the teachers."[57] Instead, she studies hard and earns high grades for her "shy mother," "carpenter-father," and "grandparents / Who cut out honor roll lists / Whenever their nietos' [grandchildren's] names appeared," as well as for herself.[58]

Like many other movement-era works, "Para Teresa" links the narrator's individual struggle to that of the collective: to her family (as represented by her parents and grandparents) and to *la familia de la raza* (Chicanas and Chicanos in general). Where the original version of the poem, first published in 1978, ends with the bathroom confrontation, a later and longer version published in 1993 jumps from the 1950s to 1975. The narrator is now twenty-eight years old; looking back on her altercation with Teresa, she realizes that, despite their differences, they had much in common as girls, for both practiced defiance. Collapsing the first-person singular with the first-person plural and drawing a clear line between "we" and "them," the narrator explains, "My contest was to prove / beyond any doubt / that we were not only equal / but superior to them. / That was why I studied. / If I could do it, we all could."[59] She situates herself within a history of racism and U.S. imperialism that oppresses all Chicanos and Chicanas (including Teresa and her homies) and claims to have acted on behalf of "my dear raza" when she showed the teachers at "Alamo which-had-to-be-its-name / Elementary" that "we were not inferior / You and I / Y las demás de tus amigas / Y los demás de nuestra gente [And the rest of your friends / And the rest of our people]."[60] Ultimately, the pachucas release the narrator and the two parties go their separate ways, yet the narrator adds, "Pero fuimos juntas [But we went together]." Although she admits that she did not understand Teresa or "accept [her] way of anger," the narrator recognizes and appreciates her foe's oppositional practices and aligns herself with her from the vantage point of the Chicano movement.[61] In the poem's concluding lines, she tells Teresa, "Te comprendo / Es más / Te respeto [I understand you / Moreover / I respect you]." Finally, she inserts *la pachuca* into *una familia de la raza* by asking Teresa, for whom she has written the poem and to whom she has dedicated it, if she may call her "hermana" (sister).[62]

Las Tres Marías

By enacting a family of hermanas, a homosocial community born in the hyperfemale and hyperfeminine space of a girls' restroom, "Para Teresa" "appropriate[s] the Chicano movement's then-official equation of the family with the nation as a basis for organized cultural resistance."[63] Similarly, via an object that invokes the highly female and feminine space of the *costurería* (seamstress's shop), Judith Baca's *Las Tres Marías* (see this book's preface) offers what the cultural critic Alicia Gaspar de Alba calls a "generational continuum" of homegirls, beginning with the pachuca of the 1950s and culminating with the chola of the 1970s. This multimedia triptych, created in 1976, consists of three 68-inch x 16-inch panels mounted on a platform: the proper left panel features a pachuca; the proper right panel, a contemporary chola; and the center panel is a mirror.[64] If this work imagines a genealogy of Chicanas, then the pachuca and chola may represent not only sisters but mother and daughter respectively. However, unlike *la familia de la raza*, which is often conceived of in racial or biological terms (*raza* literally means "race" or "breed"), the family that *Las Tres Marías* envisions is far from biological, natural, or essential. Instead, it mutates constantly, for the person standing before its mirror changes. I may stand before it, then walk away and be replaced by you or another viewer. And if I stand before the mirror again, I am not the same person who stood before it previously, for I have changed (even if only by the experience of having already stood before this work of art).

In her insightful reading of *Las Tres Marías*, Gaspar de Alba imagines the ways that an array of viewers, including a "mainstream" one, a pachuco, a cholo, a white lesbian, a "Chicana lesbian of the butch/femme school," a closeted lesbian, and a "staunch 'Hispanic,'" might identify or counter-identify with Baca's pachuca and chola.[65] Her list of possible viewers points to a multiplicity of interlocking identity categories or positions including race, gender, class, and sexuality, to the heterogeneity and instability of identity, to a spectatorship fraught with complexity and contradiction, and to the constitution or production of subjectivity via the gaze. Will a pachuco and cholo "find affinity and recognition in" the pachuca and chola (ostensibly on the basis of race or class), as Gaspar de Alba speculates, or will they counteridentify with them due to gender differences? Likewise, will a white lesbian "feel alienated" by the pachuca and chola because she is white and they are not, or will she align herself with them along the lines of gender?[66] Might these (and other) viewers *dis*identify with the pachuca and chola?[67] Like the Lacanian mirror stage, Baca's mirror may function as the outset of difference and alienation as it exposes lack or absence (for example, of similarity, identification, affinity, or community).[68] Depending on whether or not she/he identifies, counteridentifies, or disidentifies with the pachuca or chola, a viewer may see herself/himself as a bridge linking the two or as a gap or wedge that mars the smooth continuum they presumably present. As a locus for (dis)identification, Baca's mirror may invite a viewer into the text or bar her/him from it.

In contemplating the ways in which various viewers might identify or counteridentify with Baca's pachuca and chola, Gaspar de Alba reads *Las Tres Marías* as a butch-femme dyad. The pachuca, she argues, connotes "a more intentionally 'feminine' sexuality," while the chola "is an almost boylike figure."[69] With her teased hair, plucked eyebrows, long fingernails, and hourglass figure, the pachuca certainly appears more feminine than the chola, who, dressed entirely in black, wears a loose sweater, trousers, and loafers. However, given the pachuca's gender transgressions, she is not easily classified as feminine. As I discuss in detail in earlier chapters, pachucas warped or defied gender norms via their speech, behavior, and appearance. They rejected "women's language" by speaking pachuco slang or a working-class inflected form of American English. They participated in masculine activities when they associated with, formed, or joined gangs, committed crimes, or simply left the confines of their homes for work or leisure. And while the pachuca's appearance may be read as an example of exaggerated femininity, it also represents a distortion of white, middle-class, and Mexican-immigrant standards of feminine beauty. In other words, it underscores the pachuca's disidentificatory relationship to normative femininity. Her comb, teased hair, and long red fingernails may signify an innocuous and frivolous femininity, but they also allude to violence and hence to the ostensibly masculine. Gaspar de Alba compares the comb in the pachuca's right hand to the pachuco's *filero* (switchblade) and observes that there are "razor blades tucked into her curls."[70] Like pachucos, pachucas were reputed to have carried knives, switchblades, or razors, sometimes in their elaborate coiffures.[71] The pachuca's red nail polish in particular invokes the blood that long nails are capable of drawing. On top of it all, Baca's pachuca is full of attitude. Like Ramona Fonseca (whose photograph we studied in chapter 2), El Pachuco of *Zoot Suit*, and countless other homies, she leans back on her right leg, cocks her hip at a left angle, and holds her head high as she drags on a cigarette and slyly returns the viewer's gaze. Neither passive nor inert, she strikes a pose and, in doing so, encroaches upon the male and masculine realm of coolness.

Giving Up the Ghost

As they shaped their own dissident femininity or rejected feminine norms altogether, pachucas came to represent a female masculinity. As Judith Halberstam argues in *Female Masculinity*, masculinity does not belong to men exclusively. She points to the butch lesbian in particular to show that masculinity can and does exist without men, and she makes the case that when masculinity is removed from men, it is denaturalized and has the potential to "successfully challenge hegemonic models of gender conformity."[72] In her discussion of butch iconicity in film, she examines the character of the female Mexican gang member played by Mercedes Mc-Cambridge in Orson Welles's film *A Touch of Evil* (1958). Halberstam observes, "In her leather jacket and next to her femme girlfriend, Mercedes is more than convincing as a tough street butch."[73] Not coincidentally, this tough street butch is also coded pachuca.

As I show in chapter 2, dominant representations of the pachuca in the 1940s portrayed her as excessively or inadequately feminine (in other words, masculine). (It is from this latter repertoire of representations that Welles and McCambridge appeared to have drawn in creating the character of the tough street butch.) Cherríe Moraga's play *Giving Up the Ghost*, first performed in 1984 and published in 1986, also offers us a character who is a butch homegirl.[74] Yet whereas *A Touch of Evil* was made under the weight of the Hays Hollywood Production Code (consequently, McCambridge's pachuca's lesbianism must be inferred), Moraga wrote her first play at the confluence of the Chicano movement, second-wave feminism, and post-Stonewall lesbian and gay pride.[75] As the literary and theater critic Yvonne Yarbro-Bejarano observes, among self-described women of color feminists, "This was a time of considerable discussion concerning the exclusionary politics of the white women's movement" and "differences among women."[76]

Giving Up the Ghost stresses differences among women—between two Chicana lesbians in particular (Marisa and Amalia) and within a single (albeit split) character (as represented by Marisa and her former self Corky). The play does not offer a linear narrative. A variation of what Yarbro-Bejarano terms *teatropoesía*—that is, "a collage of poetry, prose, music, dance, and pantomine"[77]—it is divided into two acts, "La Pachuca" and "La Salvadora," and composed of monologues, many of which are written in free verse, by three characters: Marisa, "a Chicana in her late 20s"; Corky, Marisa's younger self, at eleven and seventeen years; and Amalia, Marisa's lover, a "Chicana in her late 40s, born in México."[78] Marisa and Amalia seem to be polar opposites, beginning with their appearance: Marisa sports jeans, tennis shoes, a dark shirt, and short hair. She is an urban Chicana, whom Amalia has nicknamed "La Pachuca," and she speaks a working-class inflected form of American English, as well as Spanglish. Amalia, in contrast, "is 'soft' in just the ways that Marisa is 'hard.' Her clothes give the impression of being draped, as opposed to worn. Shawl-over-blouse-over-skirt—all of Mexican Indian design. Her hair is long and worn down or loosely braided."[79] In addition to invoking the Indian, another important archetype in movement-era Chicano cultural production, she is associated with the rural—in particular, the desert. Moreover, she speaks standard (grammatically correct) English and Spanish. In short, Marisa is butch and Amalia is femme.

Like *Las Tres Marías*, *Giving Up the Ghost* uses the figure of the homegirl to explore a dissident femininity and female masculinity. Before she was "La Pachuca" and a butch lesbian, Marisa was Corky, a tomboy who "acts tough" and "dresses in the 'cholo style' of her period (the '60s): khakis with razor-sharp creases; pressed white undershirt; hair short and slicked back."[80] As an eleven-year-old, Corky "pack[s] a blade" and carries herself "bato-style."[81] In one instance, she "throws her chin out to" Marisa as a form of acknowledgment.[82] Indeed, the juxtaposition of Corky's "bato style" and Marisa's butchness puts into relief the structural similarity between a racialized cool and butch lesbian (female) masculinity.[83]

According to Yarbro-Bejarano, Corky identifies with "the masculine gender role" by assuming "the tough stance of the cholo" due to her "sense of the powerlessness of her sex [. . .] race, and culture . . . vis-à-vis the dominant culture."[84] Her "bato style" and incipient butchness converge in her self-perception as "big 'n' tough 'n' a dude." As a child, Corky believed that she enjoyed the same freedoms as her male counterparts, including "their freedom to really see a girl / kinda the way you see / an animal you know?" Her counteridentification with and objectification of girls and women is apparent in the predatory fantasies she concocted with her male friend Tudy. Inspired by a scene in a western movie, the two children pretended to be cowboys who captured "these chicks," bound them, and forced them to strip.[85] Later, she and Tudy recruited Chrissy, a three-year-old girl, as "the perfect victim / for our sick little fantasies." However, when it became clear to both girls that "somet'ing was wrong with what we was up to," Corky interrupted the staging, which had quickly devolved into an actual violation, and she and Tudy fled.[86]

The violent scenarios that Corky fabricated with Tudy foreshadow her own brutal induction into adolescence and womanhood. Her self-perception as a big, tough dude was shattered when she was raped at the age of twelve by a man posing as a custodian at her school. As a seventeen-year-old, she recounts this painful memory, prefacing her charged monologue with an admission: "Got raped once. / When I was a kid. / Taken me a long time to say that was exactly what happened." Underscoring her rejection of a female or feminine identity, she acknowledges that she had never worried about being raped, for she believed it happened to "other women and the people I loved."[87] Then she narrates what the historian Emma Pérez has termed "'the molestation memory,' or 'memory of origin,'" the moment "when girls recognize they do not have sociosexual power in relation to men."[88] Corky recalls the physical and psychic trauma she suffered as the rapist "hit me with it" and forced his penis into her vagina. "A hole!" she shouts. "HE MADE ME A HOLE!"[89] Here, the vagina, once a site of and source for autoerotic and lesbian pleasure for Corky, becomes both metonym and metaphor. The rape reduced this "tough cookie" who did not see herself as a girl or woman to a single body part: a hole. As such, this body part, a marker of biological femaleness, also represents a void and symbolizes the violent dissolution of her self-image and psyche. She describes herself and her vagina as "a face / with no opening / a face with no features."[90]

In many ways, *Giving Up the Ghost* is a butch coming-of-age story. Via Corky's and Marisa's monologues, which function much like flashbacks in a film, it recounts the former's evolution into the latter. But the play does not celebrate this transformation. Instead, it emphasizes the process, so often violent and traumatic, by which girls, including tomboys, are turned into women. As Halberstam reminds us, this process usually occurs during adolescence, a period of gender conformity. While adolescence for boys may "represent . . . a rite of passage (much celebrated in Western literature in the form of the bildungsroman), and an ascension to some version (however attenuated) of social power," for girls, especially masculine ones, it is "a lesson in restraint, punishment, and repression."[91] The violence of the process by which girls are transformed into compliant women is captured in Corky's monologue about the rape, which, she bitterly notes, "only convinced me of my own name. / From an early age you learn to live with it, / being a woman . . . / I only got a head start over some."[92]

Yarbro-Bejarano asserts that "Corky's experience of rape confirms for Marisa her culture's definition of female as 'taken' (*chingada*)," as pawnable and, therefore, always already disloyal.[93] In other words, for Corky/Marisa, being a woman means being vulnerable as well as injured. If trauma, as Sigmund Freud has contended, involves the "breach of the protective barrier" of the psyche, then Corky/Marisa struggles to repair and to reinforce herself by claiming masculinity and disavowing femininity (including the memory of the rape).[94] Rather than expose herself to further penetration as a susceptible *chingada* (fucked one), she endeavors to become an impervious *chingón* (fucker). In fact, she claims to admire men for their nearly impermeable genitalia: "I thought . . . how lucky they were / that they could release all that stuff, / all that pent-up shit from the day / through a hole / that nobody . . . could get into."[95]

Yet just as she is haunted by the ghosts of Corky and Amalia and by her own memories, Marisa is still haunted by that which she has repressed: her femaleness and femininity. While Corky's self-perception is violently undermined by the rape, Marisa's is shaken by her relationship with Amalia, an ostensibly heterosexual femme. But as Marisa points out, "Hay un hombre en esa mujer" (There is a man in that woman). Even in sex, she senses that Amalia dominates her: "I move on top of her, she wants this / and she is full of slips and lace and stockings / and yet it is *she* who's taking *me*." Indeed, throwing into question who literally wears the pants, Amalia initiates sex by ordering Marisa to remove her (Marisa's) pants. Marisa obeys her lover, who is a generation older and who also happens to be her teacher. Accentuating their age difference, as well as their teacher-apprentice / mother-daughter relationship and the power imbalance it has produced, Marisa declares, "Me siento como un joven lleno de deseo" (I feel like a kid full of desire).[96]

Giving Up the Ghost underscores the precariousness of sexual identity as it exposes "masculine," "feminine," "lesbian," "heterosexual," "butch," "femme," "man," and "woman" as slippery and protean signifiers. Furthermore, it highlights the split subject of sexuality. This is a play in which a butch lesbian finds that she is both desiring subject and object of desire; in which a femme shows active sexual desire and "takes" her butch lover; in which a seemingly heterosexual woman enters a lesbian relationship; and in which "big macho" men are infantilized. Recalling her male lovers, Amalia complains that what they called "*making love . . . was like having sex with children.*" She even likens one especially inept sexual partner to her son and laments, "I should have taken better care with him. / Men go from boys to viejos [old men] / *(sighing)* so soon." From boys to old men to corpses, Amalia compares her string of disappointing male lovers to "un río de cuerpos muertos" (a river of dead bodies). In summary, *Ghost* disassociates the virile and active from the masculine and the powerless and the passive from the feminine. It emphasizes that the two genders (masculinity and femininity) do not always correspond to the biological sexes (male and female) and thus it throws into question these very binaries. As Marisa observes, "It's odd being queer. / It's not that you don't want a man, / you just don't want a man in a man. / You want a man in a woman."[97]

"Later, She Met Joyce"

I find it significant that *Giving Up the Ghost* uses the figure of the pachuca, a sign of dissident femininity and (female) masculinity, to interrogate and destabilize—in other words, to queer—heteronormative gender and sexuality. Yet, as Yarbro-Bejarano points out, while "sexuality shifts" in the play, race, class, and culture remain relatively stable referents.[98] This is not the case in Moraga's poem "Later, She Met Joyce."[99] Like *Ghost*, "Joyce" is about a pachuca. It, too, eulogizes a girl who has all too quickly become a woman. And like the play, the poem features two very different female characters, Cecilia and Joyce, and relates the flowering and demise of their relationship.

In the poem's first section, the reader learns that the girls meet in Catholic school, where they form "their own girls' gang with code words & rhymes / that played itself coolly / on *this* side of trouble." In describing Cecilia and Joyce as a "girls' gang," Moraga highlights their tight bond yet also foreshadows what may become of Joyce. In addition, their "code words" point to the intimate nature of their friendship and may signal subtle flirtation. That their relationship "played itself coolly / on *this* side of trouble" indicates that it veers close to a lesbian romance, but restraint (playing it cool) keeps it platonic. However, by the end of this section, the homoerotic charge between the girls is more obvious. After being "separated by the summer," they reunite on the front porch of a house, a bygone locus of heterosexual courtship. Unable to play it cool any longer, Cecilia rushes "straight into Joyce's / arms and she would never forget the shape / of the girl's chest, a good one / and a half year's older." Here, Moraga describes Joyce's body in sexual terms: she is not only "a good one and a half year's older" and thus more physically developed than Cecilia, whose own chest is still "small," but her bosom is "a good one" as well. The girls weep as they embrace and Cecilia realizes, "*so this is love.*" It seems the feeling is mutual for Joyce; Moraga writes, "It was the first time for both of them."[100]

In section 2, the reader learns that Joyce does not return to Catholic school in the fall and the two girls have separated once again. When they finally reencounter one another, Joyce has grown into a young woman and "turned / pachuca." While Cecilia greets her long-lost friend with a simple "Hi," Joyce responds, "Eh, ésa, 'ow you doing? Whadchu say, man?" Her hair is "teased high off her head" and she wears thick turquoise eyeliner, a pair of "suedes" (loafers), and "a big winter coat." Cecilia realizes that her former friend is of "*a difernt claz o' people* / that had something to do with your tongue / going thick on you, wearing / shiny clothes and never getting / to college." Despite their childhood bond, the two girls have clearly gone in separate directions. This is accentuated in the juxtaposition of the final two sections. The second section ends with Joyce "walking away / talking about the 'guyz' / she would like to have / ride her low / through the valley floor." Meanwhile, in the third and final section, Cecilia is "picked / by the smart / white / girls / for president."[101]

"Later, She Met Joyce" is about a relationship forged across and eroded by class and race differences. To put it in quite hackneyed terms, it is about love across "the tracks": Joyce, it appears, comes from the "wrong" (poor) side of the proverbial train tracks; she lives "so far away / into the bordering / town."[102] Cecilia, in contrast, appears to enjoy the middle-class privilege of a prolonged youth. As the sociologist Julie Bettie has pointed out, middle-class youths "experience an extended adolescence by going to college, while working-class [youths] across race/ethnicity begin their adult lives earlier."[103] Small and childlike still, Cecilia is ensconced in school, the socially sanctioned domain of childhood and adolescence. She is accepted and rewarded not only by "the smart white girls"—presumably her classmates—when they elect her president but by the institution in general, an instrument of socialization (in other words, assimilation and conformity). Joyce, on the other hand, is "a fat half-breed / that flunked close to twice." She does not return to Cecilia's school (and may have dropped out altogether) and does not appear to be college-bound. In short, she does not linger in childhood and seems to have been catapulted into adulthood, as evidenced by the fact that she is already sexually active (with the "guyz") and quite possibly pregnant. In her big coat, she "look[s] more like a momma / than her childhood friend. Rounder than Cecilia had ever seen her."[104] Whereas *Giving Up the Ghost* portrays the homegirl as a tomboy and butch lesbian, in "Joyce" the pachuca is very female and feminine with her bulging chest and belly, high hair, and loud makeup. Indeed, the big coat that Joyce dons collapses the pachuca with a premature womanhood: it simultaneously invokes the long, identifying finger-tip coats that the first generation of pachucas wore in the early 1940s and alludes to its wearer's pregnancy.

A *Familia* from Scratch

Moraga's poem and play do not idealize *la pachuca* or relationships between Chicanas. In the former, it is clear that a wide chasm separates Cecilia and Joyce. Indeed, Joyce is nowhere to be found in the poem's concluding stanza. Similarly, in the latter, Marisa is left standing alone. The ghosts of her past do not join her on stage. Yet, her solitude does not necessarily signal that she is now a coherent and closed individual. With determination, she declares, "It's like making familia from scratch / each time all over again . . . with strangers / if I must. / If I must, I will."[105] In other words, Marisa will reach out to others.

In a reading of *Giving Up the Ghost*, Norma Alarcón critically assesses "the fantastic cultural silence, religious or Freudian, with regard to what the girl's position is in the Holy Family or Oedipal triad."[106] The girl-child, she points out, has no place in the prototypical Christian family (Joseph, Mary, and Jesus) or its Freudian parallel, the Oedipal triad. Having assumed a masculine position at an early age, Corky/Marisa, like Freud's boy-child, identifies her mother as object of desire. "That's what you always learn to want first," Marisa explains. "Maybe the first time you see / your Dad touch your Mom / in that way." As a young woman, she substitutes her mother as object of desire with Amalia, another unattainable maternal figure. Like the messiah, the Holy Family's boy-child, Marisa longs to rescue Amalia from her history of injury and loss. Regarding their love affair, she reminisces, "And just as I pressed my mouth to her, I'd think . . . / *I could save your life*." And like Freud's boy-child, she wishes to replace her father; she admits that she even "wished [him] dead" so she could rescue her mother in the same way her friend Marta "save[d] her mother from the poverty / her dead father left behind" by buying her a house.[107] Despite having been rebuked by her family for being a lesbian, Marta demonstrated that she was more reliable than her irresponsible father and more loyal than her own lackadaisical brother.

Yet, unlike Freud's boy-child, Marta's brother, and *Zoot Suit*'s Hank Reyna, Marisa and Marta are not sons. They are daughters and, as such, neither is promised, according to the terms of the Freudian compact, the power of patriarchy (and a woman of her own) in exchange for relinquishing her mother as object of desire. Moreover, they are lesbians and, as such, they "break . . . from the legacy [of virgin, devoted wife, and unself-ish, dedicated mother.] In doing so, [they] forfeit [their] place in the *fa-milia* and in the Latino heterosexual community."[108] Consequently, Marisa must make "familia from scratch." She must imagine a community be-yond the Holy Family or Oedipal triad, neither of which she, as daughter and lesbian, can enter as husband-father or wife-mother. In other words, she must conceive of and construct community beyond heteropatriarchy. In the words of the film and theater critic Teresa de Lauretis, she must endeavor to "reconstitute . . . a family no longer patriarchal, but politi-cal, feminist and anti-racist."[109] The family/families she creates will not be based on filiation—that is, on patriarchal relationships. As such, it/they cannot be biological and, therefore, "organic" or "natural." Instead, the family/families Marisa fabricates will be based on *affiliation*.[110]

As the psychologist Aída Hurtado reminds us, a family is not neces-sarily a biological grouping but "a set of social relations revolving around intangibles such as privileges and responsibilities."[111] In the heteropatri-archal *familia de la raza,* the privileges of fathers and sons are obvious. In contrast, *la familia de la raza* envisioned by *Giving Up the Ghost* is neither heterosexual nor patriarchal. It consists of Chicana lesbians—those who have been excluded from and by the cultural nationalist configuration of the Chicano family and, all too often, from and by individual Chicano fam-ilies as well. *La Pachuca* (Marisa) cannot and does not replace *el pachuco* as son or father, claim for herself his/their privileges, and, thus, replicate patriarchal power relations (in which the male/masculine is distinguished from, dominates, or erases the female/feminine). A butch lesbian, she, like Baca's pachuca, conflates masculinity and femininity as she assumes the simultaneously masculine and feminine role of *la salvadora* (the sav-ior), the title of the play's second and final act. Accepting the putatively masculine—yet uncannily feminine—responsibilities of the butch lesbian (for example, protecting and providing), she endeavors to "love . . . and heal . . ."—in other words, to save—"the women of her race," beginning with herself.[112]

A Long Line of *Vendidas*

Marisa's position as both pachuca and lesbian highlights her status as, in Moraga's words, an "institutionalized outcast."[113] Excluded from the het-eronormative family and, by extension, the Chicano cultural nation (qua *familia de la raza*), she is a "noncitizen" or "alien" of sorts. To paraphrase the sociologist M. Jacqui Alexander, "Not just (any) *body* can be a citizen . . . for some bodies have been marked by the state"—as well as the cultural nation—"as non-procreative, in pursuit of sex only for pleasure, a sex that is non-productive of babies and of no economic gain. Having refused the heterosexual imperative of citizenship, *these* bodies, according to the state"—and here I would add the Chicano cultural nation—"pose a profound threat to the very survival of the nation."[114]

In her landmark essay "A Long Line of Vendidas," Moraga expounds on the perceived threat of feminism and lesbianism to the survival of the Chicano nation:

> The woman who defies her role as subservient to her husband, father, brother, or son by taking control of her own sexual destiny is purported to be a "traitor to her race" by contributing to the "genocide" of her people—whether or not she has children. In short, even if the defiant woman is *not* a lesbian, she is purported to be one; for, like the lesbian in the Chicano imagination, she is *una Malinchista*. Like the Malinche of Mexican history, she is corrupted by foreign influences which threaten to destroy her people.[115]

As I note earlier, in the wake of the Sleepy Lagoon incident, the Spanish-language newspaper *La Opinión* branded pachucas "*malinches,*" thereby collapsing them with the most notorious traitor in all of Mexican history and lore. Like La Malinche, the World War II–era, second-generation pachuca who spoke substandard Spanish, who ventured unchaperoned from the home and barrio for work or play, who helped to cultivate a distinctly working-class, Chicana style, who expressed a budding sexuality by jitter-bugging in dancehalls (sometimes with men of other races and ethnicities), or who was masculine because she joined a gang, wore *el tacuche,* or threw a punch, appeared to have rejected the patriarchal authority of the Mexican American family and the customs, values, and expectations of her parents' generation. In effect, this young woman committed a sort of cultural "genocide." That Moraga's pachucas are lesbians is more than a simple coincidence, for both *la pachuca* and the lesbian are queer in that they signify excess: both exceed the limits of the heteropatriarchal family.

The literary and artistic works I discuss in detail in this chapter foreground the figure of the pachuca to explore relationships between Chicanas—however flawed. By focusing on girls/women (as sisters, mothers, daughters, or lovers), they present an alternative to the heteronormative *familia de raza.* Each represents a gynocentric analogue to the fraternity of *carnales* idealized by contemporary Chicano cultural nationalists (and later cultural workers, who continue to envision Chicano cultural identity, community, and history in very hackneyed terms as a heteropatriarchal family drama).[116] The lesbian pachuca in particular underscores the heterosexist underpinnings of Chicano cultural nationalism and its valorization of the heteronormative family.

Additionally, as a character in a play and poem, the lesbian pachuca highlights the value of fiction and art in exposing the heterosexist focus of much scholarship on the Mexican American family. She shows the important role cultural artifacts play in generating, nurturing, and sustaining new subjects, new communities, and new collective memories. And she implores scholars in Chicana and Chicano studies, especially those of us who study the zoot subculture, not only to critique the heteronormative family but to look beyond it and thus to decenter it as a stable category of analysis.

Finally, by complicating relationships between and among Chicanas and Chicanos, the literary and artistic works I study here emphasize the constructedness and instability of community. None of these works presents us with a monolithic Chicano collective identity marked by unity, homology, and plenitude. In "Para Teresa," the narrator aligns herself with her childhood nemesis only after decades have elapsed and in the context of the Chicano movement. (In fact, in the 1978 version of the poem, their imaginary reconciliation never takes place, although the poem is still named for and dedicated to Teresa.) And in Moraga's play and poem, Chicanas forge an intense but ultimately fragile bond with one another. The vision of a cohesive Chicano community is further undermined by the fact that Corky is raped by a Chicano, a man she likens to her father; the screwdriver that he brandishes as a weapon reminds her of her father's. If the Chicano imaginary is conceived of as a family, then the rape may be read as an act of incest as well. For Corky, the larger Chicano family depicted by *Giving Up the Ghost* is far from a refuge.

The precariousness of alliance and community is also especially evident in *Las Tres Marías,* another text in which the spectator plays a relatively prominent role. As I discuss above, the person who stands before Baca's mirror changes constantly. Yet where Chicano cultural nationalism was predicated upon and demanded mimesis, a "one-on-one correspondence between the subject and its reflection in a mirrorlike duplication,"[117] this mirror does not necessarily promise homology. Instead, like Lacan's mirror phase, it can provide a basis for alienation and misrecognition, especially if the person standing before it does not identify with the chola and pachuca.

Regardless of whether or not *Las Tres Marías*'s viewer links or divides the pachuca and chola who flank her/him, the tripartite community this work envisions and allows for mutates. Similarly, as Yarbro-Bejarano points out, in Moraga's play, the character of The People (the members of the audience) changes with each performance. She notes that, since 1984, "*Ghost* has played before a variety of . . . audiences," including some that were primarily women and others that were "made up of both men and women" (predominately Chicanos and Chicanas).[118] And just as the mirror in *Las Tres Marías* may prompt some viewers to identify with or to reject the pachuca or chola, Moraga's play "offers different audiences (Chicana/o, feminist, gay/lesbian) different points of entry" due to its emphasis on "fluid, contradictory, and multiple" identities and sexualities. At the same time, it defers "empathy and catharsis" with its nonnarrative structure and lack of a single, unitary protagonist.[119]

Furthermore, both Moraga's and Baca's works hail the spectator as an active participant in the production of meaning. Indeed, in *Ghost*, the three speaking characters (Marisa, Corky, and Amalia) direct their monologues to The People, a silent character. By including the members of the audience in the play's cast, Moraga positions them more as witnesses rather than as voyeurs.[120] Discussing the play's various audiences, Yarbro-Bejarano claims that "when 'The People' . . . are all women, the possibility of women's community hinted at in the play is reinforced by the interaction among women of different racial, cultural, and socioeconomic backgrounds in the audience."[121] When Marisa and Corky direct their monologues to an all-Chicana audience (or to the Chicanas in the audience), de Lauretis equates The People with "the 'other person' in the mirror" (à la Lacan's mirror stage).[122] And when the audience is composed mainly of Chicanas *and* Chicanos, Yarbro-Bejarano asserts that "the text opens up intracultural dialogue on the topics of gender and sexuality."[123] In other words, the meaning of *Giving Up the Ghost* is never stable; it shifts with each audience and performance. Likewise, the meaning of *Las Tres Marías* is never the same, for the person at its literal and figurative center changes. As both Yarbro-Bejarano's and Gaspar de Alba's illuminating readings of these works show, a number of variables, including the race, class, gender, and sexuality of the spectator, "determine the reception of the text" and shape its meanings.[124]

In *Imagined Communities*, Benedict Anderson argues that the nation "is conceived as a solid community moving steadily down (or up) history."[125] The communities imagined by Hernández's, Baca's, and Moraga's works are not solid. Instead, they are fragile, messy, temporal, and imperfect. As such, they have little in common with those movement-era texts that conceived of the Chicano cultural nation as an eternal and essential heterosexual, patriarchal family or fraternity. Long before the terms "transnational(ism)" and "postnational(ism)" gained widespread currency in the humanities and social sciences, these feminist works looked to *la pachuca*—a figure excoriated, ridiculed, or shunned by both official and unofficial nationalisms, from the World War II period to *La Causa*—to reconfigure alliances and to imagine extranational group identities. This homegirl draws attention to the home and its boundaries as she redefines the family they purport to keep.

Epilogue

HOMEGIRLS THEN AND NOW,

FROM THE HOME FRONT TO THE FRONT LINE

> The nation-state at war generates nationalism of the highest
> order in order to mobilize its citizens to arms and sacrifice.
> War nationalism is pervasive and demanding. Drawn in stark
> terms and heavily dependent upon symbol and ritual, it resists
> complexity and nuance. It is intolerant of dissent and leaves lit-
> tle, if any, room for competing ideologies. Yet, from a different
> angle, wars have also provided opportunities for immigrants
> and racial minorities to demonstrate their loyalty and to win
> full acceptance and citizenship in the nation.
> MAE M. NGAI, *IMPOSSIBLE SUBJECTS*[1]

Since the early 1990s, the figure of the pachuca has largely
been replaced in Chicana cultural production and U.S. popular
culture by that of her heir in the late twentieth century and the
twenty-first, the Latina gang member. In 1994, this figure garnered
widespread attention with the release of Allison Anders's film *Mi
Vida Loca*. Shortly thereafter, she took center stage in Yxta Maya
Murray's novel *Locas*, Mona Ruiz's autobiography *Two Badges*, and
Gini Sikes's ethnographic *8 Ball Chicks: A Year in the Violent World
of Girl Gangsters*. More recently, she has figured prominently in
scholarly monographs, among them Monica Brown's *Gang Nation:
Delinquent Citizens in Puerto Rican, Chicano, and Chicana Narratives*
and Marie "Keta" Miranda's *Homegirls in the Public Sphere*. These
works demonstrate that the meanings of the Latina homegirl—a
figure that has come to represent fear, confusion, frustration, respect, admiration, pity, or titillation—continue to shift and to circu-
late. They prompt us to ask: What do Latina homegirls of the late
twentieth century and the early twenty-first have in common with

pachucas of the 1940s and 1950s and how are they different? How do they echo their predecessors' challenges? What new challenges do they offer and face? And what can they tell us about the world they have inherited—in particular, about new genders and sexualities? New racial formations? New Latina (as opposed to Chicana) imaginaries? New (im)migration patterns? New Americans? And new wars?

I write this epilogue in the midst of the so-called war on terror. The U.S. military continues to occupy Iraq and Afghanistan, where servicemen and women from the United States and a host of other countries are killed or maimed every day; Osama bin Laden is still at large; George W. Bush remains president of the United States of America; the Taliban have resurged in parts of Afghanistan; and countless Iraqi and Afghani men, women, and children are murdered, injured, displaced, or disappeared on a daily basis. As I close this book, I ask: What can World War II teach us about the current war? How does the current war produce and police American nationalism in ways similar to or different from previous wars? How is the nation-state mobilizing citizens and non-citizens to arms and sacrifice? What new or old symbols and rituals does this war offer? And what roles do minority subjects—namely, women, people of color, and Latinas in particular—play in the unfolding national drama and global conflict?

Admittedly, these are big questions—big enough to fill many other books—and I cannot do them justice in this brief epilogue. However, I have opted to end with them in order to draw attention to the political and social milieu in which I have completed this work. By juxtaposing the World War II–era pachuca and the war on terror's Latina soldier, I also hope to show what these figures share in common and to make visible the ways in which they illuminate and diverge from each other.[2] While the war on terror has renewed old debates in the United States—for example, those related to immigration and the porosity of the U.S.–Mexico border—it has also brought unprecedented attention to U.S. servicewomen and has introduced a new icon to the American cultural landscape: the Latina GI.[3] What does this figure have in common with the World War II–era pachuca and how is it different? What does it say about and to the United States in the midst of the war on terror? And what can it tell us about the deployment of race, gender, and sexuality in the service of nationalism and imperialism in the early twenty-first century, a moment characterized not only by post-nationalism and transnationalism but jingoism, nativism, protectionism, and fundamentalism as well?

This book links the World War II period and Chicano movement because, as I state in my introduction, "both were characterized in great part by heightened nationalist consciousness, either statist or insurgent." Similarly, M. Jacqui Alexander has identified the early twenty-first century as a "hypernationalist" moment—despite and because of neoliberalism, which has been defined as "an economic doctrine with a negative relation to state power, a market ideology that seeks to limit the scope and activity of governing," and "a new relationship between government and knowledge through which governing activities are recast as non-political and non-ideological problems that need technical solutions."[4] According to Alexander, hypernationalism entails

> the manufacture of an outside enemy to rationalize criminalization and incarceration; the internal production of a new citizen patriot; [and] the creation and maintenance of a permanent war economy, whose internal elements devolve on the militarization of the police and the resultant criminalization of immigrants, people of color, and working-class communities through the massive expansion of a punishment economy at whose center is the prison industrial complex.

In addition, she maintains that the early twenty-first century is a "neo-imperial" era, with "neo-imperial" referring "to the constitution of a new empire, accelerated militarization, and war on the part of the United States."[5] Alexander upholds the U.S. invasion of Iraq in 2003 as evidence of U.S. hypernationalism and neo-imperialism.

Neoliberalism. Hypernationalism. Neo-imperialism. These are the terms that describe and produce the world young Latinas and Latinos have inherited in the early twenty-first century. They are also the terms with which we scholars in American, ethnic, feminist, and sexuality studies must increasingly locate and understand our subjects. We must see minority and minoritarian subjects in relation not only to nations and nationalisms, the groups and contexts with which they have generally been associated, but to the imperial and global as well. At the same time, we must constantly interrogate and reconsider these neologisms. How "hyper" is nationalism in the early twenty-first century and what distinguishes it from World War II–era jingoism? How new is neo-imperialism when, as Alexander argues, it "is constituted . . . through those state apparatuses . . . that are aimed at constituting a nation that is based in an originary nuclear family in ways that couple the nuclear with the heterosexual"?[6] How new is the "citizen patriot"? Is s/he a citizen and what makes her/him a patriot?

Like all wars waged by the United States since the Second World War, the war on terror has had a profound impact on Latinas and Latinos, regardless of citizenship status. Via what James Der Derian terms "the military-industrial-media-entertainment network," this war offers us disturbingly uncanny images, new Latina and Latino icons, and old ones reminiscent of their World War II antecedents.[7] Before looking at the figure of the Latina GI, a relatively new archetype, I turn first to some much older ones.

As was the case in World War II, Latinas and Latinos continue to represent an alien menace and social burden on the home front, as evidenced by the passage of two congressional bills in 2005 and 2006: the Border Protection, Antiterrorism, and Illegal Immigration Control Act (H.R. 4437) and the Comprehensive Immigration Reform Act (S. 2611). Like the Homeland Security Act of 2002, which dissolved the Immigration and Naturalization Service and transferred its functions to the newly formed Department of Homeland Security, both measures link immigration—in particular, undocumented immigration from Mexico—to terrorism and call for the fortification of the southern border of the United States, even though none of the 9/11 hijackers was undocumented or Latino and none entered this country via Mexico.

Additionally, in May 2006, Lockheed Martin, Raytheon, and Northrop Grumman, three of the largest defense contractors in the United States, announced that they would submit bids for a multibillion-dollar federal contract to build a "virtual fence" along the U.S.–Mexico border. To secure the international divide, they would use "some of the same high-priced, high-tech tools these companies have already put to work in Iraq and Afghanistan, such as unmanned aerial vehicles, ground surveillance satellites and motion-detection video equipment."[8] In brief, some politicians and businesses seek to profit from "Afghanizing" or "Iraqizing" the U.S.–Mexico border, rendering the immigrant a perennial suspect and transforming illegal immigration into an act of domestic terrorism.

The figure of the seditious Latino gangster qua domestic terrorist, as represented, for example, by José Padilla, also continues to pose a threat to national security, much like the World War II–era pachuca and pachuco. Padilla, who was born in Brooklyn, New York, in 1970 to Puerto Rican parents, was a member of a gang as an adolescent in Chicago. He converted to Islam while in prison and, upon returning from a trip to Pakistan in May 2002, he was arrested at Chicago's O'Hare Airport on suspicion of plotting a "dirty bomb" attack in the United States.[9] Amid rumors that Al-Qaeda sought to recruit Central American gangsters—notably, members of El Salvador's notorious Mara Salvatrucha gang—to carry out attacks on American soil, he was held in military custody as an enemy combatant and was eventually charged with "conspiring to murder, maim, and kidnap people overseas."[10]

As a former gangster, would-be terrorist, or terrorist sympathizer, Padilla, a U.S. citizen, embodies fears of the nation's internal and foreign dangers. Like the young Asian and black Britons who carried out the deadly public transit bombings in London on July 7, 2005, he represents the "bad"—that is, treacherous and untrustworthy—minority. In Alexander's words, he is the "dark inside threat that must be cordoned off, imprisoned, expulsed and matched simultaneously with the extinction of the dark external threat in order that the borders of the fictive, originary nation might be properly secured."[11]

In contrast, the Latina or Latino soldier, especially the slain Latina or Latino soldier, has been upheld as a model minority during the war on terror. Latinos served in disproportionate numbers during World War II. Along with Latinas, they continue to fill the ranks of the U.S. military.[12] Yet where the World War II–era Mexican American GI entered a racially segregated military and had to demand a dignified place in American society, the war on terror's literally self-sacrificing Latina or Latino soldier has become an exemplar of American egalitarianism and democracy.

Take, for example, Marine Lance Corporal José Antonio Gutiérrez and Private First Class Lori Piestewa, the first male and female U.S. military casualties in "Operation Iraqi Freedom." A Guatemalan immigrant, Gutiérrez joined the U.S. Marines after 9/11 and was killed in Iraq by enemy fire in March 2003. He was awarded U.S. citizenship posthumously and was heralded as an "American hero" and the embodiment of the American Dream.[13] Piestewa, a Hopi Chicana, was also killed in Iraq in March 2003 when the convoy in which she was traveling, along with her best friend Private First Class Jessica Lynch and Specialist Shoshana Johnson, was ambushed.[14] Upon Piestewa's death, Squaw Peak and Squaw Peak freeway, a mountain and highway near her hometown of Tuba City, Arizona, were renamed in her honor.[15] And while Lynch's capture and rescue were the subject of the controversial made-for-TV movie *Saving Jessica Lynch* in 2003, Piestewa's two small children, her parents, and their rented "over-stuffed mobile home" on the Navajo Reservation were featured two years later on the reality show *Extreme Makeover: Home Edition*.[16]

The discourse surrounding these young men and women should prompt us to reexamine the ways that the concepts of family and home, especially as homeland and home front, have been remobilized in the interests of (hyper-)nationalism and (neo-)imperialism. What drove these youths—none of whom was rich—from their homes to the front lines of the war on terror? What and whom did they leave behind? And what was gained by their departure and losses? I find it tragically ironic that Gutiérrez, an orphan who came to the United States as an undocumented immigrant and who was literally homeless before being taken in by a foster family, found what one journalist called "another family" in the U.S. Marines and was embraced not only as an American hero but simply as an American after being killed in Iraq.[17] Moreover, I am troubled by the renaming of Squaw Peak and Squaw Peak freeway. While meant to honor Piestewa and to provide Native Americans with long overdue compensation for the embarrassing legitimization of a racist and sexist epithet, this gesture appropriates a Native American woman's name and memory in the service of U.S. imperialism, not only in Iraq but in North America as well—in particular, in Arizona, a place where the past, present, and future of American Indians, Mexicans, and Mexican Americans have actively been distorted, if not erased altogether.[18]

9/11 and its aftermath, including the war on terror, offer both familiar and new icons, from the "idealized image" of New York City's firemen, to the burkha-clad Afghan woman ("an easy icon"), to Lynch, who has been described as "that archetypal blonde-in-peril" and "all-American, small-town, girl-next-door," to Padilla, Gutiérrez, Johnson, and Piestewa.[19] Although this war is by no means the first in which Latinas have served, it has brought unprecedented attention to the Latina GI and new "Adelita," as represented in part by Piestewa, Johnson (the daughter of an African American and Panamanian immigrant), and Lieutenant Emily J. T. Perez, the sixty-fourth woman from the U.S. military to be killed in Afghanistan or Iraq.[20] In fact, some of the first and most troubling images from the front lines of the war on terror were of these women. After their capture on March 23, 2003, Al Jazeera broadcast a video of an injured and frightened Johnson and a fatally wounded Piestewa. Three weeks later, images of Johnson being escorted out of Iraq by U.S. Marines were seen around the world. And shortly after her violent and untimely death in Kifl, south of Baghdad, Perez was upheld by the mainstream American media as a model "G. I. Jane" and representative of the "class of 9/11."[21]

The discourse surrounding these servicewomen reconfigures women's and racial-ethnic minorities' relationships to the nation-state. While Perez was a platoon leader and West Point graduate with a promising military career ahead of her, Piestewa and Johnson were enlistees. Moreover, both were single mothers who left children behind when they went to Iraq. As soldiers and mothers, they blur the line between the arena of politics and war, and the private, ostensibly peaceful, domestic sphere in need of protection.

As I note in the introduction, during World War II some racial and ethnic minorities, including resident aliens, attempted to claim full citizenship for themselves and their racial and ethnic groups by joining the military and fighting on behalf of the United States. Its rigid hierarchy of command notwithstanding, the U.S. military has been lauded as a site of egalitarianism and meritocracy in which racial, ethnic, and class differences (more so than gender and sexual ones) supposedly matter little. General Colin Powell (secretary of state at the start of the Iraq War), Lieutenant General Ricardo Sánchez (former commander of U.S. ground forces in Iraq), and General John Abizaid (former commander of the United States Central Command) are looked to as proof not only of the military's ability and desire to absorb and capitalize on racial and ethnic difference but of American democracy in general.[22] Meanwhile, advertising campaigns for the Army, Navy, Marines, and Air Force feature black and brown servicemen and women. Immigrant Latinas and Latinos in particular are targeted via websites in Spanish and lured into the armed forces with offers of not only college tuition but crash courses in English and promises of U.S. citizenship.[23]

The war on terror shows us that the U.S. military has also appropriated certain liberal feminist political agendas, despite charges that servicewomen are subjected to systematic sexual harassment and assault (known as Military Sexual Trauma).[24] As Veronique Pin-Fat and Maria Stern point out, Lynch, a white woman, served as "a public reminder of what the United States was fighting for" in at least two capacities.[25] Dubbed a "female Rambo" and "G. I. Jane," she was upheld as the antithesis of the oppressed Muslim woman, who has been portrayed and perceived as the quintessential victim of a misogynist and fundamentalist enemy.[26] Yet at the same time, Lynch was depicted as weak, vulnerable, and in need of rescuing. Although she insisted that she was not sexually abused as a prisoner of war, reports circulated that the "petite blonde" and "soft-spoken soldier" had been beaten and raped by her Iraqi captors.[27] Her femininity—in particular, her status as sex object—was further emphasized after her return to the United States when Larry Flynt, publisher of *Hustler* magazine, announced that he had acquired photographs in which Lynch appeared topless. However, Flynt, a vociferous critic of President Bush and the war in Iraq, said that he would not publish these photos because "Jessica Lynch is a good kid. . . . She's just a victim of the Bush administration, who is using her to justify the war in Iraq and force-feed us a Joan of Arc."[28] As a victim of the Iraqi enemy, the Bush administration, and, finally, a notorious "porn king," Lynch came to embody female and feminine helplessness—in other words, ladyness.[29]

The reinscription of heterosexual gender norms is also apparent in the unforgettable photographs of white U.S. servicewomen torturing male Iraqi prisoners at Abu Ghraib. In spite of claims that they would be read as evidence of American "gender equality" and thus "everything that the Islamic fundamentalists believe characterizes Western culture,"[30] and that they would be used "as a potent argument against modernization and the emancipation of women,"[31] these images articulated misogyny, homophobia, racism, and classism as they emasculated Arab and Muslim men, pathologized homosexuality, and depicted "white trash" women as sexually depraved. Indeed, in the words of one observer, they exemplified "porno torture."[32] And as Jasbir K. Puar observes, the infamous photo of Private First Class Lynndie England "leading a naked Iraqi on a leash. . . . hints at the sexual perversions associated with s/m."[33] Eventually, England, a divorcée and single mother, would be implicated in making a pornographic film with another Abu Ghraib guard and convicted of committing an "indecent act" (among other crimes). The Bush administration insisted that she was an aberration—one of a handful of rogue reservists who had acted independently of supervisors. As a consequence, she received a dishonorable discharge from the Army and was sentenced to three years in prison.

The current war differs from previous wars in that there are more women serving in the U.S. military and, more than ever, these women are exposed to violence.[34] Some things, however, remain the same. For example, the tired recodification of U.S. servicewomen as either virgins (Lynch) or whores (England) maintains gender norms as it consolidates and links nation and empire. In particular, it keeps the female soldier who too closely resembles the ideal (male and masculine) soldier—namely, the butch lesbian—at bay. Like Rosie the Riveter and the World War II–era WAC, the war on terror's servicewoman's femininity and heterosexuality must be accentuated and produced, for, as *la pachuca*'s exclusion from the American and Chicano imaginaries has shown us, normative gender and heterosexuality are indispensable to the project of nation building.

As if reminding Americans of their femininity, *Glamour* magazine honored Lynch, Johnson, and Piestewa at its 2003 "Women of the Year" awards ceremony, to which, one commentator noted, Lynch wore a "black gown embroidered with red roses."[35] Johnson is black and although her appearance received much less attention than Lynch's (in fact, Johnson received much less attention than Lynch *period*), by and large, minority servicewomen have not been less feminized or sexualized than their white counterparts in the war on terror. For example, Mike McNeilly's controversial sixty-foot mural *Liberty and Justice 9–11*, which appeared on the side of a prominent building in Los Angeles in October 2001, featured a young, female, black or brown Marine brandishing an M-16 and wearing not only a camouflage helmet but lip gloss, eyeliner, and mascara. Additionally, in its May 2005 issue, *Latina* magazine welcomed a group of women soldiers—"most of them Hispanas, all of them heroes"—home from Kuwait with free makeovers.[36] In the before-and-after photographs, the servicewomen pose first in their fatigues, then in civilian dress.

These images of "GI Juana" as both patriotic and pretty provide scholars in American, Chicana, feminist, and sexuality studies with a template for investigating and better understanding "the deployment of gender and sexuality in nation-state formation" and "the manufacture of citizenship normativized within the prism of heterosexuality" in the twenty-first century.[37] This template is new, but given the lessons of World War II (for example, the active feminization of women workers and servicewomen), it is also familiar. As they reify gender and sexual norms, these images incorporate the Latina GI into the nation in the service of war and empire. Unlike the World War II–era pachuca, an internal enemy, it appears that this figure is welcome in the United States, at least and perhaps exclusively as a soldier on the front line—in other words, as an *external* citizen-patriot. Paradoxically, in the war on terror, GI Juana has been domesticated by being outsourced. She has won a hard-earned place in the homeland by going to Kabul and Baghdad.

By examining the racial, class, gender, and sexual dimensions of citizenship, this book attempts to chart the stark and nuanced ways nationalisms are produced and maintained. Chapter 4 highlights the ways that Chicana feminist writers and artists have reinserted *la pachuca* into Chicana and Chicano communities and narratives and thus redefined these communities and narratives and their subjects. Using what Gloria Anzaldúa terms "feminist architecture," the writers and artists I study have returned the homegirl to her home and have constructed new homes and families for her. In doing so, they have exposed citizenship—that is, membership in a larger group—as a masculinist and heterosexist project. Furthermore, they have fabricated a "new culture" (to quote Anzaldúa again) by transforming *la familia de la raza* or moving beyond it. However, this new culture is not nostalgic, utopic, closed, or complete and is marked just as much by difference and conflict as similarity and harmony.

Without erasing her aberrant femininity, masculinity, and lesbianism, the feminist, movement-era, literary and artistic works I focus on "domesticate" *la pachuca*. Carmen Lomas Garza's 1989 goache *Las Pachucas, Razor Blade 'do* does the same. This late- or postmovement work of visual art does not locate pachucas on the street, where Latina and Latino youth are all too frequently portrayed in and by dominant media. Instead, we find them in a cozy bedroom in the midst of a highly feminine and seemingly harmless ritual: dressing up to go out. One pachuca sits at a vanity while another stands behind her and does her hair. Meanwhile, a girl surrounded by what appear to be magazines watches the two of them from the bed.

As this book illustrates, violence, material and discursive alike, plays a significant role in narratives about pachucas. It is apparent in "Para

31. *Las Pachucas, Razor Blade 'do.* Gouache painting, 19-1/2 x 27-1/2 inches. COPYRIGHT 1989, CARMEN LOMAS GARZA. PHOTO BY WOLFGANG DIETZE. COLLECTION OF SONIA SALDÍVAR-HULL AND FELIX HULL, AUSTIN, TEXAS.

Teresa," *Giving Up the Ghost,* "Later, She Met Joyce," *The Wedding,* "and when I dream dreams," "Los Corts (5 Voices)," "El Louie," "Kid Zopilote," and "El Hijo Disobediente." Indeed, it plays a very real role in not only poems, stories, plays, novels, and songs but the everyday lives of homegirls and homeboys, many of whom have been dispatched to Iraq and Afghanistan. [38]

The second half of the title of Garza's painting, *Razor Blade 'do,* alludes to violence: as one pachuca styles the other's hair into a bouffant, she inserts razor blades into it. The razor blades signal that these two young women may confront or cause violence. Perhaps they will find themselves in a *pleito* (fight) on the street, the subject of another one of Garza's works. [39] At the very least, these pachucas anticipate the need to arm themselves as they prepare for what may be a night out on the town. Yet the domestic space in which we find them is not quite an unambiguously safe haven. Sharp objects that hint at aggression and injury abound in this not atypical, working-class Mexican American bedroom: a cat exposes its claws as it cleans itself on the floor and a framed picture of Our Lady of the Sorrows hangs above the bed. With a mournful facial expression, the Virgin

Mary points to her heart, from which seven daggers, reminiscent of *fileros* (switchblades), radiate.

Like *Las Pachucas, The Woman in the Zoot Suit* points to the pervasiveness of violence. This book shows that it lurks both in public and private, on the street, on the newspaper page, in the courtroom, on the front line, on the home front, at home, and within the family. Pachucas' exclusion from their literal and symbolic homes, such as the nation-state, *la familia de la raza,* or, to invoke raúlsalinas's "Homenaje al Pachuco (Mirrored Reflections)," their and our textbooks, constitutes an act of "domestic" violence and exposes the deployment of race, class, gender, and sexuality in the formation of both official and insurgent nationalisms. Yet the Latina GI's inclusion in the nation and empire is also violent, as the war on terror has shown us. *La pachuca*'s exclusion from the nation and the Latina GI's *inclusion* in it show that "all nationalisms"—be they statist or cultural—"are gendered, all are invented," and, despite the meaning, inspiration, protection, and solace nations offer, "all [nationalisms] are dangerous."[40]

The Woman in the Zoot Suit stresses the importance of not only nation but culture. It treats culture, including words and images, as contested terrain and "history-in-the-making."[41] I open this book with two movement-era works, then look to older cultural artifacts, including songs, short fiction, newspaper articles, and a trial transcript. I close it with Garza's more recent *Las Pachucas* in order to trace a genealogy of texts that reimagine and resituate the once ignored and vilified pachuca. In addition, I offer a less obvious genealogy, one that links the World War II–era pachuca and the war on terror's Latina GI. Like many of the works I study, this book is an intervention. My hope is that the gynocentric lineages it fabricates will make us more aware of the constructedness and malleability of national imaginaries and remind us of the importance of dissent and competing ideologies.

NOTES

Preface

1. But the worse thing was / that in all their / sociological / anthropological / psychological / and historical / heaps and piles of bogus bullshit / Our sister—the Pachuca—of / equal suffering / that dear little sister / who also bore the brunt / on her entire face / remained in their textbooks / ANONYMOUS. raúlsalinas, *Un Trip through the Mind Jail y Otras Excursions*, 106; my translation.

2. Regarding the subgenre of "pachuco poetry," see Zamora, "Mythopoeia of Chicano Poetry." In everyday speech, a "homeboy" or "homegirl" (or "homie") is a friend or acquaintance, usually from a particular neighborhood. In this book, "homeboy" and "homegirl" may refer to young, poor, or working-class urban Latinas and Latinos in the United States. They may also refer to gang members more specifically.

3. "'Zoot suit' murder case" is from "Jury's Gang-Case Verdict Disproves 'Persecution,'" *Los Angeles Times*, January 14, 1943.

4. I base my description of the zoot suit as worn by young Mexican American women in the 1940s on a number of contemporary sources, including photographs, as well as on interviews I conducted with Mexican American women who either wore zoot suits or who came of age when the zoot suit was popular among young Mexican Americans. I discuss these interviews in more detail in chapter 1.

5. My broad conceptualization of the state is indebted to Louis Althusser's concepts of the ISA and RSA. According to Althusser, both ideological and repressive state apparatuses (ISAS and RSAS respectively) constitute the state. ISAS include the press, churches, schools, trade unions, political parties, and the arts. Where ISAS manufacture and maintain state power via ideology, RSAS, such as the military and police, do so via direct violence. See Althusser, "Ideology and Ideological State Apparatuses (Notes towards an Investigation)." I provide a more detailed definition of the state in note 6.

6. By "state," I refer to institutions that work together in articulating nation (a politically organized body) and nationalist identity, such as the military, government (local, regional, and national), law enforcement agencies, schools, and newspapers. However, I do not conflate "state" and "nation," as some nationalisms—for example, what David Lloyd calls "insurgent nationalisms"—

are not articulated with or by a state. I treat Chicano cultural nationalism as an insurgent nationalism. See Lloyd, "Nationalisms against the State."

Furthermore, even though city, county, and federal authorities responded differently to zoot suits, the Zoot Suit Riots, and the Sleepy Lagoon incident, I group these entities beneath the rubric of "the state." As Yuval-Davis and Anthias point out, the state, which consists of "a body of institutions," is "neither unitary in its practices, its intentions nor its effects." Still, they and I retain the concept of the state, for it "refers to a particular 'machinery' for the exercise of 'government' over a given population. . . . [T]he state can harness a number of different processes, including ideological ones, through juridical and repressive mechanisms at its command," be they at the local, regional, national, or even international level. See Yuval-Davis and Anthias, *Woman-Nation-State*, 5.

7. Here, I am heeding Angela McRobbie's critique that culture is all too often seen as "texts, images and representations rather than as social relationships." See McRobbie, "New Times in Cultural Studies," as quoted in Enstad, *Ladies of Labor, Girls of Adventure*, 12.

8. Cathy Horyn, "What They Wore to the Post-Revolution," *New York Times*, April 8, 2007, section 4, 3.

9. Bowen, *Why the French Don't Like Headscarves*, 155. Also see Benhabib, *The Rights of Others*; Keaton, *Muslim Girls and the Other France*; Mahmood, *Politics of Piety*; Scott, *The Politics of the Veil*; and Scott, "Symptomatic Politics." Regarding the significance of the *hijab* in the United States, see Ruth LaFerla, "We, Myself, and I," *New York Times*, April 5, 2007.

10. Although the term predates the twentieth century, *chola* generally refers to a late-twentieth-century Mexican American homegirl.

11. A cha-cha (probably short for *muchacha* or "girl" in Spanish) was a working-class or lower-middle-class Latina who participated in what was called the "disco" subculture in Southern California in the 1980s. This subculture revolved around certain types of dance music (hip hop, R & B, high energy, house, new wave, techno, and what is now commercially known as "freestyle"), DJs, car clubs, *clicas* (cliques or clubs), house parties, and dances (for example, "Rock of the '80s" in Pico Rivera).

To my knowledge, there is very little, if any, scholarship on the vibrant Southern California disco subculture of the 1980s. However, the Los Angeles–based performance artist María Elena Fernández paid homage to the cha-chas of her adolescence in her performance *Confessions of a Cha-Cha Feminist* (2001). Furthermore, the "*chicas*" about whom Julie Bettie writes in her very compelling study of girls at a California high school in the 1990s, *Women without Class: Girls, Race, and Identity*, are reminiscent of the cha-chas of my youth. Also see http://askachola.com/ (visited April 27, 2008) for a more recent invocation of the chola/cha-cha.

Introduction

1. "Clashes Few as Zoot War Dies Down," *Los Angeles Times,* part 1, 1 and sec. B, June 11, 1943.

2. Ibid., A.

3. Regarding race and public space during World War II, see Alvarez, *The Power of the Zoot;* Avila, *Popular Culture in the Age of White Flight;* Boris, " 'You Wouldn't Want One of 'Em Dancing with Your Wife' "; Escobedo, "Mexican American Home Front"; España-Maram, "Brown 'Hordes' in McIntosh Suits"; García, *A World of Its Own;* Macías, "Bringing Music to the People"; and Pagán, *Murder at the Sleepy Lagoon.*

4. "Half American" is from a letter to the editor as published in the *Pittsburgh Courier* on February 7, 1942. See http://www.yurasko.net/vv/courier.html (visited February 15, 2007).

5. Kessler-Harris, *Out to Work,* 273.

6. My understanding of gender, labor, and sexuality during World War II is indebted to a number of scholarly works, including Anderson, *Wartime Women;* Bailey and Farber, *The First Strange Place;* Bérubé, *Coming Out under Fire;* Bérubé, "Marching to a Different Drummer"; Campbell, *Women at War with America;* Chafe, *The American Woman;* Costello, *Virtue under Fire;* Dabakis, "Gendered Labor"; Delano, "Making Up for War"; D'Emilio, *Sexual Politics, Sexual Communities;* Erenberg and Hirsch, eds., *The War in American Culture;* Escobedo, "The Pachuca Panic"; Faderman, *Odd Girls and Twilight Lovers;* Gluck, *Rosie the Riveter Revisited;* Hartmann, "Prescriptions for Penelope"; Margaret Higonnet et al., eds., *Behind the Lines;* Honey, *Creating Rosie the Riveter;* Kennedy, *Freedom from Fear;* Kessler-Harris, *Out to Work;* Lingeman, *Don't You Know There's a War On?;* Meyer, *Creating G. I. Jane;* Milkman, *Women, Work, and Protest;* Perrett, *Days of Sadness, Years of Triumph;* Rivas-Rodríguez, *Mexican Americans and World War II;* Ruiz, *From Out of the Shadows;* and Rupp, *Mobilizing Women for War.*

7. According to Cosgrove, the category "juvenile delinquent" emerged during World War II. See Cosgrove, "The Zoot Suit and Style Warfare," 80. Regarding the emergence of the label "adolescent" in the early twentieth century, see Moore et al., *Homeboys,* 215.

8. Redl, "Zoot Suits," 260.

9. McWilliams, *North from Mexico,* 219.

10. Regarding Mexicans and Mexican Americans in early twentieth-century Los Angeles, see Escobar, *Race, Police, and the Making of a Political Identity;* Molina,

Fit to Be Citzens?; Romo, *East Los Angeles*; and Sánchez, *Becoming Mexican American*. Regarding early-twentieth-century Mexican American history more generally, see Foley, *The White Scourge*; Griswold de Castillo and de León, *North to Aztlán*; Montejano, *Anglos and Mexicans in the Making of Texas, 1836–1986*; and Ruiz, *From out of the Shadows*.

11. Stegner, *One Nation*, 117.

12. Paz, *The Labyrinth of Solitude and Other Writings*, 15.

13. Ibid., 14.

14. Sánchez, *Becoming Mexican American*, 13. Los Angeles is the site of this study not only because of its relatively high Mexican American population but because of changes it underwent during World War II. I discuss these changes below.

15. Macías, "Bringing Music to the People," 695. Like jazz, the zoot suit was not strictly a U.S. phenomenon. For example, the Mexican comedian Tin Tan (*né* Germán Valdés) launched his career as a pachuco-slang-speaking radio actor in the border city of Juárez and wore outrageous zoot suits in his stage performances in Mexico City in the early 1940s. Meanwhile, young jazz fans in Paris known as *les Zazous* adopted a style inspired in part by American zooters. And by the end of World War II, a variation of the zoot look had spread to youths in Britain. Regarding *les Zazous*, see Fishman, *The Battle for Children*, 67–69, and Shack, *Harlem in Montmartre*, 119. Regarding the popularity of the zoot suit in Britain, see Chibnall, "Whistle and Zoot."

16. Works that examine the zoot subculture's affront to Jim Crow include Alvarez, *The Power of the Zoot*; Escobedo, "Mexican American Home Front"; Escobedo, "The Pachuca Panic"; Macías, "Bringing Music to the People"; and Pagán, *Murder at the Sleepy Lagoon*.

17. Redl, "Zoot Suits," 260.

18. Nash, *The American West Transformed*, 62–65. Also see Escobar, *Race, Police, and the Making of a Political Identity*.

19. "Haircut Style Discussions Delay Gang Slaying Trial," *Los Angeles Times*, October 27, 1942, 10.

20. Escobedo, "Mexican American Home Front," 70.

21. Ibid.

22. Pagán, *Murder at the Sleepy Lagoon*, 38.

23. Ibid., 37.

24. Ibid., 39.

25. Moore, *Homeboys*, 57.

26. Ibid., 37.

27. In Los Angeles, the zoot suit probably reached the height of its popularity among Mexican Americans in the early 1940s, what Mary López, one of my

interviewees, called "the pachuco time." Variations of the ensemble remained popular through the 1950s.

28. Author's interview with Mary López, June 7, 2002, Oakland, California.

29. Carlos Amezcua, "Origenes de 'Pachucos' y 'Malinches,'" *La Opinión*, August 26, 1942, 2. All translated excerpts from this article are my own.

30. Alcalá, "From Chingada to Chingona," 34.

31. My discussion of Malintzin and the legend of La Malinche draws from a number of sources, including Alarcón, "Traddutora, Traditora"; Alcalá, "From Chingada to Chingona"; Del Castillo, "Malintzín Tenepal"; and Díaz del Castillo, *The Conquest of New Spain.*

32. Alarcón, "Traddutora, Traditora," 72.

33. Paz, *The Labyrinth of Solitude and Other Writings,* 85.

34. Ibid., 85–86.

35. Alarcón "Traddutora, Traditora." The discourse on Malinche/Malinalli/Malintzin/Marina is extensive in Chicana studies, and for the sake of brevity I will not list all sources here. However, in addition to Alarcón's "Traddutora, Traditora," see Alarcón, "Chicana's Feminist Literature"; Alcalá, "From Chingada to Chingona"; Anzaldúa, *Borderlands/La Frontera;* Candelaria, "La Malinche, Feminist Prototype"; Del Castillo, "Malintzín Tenepal"; Pérez, "Sexuality and Discourse"; and Sánchez, *"Shakin' Up" Race and Gender.*

36. Lipsitz, *American Studies in a Moment of Danger* (emphasis original), 169.

37. My definition of the Chicano movement draws from a variety of sources, including Chabram-Dernersesian, "I Throw Punches for My Race, but I Don't Want to Be a Man"; Chávez, *¡Mi Raza Primero! (My People First);* Chávez, "Despierten hermanas y hermanos"; Espinoza, "'Revolutionary Sisters'"; Espinoza, "'Tanto Tiempo Disfrutamos . . .'"; Griswold del Castillo et al., eds., *Chicano Art: Resistance and Affirmation, 1965–1985;* Lipsitz, *American Studies in a Moment of Danger;* Mariscal, *Brown-Eyed Children of the Sun;* Muñoz, *Youth, Identity, Power;* Oropeza, *¡Raza Sí! ¡Guerra No!;* Rodríguez, "Reimagined Communities"; and Rosales, *Chicano!* The National Farm Workers Association would become the United Farm Workers union. Accounts that look to the formation of the UFW as an, if not the, origin of the Chicano movement include Goldman and Ybarra-Frausto, "The Political and Social Contexts of Chicano Art"; Rosales, *Chicano!;* and Sánchez, *Contemporary Chicana Poetry.*

38. There were many actors in the Chicano movement, but Chicana and Chicano baby boomers played an especially salient role, as evidenced by the increase in student activism beginning in the late 1960s; for example, the high school "blow outs" (1968–69) in which students in Los Angeles and other Southwestern cities marched out of their schools en masse to demand changes in their education; the Third World Strike (1968–69) at San Francisco State University

and the University of California, Berkeley; the National Youth Liberation Conference in Denver (1969); and the formation of the national student organization Movimiento Estudiantil Chicano de Aztlán (MECHA) in 1969. While I do not care to declare the Chicano movement over or dead or to divide it into various "waves" (similar to first-wave, second-wave, and third-wave feminisms), in order to hone my focus, I identify it with the generation of artists, intellectuals, and activists who came of age in the 1960s, 1970s, and early 1980s. For this reason, I limit my discussion of the Chicano movement to this period.

39. Nieto-Gómez, "La Femenista," 87.

40. Ibid., 90.

41. Ibid.

42. Ibid., 88.

43. See, for example, Alexander, "Not Just (Any) Body Can Be a Citizen"; Alexander, *Pedagogies of Crossing;* Butler, *Antigone's Claim;* Gilroy, "It's a Family Affair; Luibhéid, *Entry Denied;* McClintock, "Family Feuds"; Pin-Fat and Stern, "The Scripting of Private Jessica Lynch"; and Yuval-Davis and Anthias, eds., *Women-Nation-State.*

44. See, for example, Espinoza, "'Revolutionary Sisters'"; Fregoso, *MeXicana Encounters;* Fregoso, "Re-Imagining Chicana Urban Identities in the Public Sphere, *Cool Chuca Style*"; Orozco, "Beyond Machismo, La Familia, and Ladies Auxiliaries"; Rodríguez, "Reimagined Communities"; Rodríguez, "Serial Kinship"; Rodríguez, "The Verse of the Godfather"; Saldívar-Hull, *Feminism on the Border;* Zavella, *Women's Work and Chicano Families;* and Zinn, "Political Familism."

45. Ramón Cisneros, "The Adventures of Kiki and El Cruiser," *Lowrider* 2, no. 1 (October 1978): n. p.

46. "The Further Adventures of Kiki and El Cruiser," *Lowrider* 2, no. 2 (November 1978): n. p.

47. This list is not meant to be exhaustive. Other movement-era literary works that feature *el pachuco* include Alurista, "Pachuco Paz"; Alva, "The Sacred Spot"; Burciaga, *Restless Serpents;* Durán, "Retrato de un Bato Loco"; Garza, "Saturday Belongs to the Palomía"; Granado, "Para Mi Jefe"; Montoya, "El Louie"; Montoya, "Los Vatos"; Navarro, "East Los Angeles"; Navarro, "To a Dead Lowrider"; raúlsalinas, "Homenaje al Pachuco (Mirrored Reflections)"; raúlsalinas, "A Trip through the Mind Jail"; Rechy, "El Paso del Norte"; Rivera, "On the Road to Texas"; Rodríguez, "Expresiones de mi barrio/Barrio Expressions"; Sánchez, *Canto y Grito Mi Liberación;* Sanchez, *Zoot Suit Murders;* Valdez, *Zoot Suit and Other Plays;* and Villanueva, *Hay Otra Voz.*

For representations of *el pachuco* in movement-era visual culture, see Griswold del Castillo et al., eds., *Chicano Art* (especially the "Urban Images" section); Luckenbill, *The Pachuco Era;* and José Montoya, *Pachuco Art.* Also see various issues of *Lowrider* magazine, especially from 1978 through the early 1980s. Judith Baca's *Zoot Suit Riots* (part of the *Great Wall of Los Angeles*); and Vincent Valdez's more recent oil painting *Kill the Pachuco Bastard!* (2001).

Within Chicana/o studies, there has been a (re)surgence in interest in pachucas and pachucos and the World War II–era Mexican American zoot subculture, as evidenced not only by my own work but also by Tovares's documentary film *The American Experience: Zoot Suit Riots* (which aired on PBS stations across the United States in 2001); the conference "The Sleepy Lagoon Case, Constitutional Rights, and the Struggle for Democracy," which was held at the University of California, Los Angeles, May 20–21, 2005 (http://www .library.ucla.edu/); and the roundtable "Perhaps the Zoot Suit concerns Profound Political Meaning" at the 2008 annual meeting of the Organization of American Historians. Also see Alvarez, "From Zoot Suits to Hip Hop"; Alvarez, *The Power of the Zoot*; Alvarez, "Zoot Violence on the Home Front"; Barajas, "The Defense Committees of Sleepy Lagoon"; Cummings, "Que siga el corrido"; Daniels, "Los Angeles Zoot"; De Lorca, "The Reality of a Myth"; Escobar, *Race, Police, and the Making of a Political Identity*; Escobar, "Zoot-Suiters and Cops"; Escobedo, "Mexican American Home Front"; Escobedo, "The Pachuca Panic"; Green, " 'Give It Your Best!' "; Macías, "Bringing Music to the People"; Márez, "Brown"; and Pagán, *Murder at the Sleepy Lagoon.*

48. I have found especially helpful Alarcón, Caplan, and Moallem's introduction to *Between Woman and Nation;* Chabram-Dernersesian, "I Throw Punches for My Race, but I Don't Want to Be a Man"; Espinoza, " 'Revolutionary Sisters' "; Fregoso, *The Bronze Screen* (especially chapter 2); García, ed., *Chicana Feminist Thought;* Gaspar de Alba, *Chicano Art, Inside/Outside the Master's House;* Moraga, *The Last Generation;* Moraga, *Loving in the War Years;* Oropeza, *¡Raza Sí! ¡Guerra No!;* and Pérez, "*El desorden,* Nationalism, and Chicana/o Aesthetics."

49. Oropeza, *¡Raza Sí! ¡Guerra No!,* 87.

50. Alarcón, "Chicana Feminism," 248.

51. See, for example, Nieto-Gómez's essay "Chicana Feminism" (1976), in which she distinguishes Chicana feminism from Anglo-American feminism and traces the history of Chicana feminism to "pre-Columbian feminists" and the seventeenth-century Mexican intellectual Sor Juana Inés de la Cruz; and Cotera's speech "Our Feminist Heritage" (1973), in which she aligns Chicana feminism with Mexican feminism. Both her and Nieto-Gómez's emphasis on Chicana feminism's distinctiveness vis-à-vis Anglo-American feminism echoes the cultural nationalist concern with the distinctiveness of Chicano culture vis-à-vis middle-class, Anglophone, white American culture. Also see

Pérez, "*El desorden*, Nationalism, and Chicana/o Aesthetics," and Ruiz, *From Out of the Shadows* (especially chapter 5), regarding the relationship of Chicana feminism and Chicano cultural nationalism.

52. Zavella, "The Problematic Relationship of Feminism and Chicana Studies," 27.

53. Chabram-Dernersesian, "I Throw Punches for My Race, but I Don't Want to Be a Man," 82.

54. Ibid.

55. Orona-Córdova, "*Zoot Suit* and the Pachuco Phenomenon," 100.

56. Valdez, *Zoot Suit and Other Plays*, 26.

57. Braddy, "The Pachucos and Their Argot," 262.

58. Grajeda, "The Pachuco in Chicano Poetry," 46.

59. There are numerous texts that address the significance of the World War II period in and to Chicano history. See, for example, Adler, "The 1943 Zoot-Suit Riots"; Alvarez, "From Zoot Suits to Hip Hop"; Alvarez, *The Power of the Zoot*; Barajas, "The Defense Committees of Sleepy Lagoon"; Daniels, "Los Angeles Zoot"; Johnson, "Constellations of Struggle"; Lorca, "The Reality of a Myth"; Escobar, *Race, Police, and the Making of a Political Identity*; Escobar, "Zoot-Suiters and Cops"; Escobedo, "Mexican American Home Front"; Escobedo, "The Pachuca Panic"; García, "Americans All"; García, *Mexican Americans*; Griswold del Castillo, *César Chávez*; Griswold del Castillo and de León, *North to Aztlán*; Madrid-Barela, "In Search of the Authentic Pachuco"; Mazón, *The Zoot-Suit Riots*; Montejano, *Anglos and Mexicans in the Making of Texas, 1836–1986*; Moore and Cuéllar, *Mexican Americans*; Morín, *Among the Valiant*; Oropeza, *¡Raza Sí! ¡Guerra No!*; Pagán, *Murder at the Sleepy Lagoon*; Rivas-Rodríguez, ed., *Mexican Americans and World War II*; Romano-V., "The Historical and Intellectual Presence of Mexican-Americans"; Romo, *East Los Angeles*; Ruiz, *Cannery Women, Cannery Lives*; Ruiz, "The Flapper and the Chaperone"; Ruiz, "Una Mujer sin Fronteras"; Ruiz, "'Star Struck'; Sánchez, *Becoming Mexican American*; San Miguel, *"Let All of Them Take Heed"*; Santillán, "Rosita the Riveter"; Scott, "The Zoot-Suit Riots"; Servín, "World War II and the Mexican-American"; Takaki, *Double Victory*; Tovares, *Zoot Suit Riots*; and Villarreal, *Arizona's Hispanic Flyboys, 1941–1945*. Also see the premier issue of the magazine *Corazón de Aztlán* (1981).

60. Leal, "Mexican American Literature," 28.

61. Ibid.

62. Villaraigosa, Los Angeles's first Mexican mayor since 1872, was elected in May 2005. While Roybal was shaped by the "Mexican American Generation" or "GI Generation," Villaraigosa is of the "Chicano Generation." As a teenager in the 1960s, he was active in the farm workers' struggle, and as an undergradu-

ate at UCLA he was a member of MECHA. See http://www.lacity.org/ (visited January 27, 2006).

63. Grajeda, "The Pachuco in Chicano Poetry," 47.

64. Santillán, "Rosita the Riveter," 119.

65. García, *Mexican Americans*, 6.

66. Ibid., 300.

67. Oropeza, *¡Raza Sí! ¡Guerra No!*, 79.

68. Fregoso, *The Bronze Screen*, 28.

69. In an interview I conducted with her at the Social and Public Art Resource Center in Venice, California, on August 1, 2000, Baca informed me that she based the pachuca in *Las Tres Marías* on a combination of pachucas she simultaneously admired and feared while growing up in Pacoima, California, during the 1950s. I thank her for talking to me about her life and work.

70. "Zoot Suiters Learn Lesson in Fights with Servicemen," part 1, *Los Angeles Times*, June 7, 1943, 1; Steiner, *La Raza*, 234.

71. Hondagneau-Sotelo and Messner, "Gender Displays and Men's Power, 214.

72. Ibid.

73. Halberstam, *Female Masculinity*, 2.

74. Villanueva, *Hay Otra Voz*, 40.

75. Chabram-Dernersesian, "I Throw Punches for My Race, but I Don't Want to Be a Man," 83.

76. Ibid.

77. Escobedo, "Mexican American Home Front," 228.

78. Santillán, "Rosita the Riveter," 138. The term "Rosita the Riveter" was first used by Santillán. Other works that discuss Mexican American women workers during World War II include Gluck, *Rosie the Riveter Revisited;* Escobedo, "Mexican American Home Front"; Quiñonez, "Rosita the Riveter"; and Takaki, *Double Victory* (especially chapter 5).

79. Quiñonez, "Rosita the Riveter," 245–46.

80. Oropeza, *¡Raza Sí! ¡Guerra No!*, 24. To date, there are few published works on Mexican American servicewomen in World War II (or any war for that matter). However, see *Spanish Speaking Americans in the War: The Southwest* as cited in Oropeza, *¡Raza Sí! ¡Guerra No!* Also see chapter 4 of Gluck's *Rosie the Riveter Revisited,* which features a 1944 photograph of Lockheed riveter Margarita Salazar McSweyn in her Civilian Defense Corps uniform. I discuss the figure of the Latina servicewoman in the war on terror in the epilogue.

81. Day, "The Pertinence of the 'Sleepy Lagoon' Case," 4.

82. Although Valdez stresses in *Zoot Suit* that at least one Mexican American girl was incarcerated as a result of her participation in the Sleepy Lagoon incident, he was nonetheless criticized for downplaying the participation of Mexican

American women—in particular, Josefina Fierro de Bright, whom I discuss in chapter 2—and highlighting the role of the Sleepy Lagoon Defense Committee secretary Alice Greenfield McGrath, a white woman, in the Sleepy Lagoon incident and trial. In the play and film, the character of Alice Bloomfield is based on McGrath. See Barajas, "The Defense Committees of Sleepy Lagoon"; Broyles-González, *El Teatro Campesino;* Corona, "Chicano Scholars and Public Issues in the United States in the Eighties"; and García, *Memories of Chicano History.*

83. Accounts that address the unfair treatment of the Mexican American girls and young women who took part in the Sleepy Lagoon incident and who testified in *People v. Zammora* include Barajas, "The Defense Committees of Sleepy Lagoon"; Escobedo, "Mexican American Home Front"; Escobedo, "The Pachuca Panic"; McGrath and Balter, *The Education of Alice McGrath;* Pagán, *Murder at the Sleepy Lagoon;* Ramírez, "The Pachuca in Chicana/o Art, Literature, and History"; and Tovares, *Zoot Suit Riots.* To Valdez's credit, *Zoot Suit,* which premiered in 1978, was perhaps one of the first works to mention their incarceration. See Valdez, *Zoot Suit and Other Plays.*

84. Bogardus, *The Mexican in the United States,* 28; Carlos Amezcua, "Origenes de 'Pachucos' y 'Malinches,'" *La Opinión,* August 26, 1942, 3.

85. According to Ruiz, the chaperone tradition disappeared in Mexican American Los Angeles in the years between World War II and the Korean War. See Ruiz, "The Flapper and the Chaperone." Also see Escobedo, "Mexican American Home Front," and Quiñonez, "Rosita the Riveter."

86. Escobedo, "Mexican American Home Front," 74.

87. Bogardus, *The Mexican in the United States,* 57–58.

88. See, for example, Escobedo, "Mexican American Home Front"; Escobedo, "The Pachuca Panic"; Fregoso, "Familia Matters," in *MeXicana Encounters,* 91–102; and my "Crimes of Fashion." Regarding pachucos' occupation of public space in wartime Los Angeles, see Pagan's *Murder at the Sleepy Lagoon.*

89. "Arena of discursive relations" is from Fraser's "Rethinking the Public Sphere," 75.

90. I take my definitions of public and private from a number of sources, among them Alexander, *Pedagogies of Crossing;* Duggan, *The Twilight of Equality;* Elshtain, *Public Man/Private Woman;* Fraser, "Rethinking the Public Sphere"; Fregoso, "Familia Matters"; Miranda, *Homegirls in the Public Sphere;* Kerber, "Separate Spheres, Female Worlds, Woman's Place"; Pin-Fat and Stern, "The Scripting of Private Jessica Lynch"; Scott and Keates, eds., *Going Public;* and Stansell's masterly *City of Women.*

91. See, for example, Alexander, "Not Just (Any) Body Can Be a Citizen"; Alexander, *Pedagogies of Crossing;* and Luibhéid, *Entry Denied.*

92. Stansell, *City of Women*, 93. Regarding New York City's "Bowery gals" of the 1830s, see Stansell, 92–94. Regarding *"las pelonas"* (Mexican American flappers) of the 1920s, see Ruiz, "The Flapper and the Chaperone"; Ruiz, "'Star Struck'"; and Ruiz, *From out of the Shadows*. Also see Enstad, *Ladies of Labor, Girls of Adventure*; Peiss, *Cheap Amusements*; and Odem, *Delinquent Daughters* regarding young, urban, working-class women, leisure, and public spectacle during the Progressive era.

93. Ruiz, "'Star Struck,'" 116.

94. Saldívar-Hull, *Feminism on the Border*, 141.

95. Alexander, "Not Just (Any) Body Can Be a Citizen," 6.

96. Fregoso, *MeXicana Encounters*, 91.

97. Anzaldúa, *Borderland/La Frontera*, 20.

98. Brubaker, *Citizenship and Nationhood in France and Germany*, 22. The historian Mae M. Ngai defines "alien citizens" as "persons who are American citizens by virtue of their birth in the United States but who are presumed to be foreign by the mainstream of American culture and, at times, by the state." See Ngai, *Impossible Subjects*, 2.

   My understanding of citizenship is also informed by Batstone and Mendicta, *The Good Citizen*; Beiner, *Theorizing Citizenship*; Bosniak, *The Citizen and the Alien*; Brubaker, *Immigration and the Politics of Citizenship in Europe and North America*; De Genova, *Working the Boundaries*; Flores and Benmayor, *Latino Cultural Citizenship*; Jopkke, *Challenge to the Nation-State*; Marshall and Bottomore, *Citizenship and Social Class*; Oboler, *Latinos and Citizenship*; Ong, "Cultural Citizenship as Subject-Making"; Ong, *Flexible Citizenship*; Rosaldo, "The Borders of Belonging"; and Rosaldo, "Cultural Citizenship and Educational Democracy."

99. Rosaldo, "The Borders of Belonging," 3.

100. I take my understanding of nation and nationalism from a number of works, including Anderson, *Imagined Communities*; Balibar and Wallerstein, *Race, Nation, Class*; Behdad, *A Forgetful Nation*; Bhabha, *Nation and Narration*; Brubaker, *Nationalism Reframed*; Calhoun, *Nationalism*; Chatterjee, *The Nation and Its Fragments*; Fitzgerald, *The Face of the Nation*; Gellner, *Nationalism*; Kohn, *The Idea of Nationalism*; Smith, *National Identity*; Smith, *Nationalism and Modernism*; Williams, *Keywords*; and Zolberg, *A Nation by Design*.

101. Pérez, "*El desorden*, Nationalism, and Chicana/o Aesthetics," 19.

102. Pérez-Torres, "Refiguring Aztlán," 110.

103. Omi and Winant, *Racial Formation in the United States*, 40.

104. If cultural visibility and full citizenship are inversely related, as Rosaldo has argued, then the visibility of Chicano/Mexican culture in the United States testifies to the exclusion of Chicanas, Chicanos, and Mexicans from the polity

and their status as alien citizens or aliens. Rosaldo explains, "Full citizens lack culture, and those most culturally endowed lack full citizenship. . . . Those people who have culture . . . occupy subordinate positions within the nation-state." See Rosaldo, *Culture and Truth*, 198–199.

In defining full citizenship, I find Peter H. Schuck's definition of citizenship helpful. Full citizens "mutually pledge their trust and concern for each other and their full participation in shared civic and civil cultures." They "owe allegiance to their polity—they may not betray it and may have to serve it—while the polity owes its citizens the fullest measure of protection that its law affords, including (except for minors and some convicted felons) the right to vote." In other words, full citizens are produced, acknowledged, and at times protected by the state and its apparatuses (for example, schools, hospitals, the legal system). They are expected to and often expect to participate fully in the social, political, and cultural organization of the community. See Schuck, "The Re-Evaluation of American Citizenship," 191.

105. Rosaldo, "Cultural Citizenship and Educational Democracy," 402.
106. Ong, "Cultural Citizenship as Subject-Making," 738.
107. "Group archetype" is from Valdez, *Zoot Suit and Other Plays*, 13.
108. Sturken and Cartwright, *Practices of Looking*, 36.
109. I have found especially insightful Chabram-Dernersesian's observation that "Chicano nationalism was . . . predicated on the necessity of mimesis: a one-on-one correspondence between the subject and its reflection in a mirrorlike duplication." See Chabram-Dernersesian, "I Throw Punches for My Race, but I Don't Want to Be a Man," 83. In addition, see Alarcón, "Traddutora, Traditora"; Butler, *Gender Trouble*; Butler, "Critically Queer"; Bhabha, *The Location of Culture*; and Lowe, *Immigrant Acts*.
110. I define cultural studies as "the analysis of symbolic, classificatory and, in short, meaning-making practices that are at the heart of all cultural production and consumption." See Evans and Hall, eds., *Visual Culture*, 3.
111. In understanding representation, I also draw from Hall's "The Work of Representation." Quotes in this sentence are from Sturken and Cartwright, *Practices of Looking*, 12 and 370.
112. I take the concept of the "spectacular subculture" from Hebdige's *Subculture*.

1. Domesticating the Pachuca

1. Valdez, *Zoot Suit and Other Plays*, 26.
2. Author's interview with Delia Chávez, Monterey Park, California, June 30, 1998.
3. Valdez, *Zoot Suit and Other Plays*, 24.
4. Fregoso, *The Bronze Screen*, 32.

5. Valdez, *Zoot Suit and Other Plays*, 25.

6. Brown, *States of Injury*, 38.

7. Regarding "the momentous impact Paredes's work has had on Chicano literature," see Saldívar, *The Dialectics of Our America*, 56. Also see Saldívar, *The Borderlands of Culture*; and Limón, *Mexican Ballads, Chicano Poems*.

8. Paz, *The Labyrinth of Solitude and Other Writings*, 14.

9. Alurista, *Nationchild Plumaroja*, "Serpiente," 14.

10. See, for example, Alvarez, *The Power of the Zoot*; Alvarez, "Zoot Violence on the Home Front"; Escobar, "Zoot-Suiters and Cops"; and Pagán, *Murder at the Sleepy Lagoon*. Works that focus on women or treat gender as a primary category of analysis include Barajas, "The Defense Committees of Sleepy Lagoon"; Escobedo, "Mexican American Home Front"; Escobedo, "The Pachuca Panic"; Fregoso, *The Bronze Screen*; Fregoso, "Homegirls, *Cholas*, and *Pachucas* in Cinema"; Fregoso, "Re-Imagining Chicana Urban Identities in the Public Sphere, *Cool Chuca Style*"; and Fregoso, *MeXicana Encounters*.

11. I interviewed the following women between 1998 and 2005: Delia "Dee" Chávez, Olga Cruz, María Elena "Helen" Gamboa (pseudonym), Carolina Juárez, Lupe Leyvas, Hortensia López, Mary López, Consuelo Loza (pseudonym), Mary Lou Ochoa, Enedina "Annie" Rodríguez, and Laura Vargas (pseudonym). Although I draw more heavily from some interviews than others, I am grateful to all of these women for sharing their time with me and for talking to me about life in Los Angeles in the 1930s, 1940s, and 1950s.

12. Yuval-Davis and Anthias, *Woman-Nation-State*, 3.

13. Steiner, *La Raza*, 232; Acuña, *Occupied America*, 255.

14. Sleepy Lagoon was north of Watts, south of Boyle Heights, and east of what is now the Harbor Freeway (Interstate 110). In reconstructing the Sleepy Lagoon incident, I draw primarily from *People v. Zammora, et al.*, Cr. 3719, District Court of Appeal, Second District, Division 1, California, October 4, 1944, 152 Pacific Reporter, 2d Series (box 11/12, folder 104, Ron López Papers, collection 0003, Chicano Studies Research Library, University of California, Los Angeles). This quote is from page 184.

15. Ibid., 185. According to Pagán, this group consisted of approximately twenty-two young men and thirteen young women. See Pagán, *Murder at the Sleepy Lagoon*, 63.

16. *People v. Zammora, et al.*, 188.

17. Ibid., 193.

18. Ibid., 186.

19. Testimony of Betty Nuñez Zeiss, *People v. Zammora, et al.*, District Court of Appeal, Second District, Division 1, California (box 7, vol. 2, Sleepy Lagoon Defense Committee, collection 107, Department of Special Collections,

Charles E. Young Research Library, University of California, Los Angeles), 480. Regarding Barrios's and Zeiss's ages, see Pagán, *Murder at the Sleepy Lagoon*, 82.

20. For more detailed information regarding the Sleepy Lagoon incident, see Barajas, "The Defense Committees of Sleepy Lagoon"; Escobar, *Race, Police, and the Making of a Political Identity*; McWilliams, *North from Mexico*; Pagán, *Murder at the Sleepy Lagoon*; and Tovares, *The American Experience: Zoot Suit Riots.*

21. "Jury's Gang-Case Verdict Disproves 'Persecution,'" *Los Angeles Times*, January 14, 1943.

22. Regarding the three female suspects, see "Three Teen-Age Girls Held in Boy-Gang Slaying Inquiry," *Los Angeles Times*, August 5, 1942, 12. Also see Barajas, "The Defense Committees of Sleepy Lagoon"; Escobedo, "Mexican American Home Front"; and Pagán, *Murder at the Sleepy Lagoon*. For more information concerning the so-called drive on Mexican gangs, see the undated letter from Captain Joseph F. Reed to C. B. Horrall, Chief of the Los Angeles Police Department (box 11/12, folder 89, Ron López Papers, collection 0003, Chicano Studies Research Library, University of California, Los Angeles). Also see Alvarez, *The Power of the Zoot*; Escobedo, "Mexican American Home Front"; Escobar, *Race, Police, and the Making of a Political Identity*; Escobar, "Zoot-Suiters and Cops"; McWilliams, *North from Mexico*; and Pagán, *Murder at the Sleepy Lagoon.*

23. Escobedo, "Mexican American Home Front," 68. Bertha Aguilar, Dora Barrios, Lorena Encinas, Juanita Gonzales, and Betty Nuñez Zeiss were sentenced to the Ventura School for Girls. Also see Escobedo, "The Pachuca Panic"; Barajas, "The Defense Committees of Sleepy Lagoon," 38; and Pagán, *Murder at the Sleepy Lagoon*, 203.

24. McGrath and Balter, *The Education of Alice McGrath*, 140.

25. In an interview in 1987, McGrath noted that none of the girls stayed at the Ventura School for Girls until they were twenty-one years of age. See ibid., 142. However, according to Escobedo, Dora Barrios and Betty Nuñez Zeiss entered the Ventura School in 1942, were paroled in 1943, and remained wards of the state until they turned twenty-one. See Escobedo, "Mexican American Home Front," 68, and Escobedo, "The Pachuca Panic."

Regarding Gonzales's age, see her testimony in *People v. Zammora, et al.,* Superior Court in the District Court of Appeal of the State of California, Second Appellate District (box 7, vol. 1, Sleepy Lagoon Defense Committee, collection 107, Department of Special Collections, Charles E. Young Research Library, University of California, Los Angeles), 201. Also see Pagán, *Murder at the Sleepy Lagoon*, 82.

Regarding the Ventura School for Girls, also see McWilliams, *North from Mexico*. For a more general discussion of public reformatories for girls and young women in California in the early twentieth century, see Odem, *Delinquent Daughters*.

26. There is discrepancy concerning the founding of the SLDC. Some maintain that the organization stemmed from El Congreso del Pueblo de Habla Española and attribute its formation to Fierro de Bright in particular. See, for example, Corona, "Chicano Scholars and Public Issues in the United States in the Eighties," 16; García, *Memories of Chicano History*, 114; and García, *Mexican Americans*, 171. However, Alice Greenfield McGrath, SLDC executive secretary, and Carey McWilliams, SLDC chairman, have credited LaRue McCormick with establishing the organization, which was initially called the Citizens' Committee for the Defense of Mexican American Youth (CCDMAY), in 1942. See McGrath and Balter, *The Education of Alice McGrath*, 116; and McWilliams, *North from Mexico*, 210. In a telephone interview I conducted with her on February 18, 1999, McGrath reiterated that McCormick was the SLDC's founder but added that Fierro de Bright was an early, active, and ongoing member. Similarly, George Shibley, defense attorney in *People v. Zammora*, stressed the indispensable role that Fierro de Bright played in the organization (box 28, folder 25, SERIES X, G, Bert Corona Papers, M0238, Green Library, Stanford University). More recently, Barajas credits McCormick with founding the CCDMAY and recruiting Fierro de Bright, Corona, and McWilliams into it. See Barajas, "The Defense Committees of Sleepy Lagoon," 40–41. I am grateful to Ms. McGrath for talking to me about her memories and insights concerning the Sleepy Lagoon incident, *People v. Zammora*, and the SLDC.

27. García, *Mexican Americans*, 155 and 171.

28. "Very effective" and "helpful" are from McGrath and Balter, *The Education of Alice McGrath*, 172. Other quotes in this sentence are from my February 18, 1999, telephone interview with Ms. McGrath.

29. I conducted my interview with Lupe Leyvas on August 3, 2000, in Montebello, California. I thank Ms. Leyvas for her candor, time, and memories.

30. Author's interview with Lupe Leyvas, Montebello, California, August 2, 2000.

31. Barajas, "The Defense Committees of Sleepy Lagoon," 49.

32. Ibid.

33. Author's interview with Lupe Leyvas, Montebello, California, August 3, 2000.

34. McGrath and Balter, *The Education of Alice McGrath*, 172.

35. Carey McWilliams, *North from Mexico*, 207.

36. Author's interview with Lupe Leyvas, Montebello, California, August 3, 2000.

37. Ibid.

38. Ibid.

39. In my February 18, 1999, telephone interview with her, Alice McGrath noted that finding a bilingual typist in the early 1940s was no easy task, explaining that at the time most Mexican Americans were discouraged from pursuing careers as secretaries. She mentions Lerma in McGrath and Balter, *The Education of Alice McGrath*, 193. Also see Barajas, "The Defense Committees of Sleepy Lagoon," 50.

40. Box 3, file 3, Sleepy Lagooon Defense Committee Collection, collection 107, Department of Special Collections, Charles E. Young Research Library, University of California, Los Angeles. According to Vicki L. Ruiz, UCAPAWA had the greatest number of Mexicans of any CIO or AFL affiliate. Additionally, 50 percent of its members were women and, by 1938, a handful of Spanish-surnamed women held leadership positions in the union, among them Angie González, Monica Tafoya, Emma Tenayuca, and Luisa Moreno, who would eventually become an international vice president. See Ruiz, *Cannery Women, Cannery Lives.*

41. Baca was at Sleepy Lagoon on August 1, 1942. She and her boyfriend, Henry Leyvas (Lupe's brother), were two of the youths set upon by the Downey Boys. She did not return to Sleepy Lagoon with Henry and the others, nor did she accompany them to the ill-fated party at Williams Ranch. Eventually, however, she testified as a witness for the defense in *People v. Zammora*. Regarding the Youth Committee for the Defense of Mexican American Youth, see box 11/12, folder 66, Ron López Papers, collection 0003, Chicano Studies Research Library, University of California, Los Angeles.

42. April 11, 1943, letter from Henry Ynostroza to Alice Greenfield (box 4, file 2, Sleepy Lagoon Defense Committee Collection, collection 107, Department of Special Collections, Charles E. Young Research Library, University of California, Los Angeles).

43. "Sleepy Lagoon Death Figures Given Freedom," *Los Angeles Times*, October 24, 1944, part 2, 1.

44. "The Sleepy Lagoon Case," *New Republic*, December 11, 1944, 795; Day, "The Pertinence of the 'Sleepy Lagoon' Case," 75 and 71.

45. McGrath and Balter, *The Education of Alice McGrath*, 140.

46. Ibid., 141.

47. Ibid., 141–42.

48. Ibid., 140. See Odem's *Delinquent Daughters* for a rich and insightful discussion of the ways parents and the state colluded in policing and punishing girls and young women in the early twentieth century.

49. Other civil disturbances occurred in Harlem, Detroit, San Diego, and Philadelphia (to list just a handful of cities). See Alvarez, *The Power of the Zoot*.

50. Mazón, *The Zoot-Suit Riots*, 87. Other valuable works on the Zoot Suit Riots include Adler, "The 1943 Zoot-Suit Riots"; Alvarez, *The Power of the Zoot*; Escobar, *Race, Police, and the Making of a Political Identity*; Escobar, "Zoot-Suiters and Cops"; Lipsitz, *Rainbow at Midnight*; McWilliams, *North from Mexico*; Pagán, *Murder at the Sleepy Lagoon*; Scott, "The Zoot-Suit Riots"; and Tovares, *The American Experience: Zoot Suit Riots*.

51. Contemporary accounts that assert that a sexual competition between white servicemen and Mexican American zooters sparked the Zoot Suit Riots include Horace Cayton, "Riot Causes," *Pittsburgh Courier*, September 25, 1943, 13; Chester B. Himes, "Zoot Riots Are Race Riots," *The Crisis*, vol. 50, no. 7 (July 1943): 200–201, 222; and "Zoot Suits and Service Stripes: Race Tension Behind the Riots," *Newsweek*, June 21, 1943, 35–40. For later accounts, see Acuña, *Occupied America*; Adler, "The 1943 Zoot-Suit Riots"; "Carnalismo en Los Califas," *La Causa*, May 22, 1972, 2; Domer, "The Zoot-Suit Riot"; Ford, *Thirty Explosive Years in Los Angeles*; Henstell, "The Zoot Suit"; McGrath and Balter, *The Education of Alice McGrath*; Meier and Ribera, *Mexican Americans/ American Mexicans*; Mirandé, *Gringo Justice*; Nash, *The American West Transformed*; Scott, "The Zoot-Suit Riots"; Sine, "Zoot Suit Riots of Los Angeles, 1943"; Turner and Surace, "Zoot-Suiters and Mexicans"; Valdez, *Zoot Suit and Other Plays*; and Wyatt, *Five Fires*.

52. Regarding mounting tension between white servicemen and Mexican American youths (especially pachucos) in Los Angeles in the months preceding the Zoot Suit Riots, also see Cayton, "Riot Causes"; Domer, "The Zoot-Suit Riot"; Escobar, *Race, Police, and the Making of a Political Identity*; Escobar, "Zoot-Suiters and Cops"; Griffith, *American Me*; Himes, "Zoot Riots Are Race Riots"; Mazón, *The Zoot-Suit Riots*; and Nash, *The American West Transformed*.

53. "Four Suspects Seized in Attacks on Women," *Los Angeles Times*, June 2, 1943, 7; "2 Girls Accuse 16 Zoot Suiters," *Los Angeles Daily News*, June 2, 1943, 7; "Zoot suit orgy" is from the *Times* story. Interestingly, both of the women who reported the rape had Spanish surnames. It is not clear if their husbands were servicemen.

54. Quotes in this sentence are from Manchester Boddy, "Views of the News," *Los Angeles Daily News*, June 8, 1943, 1; "Los Angeles Barred to Sailors by Navy to Stem Zoot-Suit Riots," *New York Times*, June 9, 1943, 23; "New Serviceman-'Zooter' Fights Follow Weekend Clashes," *Los Angeles Herald-Express*, June 7, 1943, A3; "Sailors Hunt Zoot-Suiters, 2 in Hospital," *Los Angeles Examiner*, June 5, 1943, 3; "Sailor 'Task Force' Hits L.A. Zooters," *Los Angeles Herald-Express*, June 5, 1943, A1; "Zoot Suiters in Hiding as Drive Starts," *Los Angeles Examiner*, June 4, 1943, 3; "Zoot Suiters Learn Lesson in Fights with Servicemen," *Los Angeles Times*, June 7, 1943, 1; and "Zoot Suit Riots," *Life*, June 21, 1943, 30–31. Also see Griffith, *American Me*, 28, 50–51.

55. "Navy-Battered Zoot Suiters Jailed by Police," *Los Angeles Examiner*, June 7, 1943, 1; "Zoot-Suit Gangs" (letter to the editor from Mary G. of San Fernando), *Los Angeles Herald-Express*, June 10, 1943, B2. Compare this letter to comments by Mildred Eusebio, a white woman who recalled that while she was living at her parents' house in Baldwin Park (a suburb in eastern Los Angeles County) during World War II, she did not go out often because she feared Mexican American zooters: "I didn't even go the movies on the week-ends because the theatres were full of [them]. . . . Some of those boys were just plain mean and nasty." This quote is from *Rosie the Riveter Revisited: Women and the World War II Work Experience*, California State University, Long Beach, University Library, Department of Special Collections, vol. 11, 40.

56. Himes, "Zoot Riots Are Race Riots," 201; Cayton, "Riot Causes," 13.

57. Himes, "Zoot Riots Are Race Riots," 200.

58. "Zoot Suits and Service Stripes," 35–36.

59. Cayton, "Riot Causes," 13.

60. See, for example, the words attributed to Tiburcio Vásquez, who, recalling the "balls and parties" he attended as a young man in California, complained that "the Americans, then beginning to become numerous, would force themselves and shove the native born [Mexican] men aside, monopolizing the dance and the women. This was about 1852. A spirit of hatred and revenge took possession of me. I had numerous fights in defense of what I believe to be my rights and those of my countrymen." See Acuña, *A Mexican American Chronicle*, 104.

61. Fregoso, *The Bronze Screen*, 132.

62. Carlos Amezcua, "Origenes de 'Pachucos' y 'Malinches,'" *La Opinión*, August 26, 1942, 2. Unless otherwise indicated, all translations of this article are my own.

63. Ibid., 3.

64. Ibid. The full sentence reads: "Lo más lamentable del caso es que las pandillas de 'pachucos' y 'malinches' están formadas de jóvenes de ascendencia mexicana" (The most deplorable aspect of the matter is that the gangs of "pachucos" and "malinches" are composed of youths of Mexican descent).

65. Alarcón, "Traddutora, Traditora," 60.

66. Alcalá, "From Chingada to Chingona," 34.

67. Alarcón, "Chicana's Feminist Literature," 184.

68. Rubin, "The Traffic in Women," 176 and 174.

69. Amezcua, "Origines de 'Pachucos' y 'Malinches,'" 2.

70. See, for example, Acuña, *Occupied America*; Adler, "The 1943 Zoot-Suit Riots"; Domer, "The Zoot-Suit Riot"; Ford, *Thirty Explosive Years in Los Angeles County*; Griffith, *American Me*; Henstell, "The Zoot Suit"; Mazón, *The Zoot-Suit Riots*; McGrath and Balter, *The Education of Alice McGrath*; Meier and Ri-

bera, *Mexican Americans/American Mexicans*; Mirandé, *Gringo Justice*; Nash, *The American West Transformed*; Scott, "The Zoot-Suit Riots"; Sine, "Zoot Suit Riots of Los Angeles"; Turner and Surace, "Zoot-Suiters and Mexicans"; Valdez, *Zoot Suit and Other Plays*; and "U.S. Navy Invasion," *La Causa*, May 22, 1970, 2. For an incisive discussion of the opening scene of *American Me*, see "Conclusion: Eastside Story Re-visited," chapter 6 of Fregoso's *The Bronze Screen*.

71. Blea, *La Chicana and the Intersection of Race, Class, and Gender*, 15.

72. Pratt, *Imperial Eyes*, 6.

73. Pagán, *Murder at the Sleepy Lagoon*, 7.

74. Cayton, "Riot Causes," 13.

75. For an example of the ways in which pachucos were perceived as a threat to the white home and family, see the interview (1982) with Mildred Eusebio in Gluck's *Rosie the Riveter Revisited* collection. Eusebio recalled that when she was living in Baldwin Park during the early 1940s, pachucos played a violent form of doorbell ditch: "They'd come knock at the door for no reason at all and just beat people," *Rosie the Riveter Revisited*, vol. 11, 39.

76. Himes, "Zoot Riots Are Race Riots," 200.

77. Griffith, *American Me*, 47.

78. Himes, "Zoot Riots Are Race Riots," 200.

79. Cayton, "Riot Causes," 13.

80. Ibid.

81. De Lorca, "The Reality of a Myth," 39–40.

82. See, for example, "Homes Invaded in Hunt for Pachucos," *Los Angeles Evening Herald-Express*, June 10, 1943, A1.

83. Griffith, *American Me*, 11.

84. Here I am drawing upon feminist scholarship that treats and criticizes the home as, in Stansell's words, "a pillar of civilization, an incubator of morals and family affections, [and] a critical alternative to the harsh and competitive world of trade and politics," and I would add, racism. See Stansell, *City of Women*, 42; Sánchez, "'Go After the Women'"; Escobedo, "Mexican American Home Front"; Fregoso, *MeXicana Encounters*; Moraga, *Loving in the War Years*; Miranda, *Homegirls in the Public*; Ruiz, "The Flapper and the Chaperone"; and Ruiz, "'Star Struck.'"

85. Al Waxman, "Column Left," *Eastside Journal*, June 9, 1943, 1; "Por la Guerra de Marinos y Pachucos," *La Opinión*, June 9, 1943, 8; "Zoot Suit Hunt on in Suburbs as Navy Clamps Ban on L.A.," *Los Angeles Examiner*, June 9, 1943, 1. Other newspaper stories about Amelia Venegas include "Policeman Is Ambushed Run Over by Zoot Auto," *Los Angeles Herald-Express*, June 9, 1943, A1; "Brass Knuckles Found on Woman 'Zoot Suiter,'" *Los Angeles Times*, June 10, 1943, A; "6 Day Zoot War Hospitalizes 112," *Los Angeles Daily News*, June 10,

1943, 1; and "U.S., Warren Act on Zoot Suits, New Outbreak of Gang Rioting," *Los Angeles Examiner*, June 10, 1943, 1. I discuss Venegas in more detail in chapters 3 and 4. Decades after the Zoot Suit Riots, *Lowrider* magazine reported that a Mexican American mother and daughter fought off two servicemen who had attacked their son and brother during the riots. See Manuel Cruz, "Gang History," *Lowrider* 2, no. 2 (1978): 32–35.

86. García, *Mexican Americans*, 172.

87. Photographs of Vera Duarte Trujillo, the "irate mother," ripping apart her son's zoot suit are on page B of the June 11, 1943, *Los Angeles Times* and page 12 of the June 11, 1943, *Los Angeles Examiner*. Also see "Mother Tears up Zoot Suit of Boy Wounded in Clash," *Los Angeles Times*, June 11, 1943, A. I discuss Trujillo in chapter 4.

88. This letter to the editor appears in Manchester Boddy, "Views of the News," *Los Angeles Daily News*, June 11, 1943, 1. The Ayres report, which has been attributed to Captain Edward Duran Ayres, head of the Foreign Relations Bureau of the Los Angeles County Sheriff's Department, is perhaps one of the most barefaced examples of biological racism to emerge in the United States during World War II, a moment when this country and its allies were combating biological racism overseas. Ayres presented the report on August 8, 1942, as testimony in the grand jury hearing that followed the Sleepy Lagoon incident and led to *People v. Zammora*. It is reprinted in Jones, "The Government Riots of Los Angeles, June 1943," 85–88.

89. "Mexican American Girls Meet in Protest," *Eastside Journal*, June 16, 1943, 5.

90. McWilliams, *North from Mexico*, 231.

91. "Mexican American Girls Meet in Protest," 5.

92. McWilliams, *North from Mexico*, 231.

93. Henstell, "The Zoot Suit," 220.

94. McWilliams, *North from Mexico*, 231.

95. See, for example, in Gluck, *Rosie the Riveter Revisited*, the interviews with Beatrice Morales Clifton (vol. 8, 46–47), Mary Luna (vol. 20, 31), Margarita Salazar McSweyn (vol. 25, 65 and 67), and Rose Echeverria Mulligan (vol. 27, 55–57). Also see the interview with Mildred Eusebio (vol. 11, 40).

96. These quotes are from Mulligan (vol. 27, 55–57) and McSweyn (vol. 25, 67).

97. Author's interview with María Elena Gamboa (pseudonym), Los Angeles, California, April 27, 1998.

98. Author's interview with Enedina Rodríguez, Monterey Park, California, April 26, 1998.

99. Author's interview with Delia Chávez, Monterey Park, California, June 30, 1998.

100. Author's interview with Consuelo Loza (pseudonym), Los Angeles, California, April 28, 1998.

101. Author's interview with Enedina Rodríguez, Monterey Park, California, April 26, 1998.

102. Author's interview with Mary López, Oakland, California, June 7, 2002.

103. Author's interview with Delia Chávez, Monterey Park, California, June 30, 1998.

104. Author's interview with Mary López, Oakland, California, June 7, 2002.

105. Author's interview with Delia Chávez, Monterey Park, California, June 30, 1998.

106. Griffith, *American Me,* 48.

107. Author's interview with Mary López, Oakland, California, June 7, 2002.

108. Author's interview with Delia Chávez, Monterey Park, California, June 30, 1998.

109. Ibid.

110. Author's interview with Mary López, Oakland, California, June 7, 2002.

111. Ibid.

112. Ibid.; author's translation.

113. Author's interview with Delia Chávez., Monterey Park, California, June 30, 1998.

114. Regarding Mexican American women and the link between physical and social mobility (namely, working outside the home) during World War II, see Escobedo, "Mexican American Home Front"; Gluck, *Rosie the Riveter Revisited;* Quiñonez, "Rosita the Riveter"; Ruiz, *Cannery Women, Cannery Lives;* and Ruiz, "'Star Struck.'" Regarding the end of chaperone tradition, see Escobedo, "Mexican American Home Front"; Quiñonez, "Rosita the Riveter"; and Ruiz, "The Flapper and the Chaperone."

115. Annie, born in 1935, is the youngest of the Gómez sisters. She has no brothers.

116. Author's interview with Enedina Rodríguez, Monterey Park, California, April 26, 1998.

117. Author's interview with Delia Chávez, Monterey Park, California, June 30, 1998.

118. Author's interview with Mary López, Oakland, California, June 7, 2002.

119. Author's interview with Delia Chávez, Monterey Park, California, June 30, 1998.

120. Fregoso, "Re-Imagining Chicana Urban Identities in the Public Sphere," 75.

121. Miranda, *Homegirls in the Public Sphere,* 45.

122. Escobedo, "Mexican American Home Front," 72.

123. Author's interview with Enedina Rodríguez, Monterey Park, California, April 26, 1998.

124. Griffith, *American Me,* 48.

125. Ruiz, "The Flapper and the Chaperone," 149.

126. I ended my interviews with questions about *Zoot Suit*, which premiered at the Mark Taper Forum in Los Angeles in April 1978 and ran for ten days. Due to its immense success, it returned for an eight-week stint the following August. In December 1978, it moved to the Aquarius Theater in Hollywood, where it ran for ten months, and after a brief run on Broadway in the spring of 1979, Universal Pictures released the film *Zoot Suit*, directed by Luis Valdez, in 1981.

127. Author's interview with Consuelo Loza (pseudonym), Los Angeles, California, April 28, 1998.

128. Author's interview with María Elena Gamboa (pseudonym), Los Angeles, California, April 27, 1998.

129. Fregoso, *MeXicana Encounters*, 91.

2. Pachuca Style and Spectacle

1. Lyrics for "A Zoot Suit (for My Sunday Gal)," by L. Wolfe Gilbert and Bob O'Brien, are from http://lyricsplayground.com/ (visited January 4, 2007).

2. Ibid.

3. Bogardus, "Gangs of Mexican American Youth," 56.

4. Griffith, *American Me*, 47.

5. See Walton, *Thread of Victory*, 78, regarding wartime complaints that a skirt that exposed the knees was immodest.

6. McRobbie, "Settling Accounts with Subcultures," 37, 43.

7. Ruiz, *From Out of the Shadows*, 53. Regarding the style and subculture of male zooters—in particular, Mexican Americans and African Americans—see Alvarez, *The Power of the Zoot*; Chibnall, "Whistle and Zoot"; Cosgrove, "The Zoot Suit and Style Warfare; Cummings, "Que siga el corrido"; Daniels, "Los Angeles Zoot"; De Lorca, "The Reality of a Myth"; Kelley, "The Riddle of the Zoot"; Macías, "Bringing Music to the People"; Márez, "Brown"; Mazón, *The Zoot-Suit Riots*; Mercer, *Welcome to the Jungle*; Noriega, "Fashion Crimes"; Pagán, *Murder at the Sleepy Lagoon*; Sanchez-Tranquilino, "Mano a Mano"; Sanchez-Tranquilino and John Tagg, "The Pachuco's Flayed Hide"; Tyler, "Black Jive and White Repression"; and White and White, *Stylin.'* Also see Tovares, *The American Experience: Zoot Suit Riots*. Scholarly works that devote considerable attention to pachucas and the roles they played in the Mexican American zoot subculture include Escobedo, "Mexican American Home Front"; Escobedo, "The Pachuca Panic"; Fregoso, "Homegirls, *Cholas*, and *Pachucas* in Cinema"; Fregoso, *MeXicana Encounters*; Fregoso, "Re-Imagining Chicana Urban Identities in the Public Sphere, *Cool Chuca Style*; and Green, "'Give It Your Best!'"

8. Espinoza, "'Tanto Tiempo Disfrutamos,'" 90.

9. Blackman and Perry, "Skirting the Issue," 78.

10. Mercer, *Welcome to the Jungle*, 119.

11. Kelley, *Race Rebels*, 166.

12. Romano-V., "The Historical and Intellectual Presence of Mexican Americans," 39.

13. Gaines, "War, Women, and Lipstick," 46.

14. Banay, "A Psychiatrist Looks at the Zoot Suit" (italics original), 81.

15. By "consumption," I refer to the buying, having, or using of commodities and leisure activities. For a fuller discussion of consumption, see Enstad, *Ladies of Labor, Girls of Adventure*, 4–5. Although Enstad's focus is working-class women in New York City at the beginning of the twentieth century, I believe much of her astute analysis of consumption, fashion, gender, and class is applicable to pachucas in Los Angeles in the early 1940s. Indeed, much of it remains relevant in the early twenty-first century.

16. Gilbert and O'Brien, "A Zoot Suit (for My Sunday Gal)."

17. Enstad, *Ladies of Labor, Girls of Adventure*, 4.

18. Veblen, *Theory of the Leisure Class*, 46.

19. Bourdieu, *Distinction*, 55.

20. Cummings, "Que siga el corrido," 101.

21. Malcolm X, *The Autobiography of Malcolm X*, 58.

22. See Kelley, *Race Rebels*, 163–65.

23. Malcolm X, *The Autobiography of Malcolm X*, 39 and 56.

24. For a brief reference to "welfare clothes," see Moore et al., *Homeboys*, 64. My father, who was born in 1924 and raised in East Los Angeles, recalled that for boys, "welfare clothes" consisted of boots, trousers or shorts, and a shirt. The quote in this sentence is from Veblen, *Theory of the Leisure Class*, 64.

25. See Enstad, *Ladies of Labor, Girls of Adventure*, 78, for a similar observation in relation to working-class American women at the beginning of the twentieth century.

26. *New York Times*, June 10, 1943, 23.

27. "Zoot Suit Girls Kick and Knife Waitress as Battle Continues," *Saint Paul Pioneer Press*, June 11, 1943, 1.

28. Veblen, *Theory of the Leisure Class*, 130.

29. Ibid.

30. Pagán, *Murder at the Sleepy Lagoon*, 7.

31. Regarding consumer culture and the Americanization of Mexican Americans in the early and mid-twentieth century, see Ruiz, "'Star Struck'"; and Sánchez, *Becoming Mexican American*.

32. Walton, *Thread of Victory*, 76. Regarding WPB Order L-224, also see Cosgrove, "The Zoot Suit and Style Warfare"; and Kelley, *Race Rebels*.

33. Griffith, *American Me*, 47.

34. "Scan Zooter Black Market," *Los Angeles Daily News*, June 12, 1943, 10.

35. *New York Times*, June 10, 1943, 23. "6 Zoot Suiters Sent to Hospital by Servicemen," *Los Angeles Daily News*, June 8, 1943, 6. Malcolm X describes how he successfully avoided the draft during World War II by wearing "the wildest zoot suit in New York" to the induction center and "talk[ing] and act[ing] high and crazy" in front of military officials. See *The Autobiography of Malcolm X*, 104–5.

36. The Ayres report is reprinted in Jones, "The Government Riots of Los Angeles, June 1943," 85–88.

37. For example, on June 9, 1943, the front page of the *Los Angeles Times* featured a story about the Zoot Suit Riots along with the headlines "FDR Warns Enemy Invasion Near" and "Over 600 Nisei at Poston Found Openly Disloyal." On the editorial page, the newspaper denounced the riots, and beneath the headline "Defeat Our Domestic Enemies First," it also condemned labor unrest.

38. Mazón discusses the paranoia that gripped the West Coast during World War II in *The Zoot-Suit Riots*. Also see newspaper stories on the alleged connection between zooters and the Axis: "6 Zoot Suiters Sent to Hospital by Servicemen," *Los Angeles Daily News*, June 8, 1943, 6; "Navy Bans All Personnel from Entire City," *Los Angeles Daily News*, June 9, 1943, 1; "Nazis Spur Zoot Riots," *Los Angeles Daily News*, June 9, 1943, 9; "Views of the News," *Los Angeles Daily News*, June 9, 1943, 12; "El Caso de los Pachucos en Manos de la Embajada," *La Opinión*, June 10, 1943, 1; "Tenney Feels Riots Caused by Nazi Move for Disunity," *Los Angeles Times*, June 10, 1943, A1; "U.S. Acts in Zoot Riots; Governor Orders Probe," *Los Angles Examiner*, June 10, 1943, 9; "Pastor Blames Fifth Column," *Los Angeles Examiner*, June 11, 1943, 12; "Watts Pastor Blames Riots on Fifth Column," *Los Angeles Times*, June 11, 1943, A1; and "Idea of Enemy Hand in Zoot Trouble Spiked by Howser," *Los Angeles Times*, June 12, 1943, A1.

39. "His Pant-elleria," *Los Angeles Times*, June 12, 1943, 4.

40. "Zoot Origins Are Traced," *Los Angeles Daily News*, June 10, 1943, 16.

41. "Campaign to Wipe Out Juvenile Gangs Speeded," *Los Angeles Times*, August 6, 1942, part 2, 2.

42. I derive the term "feminine patriot" from "Let Victory Go to Your Head," *Los Angeles Examiner*, August 2, 1942, 10.

43. Honey, *Creating Rosie the Riveter*, 6–7. Also see Rupp, *Mobilizing Women for War*, for a comparison of representations of women in American and German propaganda during World War II.

44. Enstad, *Ladies of Labor, Girls of Adventure*, 27.

45. "Feminine Charm Is Measured by Good Grooming, Daintiness," *Los Angeles Examiner*, August 6, 1942, 16.

46. Lingeman, *Don't You Know There's a War On?*, 153–54.

47. Ibid.

48. Quoted in Faderman, *Odd Girls and Twilight Lovers*, 122.

49. Quoted in Bérubé, "Marching to a Different Drummer," 91.

50. Faderman, *Odd Girls and Twilight Lovers*, 122. Also see Bérubé, "Marching to a Different Drummer"; Bérubé, *Coming Out under Fire*; Costello, *Virtue under Fire*; D'Emilio, *Sexual Politics, Sexual Communities*; and Meyer, *Creating G. I. Jane*.

51. Meyer, *Creating G. I. Jane*, 151. Regarding military officials' tolerance of butch and lesbian servicewomen during World War II, see Bérubé, *Coming Out under Fire*; Bérubé, "Marching to a Different Drummer"; and Faderman, *Odd Girls and Twilight Lovers*.

52. Lingeman, *Don't You Know There's a War On?*, 150.

53. Escobedo, "Mexican American Home Front," 149.

54. Rupp, *Mobilizing Women for War*, 156.

55. Enstad, *Ladies of Labor, Girls of Adventure*, 10.

56. Regarding "sex delinquency" among girls and young women during the Second World War, see Anderson, *Wartime Women*; Bailey and Farber, *The First Strange Place*; Burgess, "The Effect of War on the American Family"; Campbell, *Women at War with America*; Lingeman, *Don't You Know There's a War On?*; Delano, "Making Up for War"; Reckless, "The Impact of War on Crime, Delinquency, and Prostitution"; and Winter, "Are Children Worse in Wartime?"

57. Burgess, "The Effect of War on the American Family," 343.

58. Campbell, *Women at War with America*, 208.

59. Lingeman, *Don't You Know There's a War On?*, 88.

60. Winter, "Are Children Worse in Wartime?" 52.

61. "One Killed and 10 Hurt in Boy 'Wars,'" *Los Angeles Times*, August 3, 1942, 1; "Black Widow Girls in Boy Gangs; War on Vandals Pushed," *Los Angeles Herald-Express*, August 3, 1942, A1.

62. "Black Widow Girls in Boy Gangs; War on Vandals Pushed," *Los Angeles Herald-Express*, August 3, 1942, A1; "One Man Slain; Girls Join in Youthful Gang Forays Here," *Los Angeles Examiner*, August 3, 1942, 1.

63. "Youthful Gang Evil," *Los Angeles Herald-Express*, August 4, 1942, B2.

64. "Ranch Killing Inquiry Opens," *Los Angeles Times*, August 5, 1942, 1; Carlos Amezcua, "Origenes de 'Pachucos' y 'Malinches,'" *La Opinión*, August 26, 1942, 2. All translations of this article are my own. For a discussion of *La Opinión*'s position regarding pachucos, the Sleepy Lagoon incident, and the Zoot Suit Riots, see Gaytán, "Pachucos and the Wartime Mexican Angeleno Press."

65. Griffith, *American Me*, 47. Quotation marks appear in Griffith's excerpt. Unfortunately, I do not know whom she may have been quoting.

66. Banay, "A Psychiatrist Looks at the Zoot Suit," 84.

67. Ibid., 81.

68. Ibid.

69. "Ranch Killing Inquiry Opens," *Los Angeles Times*, August 5, 1942, 1.

70. "Girl 'Zoot Suiters' Gird to Join Gangland Battle," *Los Angeles Herald-Express*, June 10, 1943, A3.

71. Banay, "A Psychiatrist Looks at the Zoot Suit," 84.

72. Amezcua, "Origenes de 'Pachucos' y 'Malinches,'" *La Opinión*, August 26, 1942, 2.

73. "Feminine Charm Is Measured by Good Grooming, Daintiness," *Los Angeles Examiner*, August 6, 1942, 16; "Let Victory Go to Your Head," *Los Angeles Examiner*, August 2, 1942, 10.

74. "Girl 'Zoot Suiters' Gird to Join Gangland Battle," *Los Angeles Herald-Express*, June 10, 1943, A3.

75. For example, Enstad argues that at the beginning of the twentieth century, "fashion without middle-class taste was not only tacky, from a middle-class perspective it was morally suspect." See Enstad, *Ladies of Labor, Girls of Adventure*, 27.

76. Ortner, "Preliminary Notes on Class and Culture," 177.

77. Enstad, *Ladies of Labor, Girls of Adventure*, 26.

78. A few of the Mexican American women I interviewed as part of this study stressed that many female zooters were not promiscuous, amoral, or delinquent. Some compared the zoot suit to the hip-hop look popular among many young people in the United States beginning in the 1980s. They noted that many young people who wear hip-hop attire are not gang members or criminals. However, as some pointed out, the look, like the zoot suit of the past, is often associated with violence and criminality.

79. "Feminine Charm Is Measured by Good Grooming, Daintiness," *Los Angeles Examiner*, August 6, 1942, 16.

80. "Girl 'Zoot Suiters' Gird to Join Gangland Battle," *Los Angeles Herald-Express*, June 10, 1943, A3.

81. Tuck, *Not with the Fist*, 217.

82. Stories that highlight pachucas' blackness include Amezcua, "Origenes de 'Pachucos' y 'Malinches'"; "Black Widow Girls in Boy Gangs; War on Vandals Pushed," *Los Angeles Herald-Express*, August 3, 1942, A1; "Sailor 'Task Force' Hits L.A. Zooters," *Los Angeles Herald-Express*, June 5, 1943, A1; "Army, Navy End War on Zooters after Wild Rioting," *Los Angeles Herald-Express*, June 8, 1943, A1; "Web of 'Zoot Suit' Gangs Spreads over Entire L.A. Area," *Los An-*

geles Herald-Express, June 8, 1943, B1; "Zoot Girls Stab Woman; State Probes Rioting," *Los Angeles Herald-Express*, June 10, 1943, A1; and "Launch State Probe of L.A. Zooter Raids," *Los Angeles Herald-Express*, June 12, 1943, A1. I must credit Green for pointing out the newspapers' emphasis on pachucas' alleged blackness. See Green, "'Give It Your Best!,'" 162.

83. Frazier, "Ethnic and Minority Groups in Wartime, with Special Reference to the Negro," 371.

84. Domer, "The Zoot-Suit Riot," 62.

85. On the attack on the lone woman, see "Zoot Girls Stab Woman; State Probes Rioting," *Los Angeles Herald-Express*, June 10, 1943, A1; "Clashes Few as Zoot War Dies Down," *Los Angeles Times*, June 11, 1943, 1; "Zoot Girls Kick and Knife Waitress as Battles Continue," *Saint Paul Pioneer Press*, June 11, 1943, 1; and "Zoot Suits and Service Stripes: Race Tension behind the Riots," *Newsweek*, June 21, 1943, 35–40. On the taunting of high school girls and the attempted carjacking, see "Launch State Probe of L.A. Zooter Riots," *Los Angeles Herald-Express*, June 12, 1943, A1. And on the strong-arm robbery of a soldier in a cafe, see "New Servicemen-'Zooter' Fights Follow Weekend Clashes," *Los Angeles Herald-Express*, June 7, 1943, A3.

86. "Girl 'Zoot Suiters' Gird to Join Gangland Battle," *Los Angeles Herald-Express*, June 10, 1943, A3. Regarding pachucas' efforts to sustain the riots, also see "Train-Attacking Zoot Gangs Broken Up," *Los Angeles Herald-Express*, June 11, 1943, A1; "Zoot Suit Girls Kick and Knife Waitress as Battles Continue," *Saint Paul Pioneer Press*, June 11, 1943, 1; and "Riots Subsiding in Zooter War, Police Declare," *Los Angeles Daily News*, June 11, 1943, 1.

87. "Train-Attacking Zoot Gangs Broken Up," *Los Angeles Herald-Express*, June 11, 1943, A1.

88. Regarding Mexican American women who wore the masculine zoot suit, see Escobedo, "Mexican American Home Front," 177; and Macías, *Mexican American Mojo*. Regarding white and black women in Buffalo, New York, in the 1940s and 1950s, see Kennedy and Davis's invaluable oral history, *Boots of Leather, Slippers of Gold*, 156. Also see the advertisement for "DRAPE SUITS, COATS AND PANTS FOR MEN, BOYS AND WOMEN" in the African American newspaper *California Eagle*, June 3, 1943, 4B.

89. "Sailor 'Task Force' Hits L.A. Zooters," *Los Angeles Herald-Express*, June 5, 1943, A1; "Army, Navy End War on Zooters after Wild Rioting," *Los Angeles Herald-Express*, June 8, 1943, A1; "Web of 'Zoot Suit' Gangs Spreads over Entire L.A. Area," *Los Angeles Herald-Express*, June 8, 1943, A1; "Girl 'Zoot Suiters' Gird to Join Gangland Battle," *Los Angeles Herald-Express*, June 10, 1943, A3.

90. On the hypermasculine pachuco, see Humphrey, "The Stereotype and the Social Types of Mexican American Youths"; and Paz, "The *Pachuco* and Other

Extremes," in *The Labyrinth of Solitude and Other Writings*. "Gamin dandies" is from "Zoot Suiters Learn Lesson in Fights with Servicemen," *Los Angeles Times*, June 7, 1943, part 1, 1.

91. Amezcua, "Orígenes de 'Pachucos' y 'Malinches'": 2.

92. On the gendering of consumer culture, see Enstad, *Ladies of Labor, Girls of Adventure*, 4–5.

93. See, for example, Adler, "The 1943 Zoot-Suit Riots"; Mazón, *The Zoot-Suit Riots;* Mirandé, *Gringo Justice;* and Wyatt, *Five Fires*.

94. Mazón, *The Zoot-Suit Riots*, 87.

95. Ibid.

96. For an insightful reading of the feminized zoot suit, see Sanchez-Tranquilino, "Mano a Mano."

97. Banay, "A Psychiatrist Looks at the Zoot Suit,": 84; Walton, *Thread of Victory*, 129; Walter Davenport, "Swing It, Swing Shift!," *Colliers* 110, no. 8 (1942): 24.

98. Banay, "A Psychiatrist Looks at the Zoot Suit," 81 and 84. Somewhat ironically, Banay's vivid description of the masculine sailor is reminiscent of images of sailors that may be found in late-twentieth-century gay male visual culture—in particular, in works by Tom of Finland (*né* Touko Laaksonen).

99. Braddy, "The Pachucos and Their Argot," 258. In the years immediately preceding the Zoot Suit and Harlem riots of 1943, black and brown zooters wore clothes, accessories, and colors that bore a resemblance to what the historian George Chauncey calls "distinctively homosexual attire," such as "tight-cuffed trousers," "half-lengthed flaring top-coats," and "excessively bright feathers in their hat-bands." See Chauncey, *Gay New York*, 52–53.

100. Bourdieu, *Photography*, 80.

101. "Lowriders Pasados," *Lowrider* 2, no. 6 (1978): 22. I thank Eduardo Pagán for bringing this photo to my attention.

102. Santillán, "Rosita the Riveter," 127.

103. Lingeman, *Don't You Know There's a War On?*, 150. Although the hippies of the late 1960s and 1970s helped to popularize pants—in particular jeans—among American women (and probably helped to make American fashion more informal in general), the fashion historian Diana Crane notes that even in the late twentieth century, "middle-class professional and businesswomen" were "not . . . permitted to don a totally mannish look but [were] still expected to retain elements of femininity in their office clothes. . . . In middle-class corporate workplaces, taboos against the use of trousers by women executives remain[ed], although these women typically [wore] jeans and other types of trousers for leisure activities." See Crane, *Fashion and Its Social Agendas*, 124.

As a professor at the University of Calfornia, Santa Cruz, where many students (and some faculty) wear shorts, flip-flops, jeans, sweat pants, and even flannel pajama bottoms outside their homes on a regular basis and in broad daylight, I sometimes find it easy to forget that workers in other professions and places must dress more formally. For example, a federal public defender I know usually wears pants to work but keeps a skirt in her office. If she must appear in court, she replaces her pants with the skirt for her clients' sake. She says that she does so because even today some judges do not regard favorably female lawyers who wear trousers in the courtroom.

104. I discuss this photo at length in chapter 1.

105. Davis, "The Butch as Drag Artiste." On the persecution of cross-dressed women in the 1940s and 1950s, also see Faderman, *Odd Girls and Twilight Lovers*, 185; Kennedy and Davis, *Boots of Leather, Slippers of Gold*; Meyer, *Creating G. I. Jane*, 150; and Nestle, *A Restricted Country*.

106. Rubin, "Of Catamites and Kings," 467.

107. It is difficult to pinpoint when the labels "butch" or *marimacha* (Spanish for "bulldyke" or "bull dagger") gained currency among Chicanas and Latinas. On the significance of these terms in the late twentieth and early twenty-first centuries, see Hollibaugh and Moraga, "What We're Rollin around in Bed with"; and Rosales, "Papis, Dykes, Daddies." Also see Rosales's film *Mind If I Call You Sir?: A Discussion between Latina Butches and Female-to-Male Transgendered Latinos* (2004). I am grateful to Horacio Roque Ramírez for referring me to Rosales's groundbreaking work.

108. Rosales, "Papis, Dykes, Daddies," 86–87.

109. Kennedy and Davis, "'They Was No One to Mess With,'" 64. Recounting her relationships with butch women, the self-proclaimed femme and lesbian writer and activist Joan Nestle has recounted, "None of the butch women I was with . . . ever presented themselves to me as men; they did announce themselves as tabooed women who were willing to identify their passion for other women by wearing clothes that symbolized the taking of responsibility." See Nestle, *A Restricted Country*, 100.

110. Of course, for some, the effect of butchness is predicated on the female crossdresser's ability to pass as a man. See, for example, Bell, "Finding the Male within and Taking Him Cruising"; Garber, *Vested Interests*; Halberstam, *Female Masculinity*; Rosales, *Mind If I Call You Sir?*; and Rosales, "Papis, Dykes, Daddies."

111. Garber, *Vested Interests*, 64.

112. Case, "Toward a Butch-Femme Aesthetic"; Garber, *Vested Interests*; Kennedy and Davis, *Boots of Leather, Slippers of Gold*; Livia, "'I Ought to Throw a Buick at You'"; Meyer, *Creating G. I. Jane*; and Nestle, *A Restricted Country*.

113. Bordo, "The Body and the Reproduction of Femininity," 25–26.

114. McAlister, *Epic Encounters*, 268. Here, McAlister is drawing upon Susan Sontag's *On Photography* (New York: Farrar, Straus and Giroux, 1977).

115. See Ruth La Ferla, "First Hip-Hop, Now Cholo Style," *New York Times*, November 30, 2003, section 9, 1. Stefani, who is from Orange County, California, has acknowledged cholas' influence on her successful clothing line L. A. M. B. See Beth Moore, "A Singer in L. A. M. B.'s Clothing, No Doubt," *Los Angeles Times*, September 14, 2005. I am grateful to Deb Vargas for forwarding this story to me.

3. Saying "Nothin'"

1. "Brass Knuckles Found on Woman 'Zoot Suiter,'" *Los Angeles Times*, June 10, 1943, 1A. "Policeman Is Ambushed, Run Over by Zoot Auto," *Los Angeles Evening Herald-Express*, June 10, 1943, A6. For more accounts of the arrest of Amelia Venegas, see "Zoot Suit Hunt on in Suburbs as Navy Clamps Ban on L.A.," *Los Angeles Examiner*, June 9, 1943, 1; "6-Day Zoot War Hospitalizes 112," *Los Angeles Daily News*, June 10, 1943, 1; and "U.S., Warren Act on Zoot Suits, New Outbreak of Gang Rioting," *Los Angeles Examiner*, June 10, 1943, 1.

2. "Policeman Is Ambushed, Run Over by Zoot Auto," A1; "Brass Knuckles Found on Woman 'Zoot Suiter,'" 1A. For photographs of Venegas, see page 3 of the June 10, 1943, *Los Angeles Daily News*; page 8 of the June 10, 1943, *Los Angeles Examiner*; page A1 of the June 10, 1943, *Los Angeles Evening Herald-Express*; and page A of the June 10, 1943, *Los Angeles Times*.

3. For discussions of the wartime African American zoot subculture, see Alvarez, *The Power of the Zoot*; Chibnall, "Whistle and Zoot"; Cosgrove, "The Zoot Suit and Style Warfare"; Daniels, "Los Angeles Zoot"; Kelley, *Race Rebels*; Tyler, "Black Jive and White Repression"; and White and White, *Stylin.'*

4. Scott, *Domination and the Arts of Resistance*, 8.

5. Kelley, *Race Rebels*, 166.

6. Galindo, "Dispelling the Male-Only Myth," 19.

7. See, for example, Bettie, *Women without Class*; Herrera-Sobek, "The Street Scene"; Mendoza-Denton, *Homegirls*; Mendoza-Denton, "Language Attitudes and Gang Affiliation among California Latina Girls"; Mendoza-Denton, "'Muy Macha'"; Mendoza-Denton, "Fighting Words"; Mendoza-Denton, "Turn-Initial No"; Mendoza-Denton, "The Anguish of Normative Gender"; Miranda, *Homegirls in the Public Sphere*; and Schalet et al., "Respectability and Autonomy."

8. My discussion of pachuco slang, caló, and tirili/tirilongo is indebted to the following works: Alvarez, "Calo"; Barker, *Pachuco*; Berk-Seligson, "A Sociolinguistic View of the Mexican American Speech Community"; Braddy, "The *Pachucos* and Their Argot"; Coltharp, *The Tongue of the Tirilones*; Coltharp, "Invitation to the Dance"; Cummings, "Que siga el corrido"; Fuentes and López, *Barrio Language Dictionary*; Gaarder, "Notes on Some Spanish Terms in the Southwest"; Galindo, "Perceptions of Pachuquismo and Use of Calo/Pachuco

Spanish by Various Chicana Women"; Galindo, "Dispelling the Male-Only Myth"; Galindo, "The Language of Gangs, Drugs, and Prison Life among Chicanas"; Galindo, "Capturing Chicano Voices: An Interdisciplinary Approach"; Galindo, "Caló and Taboo Language Use among Chicanas"; González, "Pachuco"; Green, "Calo, Pachuco, and Lunfardo"; Griffith, "The Pachuco Patois"; Hinojos, "Notes on the Pachuco"; Hutter, "El Milagrucho"; Katz, "The Evolution of the Pachuco Language and Culture"; Mazón, *The Zoot Suit Riots*; Ornstein-Galicia, "Chicano Caló"; Ortega, *Caló*; Pagán, *Murder at the Sleepy Lagoon*; Polkinhorn et al., *El libro de caló*; Rosensweig, *Caló*; Sánchez, "Chicano Spanish"; and Sánchez, *Chicano Discourse*.

9. Mazón, *The Zoot-Suit Riots*, 3.

10. Pagán, *Murder at the Sleepy Lagoon*, 37.

11. Barker, *Pachuco*, 13.

12. Galindo, "Dispelling the Male-Only Myth," 5.

13. "Youthful Gang Secrets Exposed," *Los Angeles Times*, July 16, 1944, part 1, 1.

14. Ibid.

15. Carlos Amezcua, "Origenes de 'Pachucos' y 'Malinches,'" *La Opinión* August 26, 1942, 2.

16. Galindo, "Capturing Chicana Voices," 221; Sánchez, *Chicano Discourse*, 127. According to Galindo, "Lexical borrowings from English are morphosyntactically and phonologically adapted to Spanish; for example, *troca* is adapted from truck." See Galindo "Capturing Chicana Voices," 221.

17. Sánchez, *Chicano Discourse*, 127.

18. "Authentic Pachuco," *Time*, July 10, 1944, 72.

19. Braddy, "The *Pachucos* and Their Argot," 261.

20. "Youth Gangs Leading Cause of Delinquencies," *Los Angeles Times*, June 2, 1943, part 2, 10.

21. Lowe, *Immigrant Acts*, 130.

22. Regarding the relationship of English to Americanness, see Franklin, "The German Language in Pennsylvania." Centuries after Franklin wrote this letter, the political scientist Samuel P. Huntington has conflated the English language and American identity in *Who Are We? The Challenges to America's Identity* (2004).

23. See "Watts Pastor Blames Riots on Fifth Column," *Los Angeles Times*, June 11, 1943, A; and "Pastor Blames Fifth Column," *Los Angeles Examiner*, June 11, 1943, 12.

24. "Web of 'Zoot Suit' Gangs Spreads over Entire L.A. Area," *Los Angeles Herald-Express*, June 8, 1943, 1.

25. For a discussion of the Cold War–era "bad boy," see Medovoi, *Rebels*.

26. Calloway *Of Minnie the Moocher and Me*, 182.

27. Clark and Barker, "The Zoot Effect in Personality," 147.

28. Alvarez, "Calo," 9.

29. Clark and Barker, "The Zoot Effect in Personality," 147.

30. Alvarez, "Calo," 9.

31. Malcolm X, *The Autobiography of Malcolm X*, 134.

32. "El Louie" was first published in 1970 in *Rascatripas*. I quote from the 1972 version. See Montoya, "El Louie."

33. Montoya, "El Louie," 174. Unless otherwise indicated, all translations of "El Louie" are my own.

34. Ibid., 175.

35. Ibid.

36. Ibid., 174.

37. Ibid.

38. Ibid., 176.

39. Ibid., 174.

40. Suárez, "Kid Zopilote," 131.

41. Ibid.

42. Ibid.

43. Ibid., 136.

44. Montoya, "El Louie," 174.

45. Ibid.

46. Ibid.

47. Suárez, "Kid Zopilote," 131.

48. Montoya, "El Louie," 175.

49. Ibid.

50. See, for example, Bruce-Novoa, *Chicano Authors*, 115; Bruce-Novoa, *Chicano Poetry*, 16; and Zamora, "Mythopoeia of Chicano Poetry," 167.

51. Arteaga, *Chicano Poetics*, 68.

52. Galindo, "Dispelling the Male-Only Myth," 6.

53. Galindo, "The Language of Gangs, Drugs, and Prison Life among Chicanas," 33.

54. Alvarez, "Calo," 12.

55. In defining "cool" and "hip," I draw from the following: Calloway, *Of Minnie the Moocher and Me*; Fraiman, *Cool Men and the Second Sex*; Frank, *The Conquest of Cool*; Golden et al., *Dictionary of American Underworld Lingo*; Leland, *Hip*; MacAdams, *Birth of the Cool*; Mailer, "The White Negro"; Majors and Bilson, *Cool Pose*; Medovoi, *Rebels*; Mezzrow and Wolfe, *Really the Blues*; Poutain and Robins, *Cool Rules*; Stearns, *American Cool*; and Thompson, "An Aesthetic of the Cool."

56. See Saldaña-Portillo, *The Revolutionary Imagination in the Americas and the Age of Development*. The quote is from Kelley, *Race Rebels*, 162.

57. X, *The Autobiography of Malcolm X*, 56.

58. Ibid., 310.

59. Majors and Billson, *Cool Pose*, 7.

60. Mailer, "The White Negro," 243.

61. Alvarez, "Calo," 9.

62. Majors and Billson, *Cool Pose*, 83. I recall that when I was in high school and college in the 1980s and early 1990s, "gay" was synonymous with uncool: regardless of sex or sexual orientation, a person was "gay" if s/he removed the mask of coolness and showed excessive emotion—in particular, excitement, sadness, or fear. For a brief discussion of gay cool, see Leland, *Hip*.

63. Alvarez, "Calo," 12.

64. Almaguer, "Chicano Men," 82.

65. Ibid.

66. Berk-Seligson, "A Sociolinguistic View of the Mexican American Speech Community," 94; Coltharp, "Invitation to the Dance," 7.

67. Coltharp, *The Tongue of the Tirilones*, 32.

68. Leland, *Hip*, 241.

69. Fraiman, *Cool Men and the Second Sex*.

70. Ponce, *Hoyt Street*, 167.

71. Galindo, "Dispelling the Male-Only Myth," 20 and 19.

72. Ibid.

73. Coltharp, *The Tongue of the Tirilones*, 32.

74. Ibid.

75. Galindo, "Dispelling the Male-Only Myth," 19.

76. "Tough-tongued" is from Chuy Varela's liner notes for *Pachuco Boogie, featuring Don Tosti* (El Cerrito, Calif.: Arhoolie Productions, 2002), 11.

77. The advertisement for the *Dictionary of Pachuco Slang* may be found in *Lowrider* 2, no. 2 (November 1978). Regarding the 1940s-themed fundraiser dances, see *Lowrider* 1, no. 11 (August 1978), 39; and *Lowrider* 2, no. 2 (November 1978).

78. For transcriptions of conversations in pachuco slang, see Barker, "Pachuco"; Coltharp, "Invitation to the Dance"; Gaarder, "Notes on Some Spanish Terms in the Southwest"; Galindo, "The Language of Gangs, Drugs, and Prison Life among Chicanas"; Hutter, "El Milagrucho"; Sánchez, "Chicano Spanish"; and Sánchez, *Chicano Discourse*. Coltharp's "Invitation to the Dance" and Galindo's "The Language of Gangs, Drugs, and Prison Life among Chicanas" feature women speaking pachuco slang. Barker's audio recording of a conversation between two men speaking pachuco slang may be found at the University of Arizona Library, Department of Special Collections, Southwest Folklore Center Manuscript Collection (SWF 009, items 85.2/C.1 and 85.2/R.1). I am grateful to Veronica Reyes and Scott Cossel of the University of Arizona Library for providing me with access to it.

79. Songs that feature pachuco slang by Lalo Guerrero and Don Tosti's Pachuco Boogie Boys, as well as other artists, may be found on *Pachuco Boogie*. "El Bracero y La Pachuca" is also on this album. I thank Anthony Macías for bringing this recording to my attention.

80. Translated by Don Tosti, Chuy Varela, and Zac Salem, liner notes for *Pachuco Boogie*, 21.

81. Ibid., 22.

82. Katz, "The Evolution of the Pachuco Language and Culture," 55.

83. Gal, "Language, Gender, and Power," 173.

84. For a discussion of the theme of women and betrayal in corridos, see Herrera-Sobek's *The Mexican Corrido* and "The Treacherous Woman Archetype."

85. During *People v. Zammora*, thirty-nine witnesses were called by the prosecution and twenty-two by the defense (certain individuals were called as witnesses by both parties). The "girl companions" who were called as the prosecution's witnesses were Bertha Aguilar, Dora Barrios, Ann Kalustian, Betty Nuñez Zeiss, Josephine Gonzáles, and her sister Juanita Gonzáles. Dora Baca and Lorena Encinas were called as the defense's witnesses. Frances Silva was also held by the police as a suspect in José Diaz's murder and testified before the grand jury in August 1942. However, unlike the others, she was not a witness in the trial. See *People v. Zammora, et al.*, Superior Court in the District Court of Appeal of the State of California, Second Appellate District (Sleepy Lagoon Defense Committee Collection, Collection 107, Department of Special Collections, Charles E. Young Research Library, University of California, Los Angeles) (hereafter cited as "court transcript"). The list of witnesses may be found in box 7, volume 1. Regarding the incarceration of some of the girls and young women at the Ventura School for Girls, also see Barajas, "The Defense Committees of Sleepy Lagoon"; Escobedo, "Mexican American Home Front"; Escobedo, "The Pachuca Panic"; McGrath and Balter, *The Education of Alice McGrath*; and Tovares, *The American Experience: Zoot Suit Riots*.

86. References to the young women's hair and clothing may be found on the following pages of the court transcript: 1336, 1345, 3720, and 3722.

87. "Jury's Gang-Case Verdict Disproves 'Persecution,'" *Los Angeles Times*, January 14, 1943.

88. Testimony of Bertha Aguilar, court transcript, 1324.

89. Court transcript, 1318–19.

90. Ibid., 1319.

91. Post, *Etiquette*, 97.

92. Ibid.

93. Ibid., 98.

94. Ibid., 86.

95. Ibid., 92.

96. Here, "perform" refers to the repetition and disruption of symbolic categories. See Butler's *Gender Trouble* and *Bodies That Matter*. Also see Bhabha, *The Location of Culture*, and Lowe, *Immigrant Acts*.

97. Lakoff, *Language and Woman's Place*, 80.

98. According to Pagán, Zacsek (a.k.a. Olga Grey) had a supporting role in D. W. Griffith's *The Birth of a Nation* and "relied on her dramatic talents and personal flair" in the courtroom. See Pagán, *Murder at the Sleepy Lagoon*, 77.

99. Court transcript, 297.

100. Ibid., 298.

101. Testimony of Bertha Aguilar, court transcript, 1235. Other instances in which the young women used incorrect grammar may be found on the following pages of *People v. Zammora*: 207, 218, 300, 403, 770, 1046, 1088, 1099, 1106, 1141, 1142, 1153, 1180, 1185, 1192, 1198, 1201, 1204, 1212–13, 1215, 1231, 1324, 1394, 1420, 1437, and 4509. Incidentally, each teenage girl had attended school up to the proper grade according to her age.

102. Testimony of Bertha Aguilar, court transcript, 1215.

103. Lakoff adds that the omission of the final g in the gerund form is generally associated with boys. See Lakoff, *Language and Woman's Place*, 80.

104. Court transcript, 1173.

105. Testimony of Bertha Aguilar, court transcript, 1212–13.

106. Galindo, "The Language of Gangs, Drugs, and Prison Life among Chicanas," 32.

107. Court transcript, 1202.

108. Ibid., 1273–74.

109. Pagán, *Murder at the Sleepy Lagoon*, 82.

110. Testimony of Bertha Aguilar, court transcript, 1212.

111. Testimony of Juanita Gonzáles, court transcript, 1043. Other examples of the young women's "forgetfulness" may be found on the following pages: 263–66, 274–79, 454, 851, 854, 917, 1023, 1026, 1095, 1107, 1204, 1211, 1222–23, 1229, and 1437–39.

112. Testimony of Juanita Gonzáles, court transcript, 207.

113. Testimony of Bertha Aguilar, court transcript, 1201–2. See pages 225, 233, 767, 787, 1095, 1182, 1185–89, 1192–95, 1197, 1199, 1204, 1211–13, 1229, 1233, 1238, 1354, 1386, 1396, and 1437–40 for other instances in which the young women refused to testify or to cooperate while in court.

114. Testimony of Dora Baca, court transcript, 4550. There are numerous complaints from the judge and lawyers about the female witnesses' inaudibility. See, for example, the following pages: 234, 258, 296–97, 403, 410, 449, 521, 527, 678, 1084, 1271, 1457, 4496, and 5483.

115. Lakoff, *Talking Power*, 90–91.

116. Kelley, *Race Rebels*, 8.

117. Leyva, "Listening to the Silences in Latina/Chicana Lesbian History," 432.

118. For a brief, albeit vivid, discussion of Aguilar's sentence at the Ventura School for Girls, see Escobedo, "Mexican American Home Front," 68–69.

119. For reasons I explain below, I am unable to disclose the identity of this speaker. Suffice it to say that my interview with this person, whom I call unidentified interviewee #1, was conducted by telephone on February 19, 2005.

120. Valdez, *Zoot Suit and Other Plays*, 25.

121. Ibid., 43.

122. Ibid., 46.

123. Ibid., 44.

124. Fregoso, "Re-Imagining Chicana Urban Identities in the Public Sphere, *Cool Chuca Style*," 84.

125. Valdez, *Zoot Suit and Other Plays*, 51.

126. Ibid., 81.

127. Broyles-González, *El Teatro Campesino*, 203. Other feminist critiques of *Zoot Suit* may be found in Fregoso, *The Bronze Screen*; Fregoso, *MeXicana Encounters*; Fregoso, "Homegirls, *Cholas*, and *Pachucas* in Cinema"; Fregoso, "Re-Imagining Chicana Urban Identities in the Public Sphere, *Cool Chuca Style*"; and Yarbro-Bejarano, "The Female Subject in Chicano Theatre."

128. Valdez, *Zoot Suit* (Universal Pictures, 1981).

129. Valdez, *Zoot Suit and Other Plays*, 90.

130. Ibid.

131. Valdez, *Zoot Suit and Other Plays*, 35.

132. Ibid.

133. George Shibley, "Sleepy Lagoon: The True Story," *New West*, January 15, 1979, 88 (box 3, folder 27, Alice G. McGrath Collection, Collection 1490, Department of Special Collections, Charles E. Young Research Library, University of California, Los Angeles).

134. See "Suit Filed against 'Zoot Suit' Producers," *Los Angeles Times*, November 23, 1979, part 4, 34 (box 24, "Zoot Suit Murders/Sanchez" folder, Carey McWilliams Collection, Collection 1390, Department of Special Collections, Charles E. Young Research Library, University of California, Los Angeles). In naming the case after Zamora, the state misspelled his surname.

135. Telephone interview with unidentified interviewee #2 (November 20, 2004).

136. Butler, *Gender Trouble*, 144. Regarding the (un)intelligibility of agency, also see Enstad, *Ladies of Labor, Girls of Adventure*, and Lipsitz, *Time Passages*.

137. Anzaldúa, *Borderland / La Frontera*, 58.

138. Ibid., 54.

139. Ibid.

140. Lakoff, *Language and Woman's Place*, 84.

141. Ibid., 85.

142. In September 2007, I was lucky to see a very moving performance of *Zoot Suit* at El Teatro Campesino in San Juan Bautista, California. The house was packed and the play's run was extended—evidence of its enduring power.

143. See, for example, Moraga, "Later, She Met Joyce"; Moraga, *Giving Up the Ghost*; Castellano, "Estos Vatos with Their Intellectual Conversation"; Tafolla, *Sonnets to Human Beings and Other Selected Works*; and Vigil, *Thirty an' Seen a Lot*. See Fregoso's *MeXicana Encounters* and "Re-Imagining Chicana Urban Identities in the Public Sphere, *Cool Chuca Style*" for a brief discussion of Tafolla's poems; and Herrera-Sobek, "The Street Scene," for an insightful analysis of Vigil's poetry. Also see Moreno, *El Milagrucho*, a short play written almost entirely in pachuco slang; and Hutter, "El Milagrucho," a linguistic analysis of this play. I discuss some of these works in the next chapter.

4. *La Pachuca* and the Excesses of Family

1. Villarreal, *Pocho*, 151.

2. Steiner, *La Raza*, 234.

3. Rubén Salazar, "Pachuco Folk Heroes—They Were First to Be Different," *Los Angeles Times*, July 7, 1970, part 2, 7.

4. Luis Valdez, "Once Again, Meet the Zoot Suiters," *Los Angeles Times*, August 13, 1978, part 5, 3. For a lengthier discussion of pre-movement and movement-era literary and artistic works that feature *el pachuco*, see my "The Pachuca in Chicana/o Art, Literature and History," especially chapter 4.

5. "A New American Play" is from the 1978 Mark Taper Forum and 1978–79 Aquarius Theater programs for *Zoot Suit* (in author's possession). I thank Will and Emma Rodríguez for saving and giving to me their programs from these productions. Although *el pachuco* has been upheld as an emblem of a distinctly American (that is, Mexican American) identity, pachuquismo was not limited to the United States exclusively. Gerardo Licón's forthcoming study of pachuquismo on both sides of the U.S.–Mexico border promises to make valuable contributions to studies of the zoot subculture(s).

6. Valdez, *Zoot Suit and Other Plays*, 30.

7. Hartmann, "The Family as the Locus of Gender, Class, and Political Struggle," 111.

8. Lipsitz, "Not Just Another Social Movement," 173.

9. See Romano-V., "The Historical and Intellectual Presence of Mexican Americans."

10. Salazar, "Pachuco Folk Heroes": Montoya, *Pachuco Art*.

11. Villanueva, *Hay Otra Voz*, 40; Granado, "Para Mi Jefe."

12. Valdez, "Once Again, Meet the Zoot Suiters."

13. Ibid.

14. Page 6 of the Aquarius Theater program.

15. Sánchez, *Contemporary Chicana Poetry*, 3.

16. Valdez, "Once Again, Meet the Zoot Suiters," 3. Regarding the connection between *carnalismo* and Chicano gangs, see Muñoz, *Youth, Identity, Power*, 76.

17. Fregoso, *The Bronze Screen*, 37.

18. Regarding the prominent role Valdez played in articulating Chicano cultural nationalism via both *Zoot Suit* and *El Plan Espiritual de Aztlán* (which he coauthored), see Fregoso, *The Bronze Screen*, especially chapter 2.

19. See Rodríguez, "Serial Kinship."

20. Gonzáles, "Chicano Nationalism," 379.

21. Zinn, "Political Familism," 459, 455, and 462.

22. Alma M. García has compiled writings by Chicana feminists, including Cotera and Nieto Gómez, from the late 1960s on. See García, *Chicana Feminist Thought*. Also see Espinoza, "'Revolutionary Sisters'" and Rodríguez, "Reimagined Communities," for discussions of Chicana feminist critiques of the patriarchal family during the 1970s.

23. See Moraga, *Loving in the War Years*; Anzaldúa, *Borderlands / La Frontera*; and Alarcón, "Making *Familia* From Scratch."

24. Orozco, "Beyond Machismo, La Familia, and Ladies Auxiliaries," 7.
    See also Chabram-Dernersesian, "I Throw Punches for My Race, but I Don't Want to Be a Man"; Espinoza, "'Revolutionary Sisters'"; Fregoso, *The Bronze Screen*; Fregoso, "Re-Imagining Chicana Urban Identities in the Public Sphere, *Cool Chuca Style*"; Fregoso, *MeXicana Encounters*; Hurtado, *Voicing Chicana Feminisms*; Orozco, "Beyond Machismo, La Familia, and Ladies Auxiliaries"; and Rodríguez, "Reimagined Communities."

25. For feminist critiques of *I Am Joaquin*, see Chabram-Dernersesian, "I Throw Punches for My Race, but I Don't Want to Be a Man," and Fregoso, *The Bronze Screen*. Also see Gaspar de Alba, *Chicano Art, Inside, Outside the Master's House*, which takes to task Rendón's *Chicano Manifesto* for its barefaced sexism and masculinism.

26. Orozco, "Beyond Machismo, La Familia, and Ladies Auxiliaries," 7.

27. "Mother Tears Up Zoot Suit of Boy Wounded in Clash," *Los Angeles Times*, June 11, 1943, A. Photographs of Trujillo are on page B of the June 11, 1943, *Los Angeles Times* and page 12 of the June 11, 1943, *Los Angeles Examiner*.

28. See "Youth Gangs Leading Cause of Delinquencies," *Los Angeles Times*, June 2, 1943, part 2, 10. Regarding the widely held belief that working-class and immigrant parents in early-twentieth-century Los Angeles were incapable of

caring for and reining in their adolescent children, see Escobedo, "Mexican American Home Front"; Odem, *Delinquent Daughters;* and Sánchez, "'Go After the Women.'"

29. "Latter-day prototype" is from Castañeda Shular et al., eds., *Literatura chicana,* 179.

30. Chávez, *¡Mi Raza Primero! (My People First),* 57.

31. Raymund Paredes dates "El Hijo Desobediente" to circa 1910 (http://college .hmco.com/english/lauter/heath) (visited June 27, 2005). For "A Pachuco Version of 'El Hijo Desobediente'" in pachuco slang and English, see Barker, *Pachuco,* 37–38.

32. Barker, *Pachuco,* 38.

33. Muñoz, *Youth, Identity, Power,* 76.

34. Fregoso, *The Bronze Screen,* 30. The disobedient pachuco-son of "El Hijo Desobediente" was resurrected in the film *Mi Familia / My Family* (1995), directed by Gregory Nava. For critiques of this film, see Fregoso, *MeXicana Encounters,* 71–90; Huaco-Nuzum, "Mi Familia / My Family"; and Rodríguez, "Reimagined Communities," 89–102.

35. Mirandé, "The Chicano Family," 755.

36. Moraga, *Loving in the War Years,* 103.

37. Escobedo, "Mexican American Home Front," 88.

38. "Brass Knuckles Found on Woman 'Zoot Suiter,'" *Los Angeles Times,* June 10, 1943, part 1, A.

39. These exceptions include the sensationalist newspaper accounts of Venegas's arrest, raúlsalinas's poem "Homenaje al Pachuco" (Mirrored Reflections), which refers to *la pachuca* as a *"carnalita,"* and Escobedo's "Mexican American Home Front."

40. Fregoso, "Homegirls, *Cholas,* and *Pachucas* in Cinema," 316.

41. Valdez, *Zoot Suit and Other Plays,* 34–35. In Mexican Spanish, the expression "*jijo*" (or *hijo*) is short for *hijo de la chingada,* which may be translated as son of the fucked one/the whore. La Malinche is also known as La Chingada.

42. Fregoso, "Re-Imagining Chicana Urban Identities in the Public Sphere, *Cool Chuca Style,*" 75.

43. Valdez, *Zoot Suit and Other Plays,* 35.

44. Drawing from Los Angeles County Juvenile Court records, Escobedo deftly shows the ways Mexican American girls who had been branded pachucas exceeded the limits of the nuclear family. In one case, a thirteen-year-old girl was sent by her parents to live with an aunt in Mexico because of her "association with pachucos on the streets of downtown Los Angeles after sundown." And in another case, a fifteen-year-old girl, whose parents had locked her in her bedroom because of "several curfew violations and nights out on the

town," crawled out a window—much like *Zoot Suit*'s Lupe Reyna—in order to meet "her pachuco friends on a nearby street corner." See Escobedo, "Mexican American Home Front," 86, and Escobedo, "The Pachuca Panic."

45. Fregoso, *The Bronze Screen*, 33.

46. Fregoso, "Homegirls, *Cholas*, and *Pachucas* in Cinema," 327.

47. See Garza, *Un Pedacito de Mi Corazón / A Piece of My Heart*; Ponce, *The Wedding*; del Fuego, *Maravilla*; Vigil, *Thirty an' Seen a Lot*; and Castellano, "Estos Vatos with Their Intellectual Conversations." For a fuller discussion of del Fuego's and Tafolla's works, see Fregoso, "Re-Imagining Chicana Urban Identities in the Public Sphere, *Cool Chuca Style*." Regarding Vigil's poems, see Herrera-Sobek, "The Street Scene."

48. Ponce, *The Wedding*, 44, 6, and 42–43.

49. Notable examples of pachuco poetry may be found in raúlsalinas, *Un Trip through the Mind Jail y Otras Excursions*; Shular et al., *Literatura chicana* (especially chapter 4, "Los Barrios de Aztlán"); and Valdez and Steiner, eds., *Aztlán*.

50. According to Fregoso, "Los Corts (5 Voices)" was written in 1975 and "and when I dream dreams" was written in 1979. Both were published in Tafolla's *Sonnets to Human Beings and Other Selected Works* (1992). See Fregoso, *MeXicana Encounters*, 94–95.

In an interview that I conducted with her via e-mail on September 30, 1999, Inés Hernández-Avila informed me that she wrote and read aloud "Para Teresa" in 1975 at Festival Floricanto in Austin. The poem was first published, albeit in truncated form, in 1978 by Scorpion Press of Tucson in the collection *Siete Poetas*. In 1993 it was published in its entirety in the anthology *Infinite Divisions*, edited by Tey Diana Rebolledo and Eliana S. Rivero. I cite both versions here and am grateful to the poet for responding to my questions about her poem and life.

51. Tafolla, "Los Corts (5 Voices)," *Sonnets to Human Beings*, 59. All translations of this poem are my own.

52. Tafolla, "and when I dream dreams," *Sonnets to Human Beings*, 96.

53. Hernández informed me that "Para Teresa" is autobiographical in my e-mail exchange with her.

54. Inés Hernández-Tovar, "Para Teresa": "grew up fighting" is from the 1993 version (332); "game of deadly defiance . . ." is from the 1978 version (31).

55. "Para Teresa" (1993), 332.

56. Ibid.

57. "Para Teresa" (1978), 32.

58. "Para Teresa" (1993), 331. All translations of this poem are mine unless otherwise noted.

59. "Para Teresa" (1993), 332.

60. "Alamo which-had-to-be-its-name / Elementary" is from the 1978 version (31); "we were not inferior . . ." is from the 1993 version (331).

61. "Para Teresa" (1993), 332.

62. Ibid., 333.

63. Espinoza, "'Revolutionary Sisters,'" 39.

64. Gaspar de Alba, *Chicano Art, Inside/Outside the Master's House*, 139 and 136.

65. Ibid., 138–39.

66. Ibid.

67. According to José Esteban Muñoz, disidentification is "the third mode [after identification and counteridentification] of dealing with dominant ideology, one that neither opts to assimilate within such a structure nor strictly opposes it." He explains, "To disidentify is to read oneself and one's own life narrative in a moment, object, or subject that is not culturally coded to 'connect' with the disidentificatory subject. It is not to pick and choose what one takes out of an identification. It is not to willfully evacuate the politically dubious or shameful components within an identificatory locus. Rather, it is the reworking of those energies that do not elide the 'harmful' or contradictory components of any identity." See Muñoz, *Disidentifications*, 11–12.

   Inspired in part by Jacques Lacan's mirror phase, I liken Muñoz's concept of disidentification to the act of looking at oneself in a mirror, which involves a process of simultaneous identification and alienation. I, for example, see my image in a mirror and I know that the person I see reflected in the glass is me. But I also know that this person is not *really* me but merely my image, a reflection. Thus, I have a disidentificatory relationship to the image (and to myself): I know that it is and isn't me at the same time.

68. According to Lacan, infants experience the mirror stage at around eighteen months of age. It supposedly establishes selfhood (ego formation) as it prompts them to distinguish themselves from other human beings (beginning with their mothers). See Lacan's "The Mirror Stage as Formative Function of the 'I' as Revealed in Psychoanalytic Experience" in *Écrits*. As Marita Sturken and Lisa Cartwright succinctly explain, "The mirror phase thus provides infants with a sense of their existence as a separate body in relationship to another body, but it also provides a basis for alienation, since the process of image recognition involves a splitting between what they are physically capable of and what they see and imagine themselves to be (powerful, in control)." See Sturken and Cartwright, *Practices of Looking*, 75.

69. Gaspar de Alba, *Chicano Art, Inside/Outside the Master's House*, 137.

70. Ibid., 136.

71. Many of my interviewees claimed that pachucas tucked razor blades into their hair. However, one, Dee Chávez, insisted that she and her friends never put razor blades in their bouffants. See chapter 1.

72. Halberstam, *Female Masculinity*, 9.

73. Ibid., 196.

74. *Giving Up the Ghost* was performed as a staged reading by the theater group At the Foot of the Mountain in 1984 in Minneapolis. The play was published in 1986 by West End Press of Los Angeles. A later version was produced by Theatre Rhinoceros in San Francisco and published by West End Press of Albuquerque in 1994. See Yarbro-Bejarano, *The Wounded Heart*. I cite the 1986 version of Moraga's play in this chapter.

75. Among other things, the Hays Hollywood Production Code banned the representation of "sex perversion" in films from 1932 to 1962. See Halberstam, *Female Masculinity*, 177.

76. Yarbro-Bejarano, *The Wounded Heart*, 31–32.

77. Yarbro-Bejarano, "The Female Subject in Chicano Theatre," 397.

78. Moraga, *Giving Up the Ghost*, 1.

79. Ibid.

80. Ibid.

81. Ibid., 4, 30.

82. Ibid., 30.

83. Both African American cool and butch lesbian (female) masculinity have been described as responses to racism and homophobia/misogyny respectively. For example, Richard Majors and Janet Mancini Billson discuss "cool pose" as a "distinctive coping mechanism that serves to counter, at least in part, the dangers that black males encounter on a daily basis. . . . By acting calm, emotionless, fearless, aloof, and tough, the African-American male strives to offset an externally imposed 'zero' image. . . . He is a survivor, in spite of the systematic harm done by the legacy of slavery and the realities of racial oppression, in spite of the centuries of hardship and mistrust." See Majors and Billson, *Cool Pose*, 5.

    Similarly, Ann Cvetkovich describes "a stone attitude" as "a form of protection against the raids and arrests that were a regular occurrence in pre-Stonewall bar culture as well as against the harassment that butch women working in factories frequently experienced. Refusing to show that one had been affected by insults, strip searches, rapes, beatings, and other forms of psychic, physical, and sexual trauma to which lesbians were subject was a significant form of butch resistance." See Cvetkovich, *An Archive of Feelings*, 67.

84. Yarbro-Bejarano, *The Wounded Heart*, 37–38.

85. Moraga, *Giving Up the* Ghost, 5.

86. Ibid., 10–11.

87. Ibid., 36.

88. Pérez, "Sexuality and Discourse," 162.

89. Moraga, *Giving Up the Ghost,* 42–43.

90. Ibid., 4 and 43.

91. Halberstam, *Female Masculinity,* 6.

92. Moraga, *Giving Up the Ghost,* 43.

93. Yarbro-Bejarano, *The Wounded Heart,* 38.

94. Freud, *Beyond the Pleasure Principle and Other Writings,* 69.

95. Moraga, *Giving Up the Ghost,* 44.

96. Ibid., 30.

97. Ibid., 23, 24, 47, 24, and 29.

98. Yarbro-Bejarano, *The Wounded Heart,* 46.

99. "Later, She Met Joyce" was first published in 1983 in Moraga's *Loving in the War Years.* The poem also appeared in *Third Woman,* 2, no. 1 (1984): 28–30, and is in the expanded second edition of *Loving in the War Years* (2000). I cite the 1983 version in this chapter.

100. Cherríe Moraga, *Loving in the War Years,* 19–20.

101. Ibid., 20–21.

102. Ibid., 19.

103. Bettie, *Women without Class,* 62.

104. Moraga, *Loving in the War Years,* 20.

105. Moraga, *Giving Up the Ghost,* 58.

106. Alarcón, "Making Familia from Scratch," 156.

107. Moraga, *Giving Up the Ghost,* 29, 57, 15, and 14.

108. Rosales, "Papis, Dykes, Daddies," 83.

109. de Lauretis, *The Practice of Love,* 208.

110. Regarding filiation and affiliation, see Haraway, *Simians, Cyborgs, and Women.*

111. Hurtado, *Voicing Chicana Feminisms,* 39.

112. de Lauretis, *The Practice of Love,* 246.

113. Moraga, *Loving in the War Years,* 125.

114. Alexander, "Not Just (Any) Body Can Be a Citizen," 6.

115. Moraga, *Loving in the War Years,* 113.

116. Here, I am thinking specifically of Gregory Nava's films *Mi Familia / My Family* (1995) and *Selena* (1997), as well as his short-lived dramatic series *American Family,* which aired on PBS in 2002. For a critique of *American Family,* see Noriega, "'American Family.'"

117. Chabram-Dernersesian, "I Throw Punches for My Race, but I Don't Want to Be a Man," 83.

118. Yarbro-Bejarano, *The Wounded Heart,* 47.

119. Ibid., 46.

120. I take the distinction between witness and voyeur from Alcoff and Gray, "Survivor Discourse."

121. Yarbro-Bejarano, *The Wounded Heart*, 47.

122. de Lauretis, *The Practice of Love*, 245.

123. Yarbro-Bejarano, *The Wounded Heart*, 47.

124. Ibid., 46.

125. Anderson, *Imagined Communities*, 26.

Epilogue

1. Ngai, *Impossible Subjects*, 171.

2. I am certainly not the first nor will I be the last scholar to compare World War II and the war on terror. This epilogue was inspired by "The Sleepy Lagoon Case: Constitutional Rights and the Struggle for Democracy," a symposium held at the University of California, Los Angeles, May 20–21, 2005, that brought together scholars and activists in a dialogue on the two wars. For more information about it, see http://www.library.ucla.edu/.

3. For one example of the increased attention American servicewomen have received from a prominent media source, see Sara Corbett's "The Women's War," the cover story of the March 18, 2007, *New York Times Magazine*, http://www.nytimes.com/ (visited May 19, 2007); and "Latina G. I.s: The Soldiers," *Latina*, December 2005, 146.

4. I take this pithy definition of "neoliberalism" from Ong, *Neoliberalism as Exception*, 3.

5. See Alexander, *Pedagogies of Crossing*, 234.

6. Ibid.

7. Derian, "9/11," 187.

8. Eric Lipton, "Defense Giants to Bid on Border Fence Contract," *Santa Cruz Sentinel*, May 18, 2006, A9.

9. Information about Padilla's life comes from "Profile: José Padilla," BBC News, November 22, 2005, http://news.bbc.co.uk/ (visited June 29, 2006).

10. Regarding the alleged link between Al-Qaeda and Central American gangs, see Jack Epstein, "General Seeks Boost for Latin American Armies," *San Francisco Chronicle*, April 30, 2004, http://www.commondreams.org/ (visited November 9, 2004); "Honduran Official: Al-Qaida Recruits Central American Gangs," NewsMax.com, October 21, 2004, http://www.newsmax.com/ (visited November 9, 2004); and Jerry Seper, "Al Qaeda Seeks Tie to Local Gangs," *Washington Times*, September 28, 2004, http://www.washingtontimes.com/ (visited November 9, 2004).

    In 2006, the U.S. Department of Homeland Security initiated "Operation Community Shield," a crackdown on members of Mara Salvatrucha and other alleged gang members in the United States. See Suzanne Gamboa, "Gang Members Arrested on Immigration Charges," *Santa Cruz Sentinel*, March 11, 2006, A8.

The quote in this paragraph is from "José Padilla, Alleged Terrorist," http://en.wikipedia.org/ (visited June 29, 2006).

11. Alexander, *Pedagogies of Crossing*, 235. Regarding the British youths responsible for the July 2005 bombings in London, see Amy Waldman, "Seething Unease Shaped British Bombers' Newfound Zeal," *New York Times*, July 31, 2005, 1.

12. According to *Latina* magazine, there were "23,500 Hispanics deployed in the Middle East" by December 2005. Approximately 2,500 were Latinas. See "Latina G. I.s," 146.

13. Brendan Miniter, "José Antonio Gutiérrez: He Was an American Hero. Now He's an American," wsj.com, April 4, 2003, http://www.opinionjournal.com/ (visited June 29, 2006). Regarding Latina/o immigrants and noncitizens serving in the U.S. military in the war on terror, see Amaya, "Dying American or the Violence of Citizenship"; Bill Berkowitz, "Latinos on the Front Lines: U.S. Military Targets Latinos for Iraq and Future Twenty-first Century Wars," *WorkingforChange*, http://www.workingforchange.com/ (visited July 22, 2004); Andrew Gumbel, "Pentagon Targets Latinos and Mexicans to Man the Front Lines in War on Terror," *The Independent*, September 10, 2003, http://aztlan.net/ (visited July 22, 2004); Raymond J. Keating, "Immigrants Fight for U.S., Deserve Welcome," *Newsday*, April 8, 2003, http://www.latinamericanstudies.org/ (visited July 22, 2004); Deborah Kong, "Casualty Lists Highlight Thousands of Non-Citizens Serving in the Army," http://www.woodtv.com/ (visited July 22, 2004); Erika Robles, "Non-Citizen Soldiers Heroes Too," *Daily Aztec*, December 9, 2003, http://www.dailyaztec.com/ (visited July 22, 2004); and Mark Stevenson, "U.S. Army Recruiter Crosses Mexico Border," *Akron Beacon Journal*, May 9, 2003, http://www.ohio.com/ (visited July 22, 2004).

14. Piestewa's mother, Percy, is Mexican American. See "Lori Piestewa," http://en.wikipedia.org (visited July 5, 2006); and "Lori Piestewa Confirmed Dead by U.S. Military," indianz.com, April 5, 2003, http://indianz.com/ (visited July 5, 2006).

15. Osha Gray Davidson, "A Wrong Turn in the Desert," *Rolling Stone*, May 27, 2004, http://www.oshadavidson.com/ (visited January 12, 2005). Regarding the controversial renaming of Squaw Peak and Squaw Peak freeway, see Robbie Sherwood and Betty Reid, "Piestewa Kin Seek End to Peak Fray," *Arizona Republic*, March 24, 2004, http://groups.msn.com/BayAreaIndianCalendar/ (visited July 22, 2004); and Judy Nichols, "Arizona 51 Is Now Piestewa Freeway," *Arizona Republic*, May 2, 2003, http://www.azcentral.com/ (visited June 29, 2006).

16. Mark Shaffer and Betty Reid, "'Makeover' Heads to Piestewa Home," *Arizona Republic*, April 13, 2005, http://www.azcentral.com/ (visited June 29, 2006).

Also see Mark Shaffer, "5,000 Flock to See Piestewa House," *Arizona Republic,* April 18, 2005, http://www.azcentral.com/ (visited June 29, 2006). *Saving Jessica Lynch* aired on NBC on November 9, 2003, seven months after Lynch's capture and rescue. See "Saving Jessica Lynch," http://en.wikipedia.org/ (visited July 13, 2006). The special two-hour *Extreme Makeover* episode featuring the Piestewa family aired on ABC on May 22, 2005, as the season finale. See Judy Hedding, "Extreme Makeover Builds a Home for the Piestewas," http://phoenix.about.com/ (visited July 13, 2006).

17. Miniter, "José Antonio Gutiérrez."

18. Regarding the erasure and distortion of Arizona's history, see Mary Pat Brady's elegant *Extinct Lands, Temporal Geographies* and "'Full of Empty.'"

19. McCalister, *Epic Encounters,* 272; Puar and Rai, "Monster, Terrorist, Fag," 127; Antonia Zerbisias, "'Saving Private Lynch' and Other Tales," *Toronto Star,* April 6, 2003, http://www.commondreams.org/ (visited June 30, 2006); and Pin-Fat and Stern, "The Scripting of Private Jessica Lynch," http://web3.infotrac.galegroup.com/ (visited July 25, 2005).

20. "Adelitas" refers to the women "who fought courageously side by side with the men" in the Mexican Revolution. See Jorge Mariscal, "Mexican American Women in Iraq: Las Adelitas 2003," *CounterPunch,* http://www.counterpunch.org/ (visited July 22, 2004). Regarding Johnson's Panamanian heritage, see Stan Goff, "The Use and Abuse of a Woman Soldier: Jessica Lynch, Plural," *CounterPunch,* December 13–14, 2003, http://www.counterpunch.org/ (visited June 27, 2005).

21. Lizette Alvarez, "Jane, We Hardly Knew Ye Died," *New York Times,* September 24, 2006, section 4, 1; Nathan Thornburgh, "A Death in the Class of 9/11," *Time,* September 28, 2006, http://www.time.com/ (visited February 12, 2007).

22. Secretary of State Condoleezza Rice has served a similar purpose. As McAlister points out, she is a "highly visible symbol. In her very person, standing by the side of the president or speaking on the evening news, she represented a vision of the United States as a place where a woman of any race might achieve extraordinary success and power." See McAlister, *Epic Encounters,* 291–92.

23. Regarding the Army's Foreign Language Recruitment Initiative, which provides recent immigrants with English-language lessons, and Executive Order 13269, which expedites the naturalization process for noncitizens in the U.S. military (signed by President George W. Bush on July 3, 2002), see Mariscal, "Homeland Security, Militarism, and the Future of Latinos and Latinas in the United States," 46.

24. Regarding sexual assault and trauma within the U.S. military, see Corbett, "The Women's War," as well as the websites for Women Organizing Women

(http://vetwow.com/) and U.S. Army Specialist Suzanne Swift (http://www
.suzanneswift.org/) (both visited July 14, 2006).

25. Pin-Fat and Stern, "The Scripting of Private Jessica Lynch."

26. "Female Rambo" is from Pin-Fat and Stern, "The Scripting of Private Jessica
Lynch." "G. I. Jane" is from Goff, "The Use and Abuse of a Woman Soldier."
Also see "Then and Now: Jessica Lynch," cnn.com/ (visited July 14, 2006).

27. "Then and Now: Jessica Lynch."

28. Doug Giebel, "Used and Used Again: Jessica Lynch and Saving American Decency," *CounterPunch*, November 12, 2003, http://www.counterpunch.org/
(visited July 14, 2006).

29. Ibid.

30. Barbara Ehrenreich, "Prison Abuse: Feminism's Assumptions Upended," *Los
Angeles Times*, May 16, 2004, M1.

31. Kelly Cogswell, "Torture and America: So This Is Us," *The Gully*, May 13,
2004, http://www.thegully.com/ (visited July 15, 2006).

32. "White trash" is from Gary Younge, "Blame the White Trash," *Guardian Unlimited*, May 17, 2004, http://www.guardian.co.uk/ (visited July 15, 2006).
"Porno torture" is from Liaquat Ali Khan, "Not One Victim Was Called to
Testify: The Invention of Porno Torture," *CounterPunch*, September 28, 2005,
http://www.counterpunch.org/ (visited July 14, 2006).

33. Puar, "On Torture," 20–21.

34. According to Corbett, one in ten U.S. soldiers in Iraq is female. Where
75,000 women served in Vietnam and 45,000 in the Persian Gulf War,
160,000 women had been deployed to Iraq or Afghanistan as of March 2007.
See Corbett, "The Women's War."

35. George Rush, "Jessica's Hustled: Porn Mag Pulls Plan to Run Topless Pics
of G. I.," *New York Daily News*, November 11, 2003, http://nydailynews.com/
(visited July 14, 2006). This Web page features a photograph of Britney Spears
flanked by Lynch and Johnson at the magazine gala. Johnson is in uniform.

36. "Inspiring Latinas," *Latina*, May 2005, 30.

37. Alexander, *Pedagogies of Crossing*, 181.

38. See, for example, Janine DeFao, "Marine Who Killed Cop Linked to Gang
Activity," *San Francisco Chronicle*, January 16, 2005, 17A.

39. See Garza's gouache *Polvo y Pelo, El Pleito (Dust and Hair, the Fight, 1987)*,
which appears in Garza, *A Piece of My Heart / Pedacito de mi Corazón*, 46.

40. McClintock, "Family Feuds," 61.

41. I take the concept of culture as "history-in-the-making" from McAlister's *Epic
Encounters*, 307.

BIBLIOGRAPHY

Oral Histories, Interviews, and Personal Correspondence

Baca, Judith F. Interview with author. Venice, Calif., August 1, 2000.

Chávez, Delia. Interview with author. Monterey Park, Calif., June 30, 1998.

Cruz, Olga. Interview with author. Los Angeles, Calif., January 13, 2005.

Gamboa, María Elena (pseudonym). Interview with author. Los Angeles, Calif., April 27, 1998.

Hernández-Avila, Inés. E-mail correspondence with author. September 30, 1999.

Juárez, Carolina. Interview with author. Oakland, California, May 11, 2002.

Leyvas, Lupe. Interview with author. Montebello, Calif., August 3, 2000.

López, Hortensia. Interview with author. Los Angeles, Calif., April 28, 1998.

López, Mary. Interview with author. Oakland, Calif., June 7, 2002.

Loza, Consuelo (pseudonym). Interview with author. Los Angeles, Calif., April 28, 1998.

McGrath, Alice. Telephone interview with author. February 18, 1999.

Ochoa, Mary Lou. Interview with author. Monterey Park, Calif., April 27, 1998.

Rodríguez, Enedina. Interview with author. Monterey Park, Calif., April 26, 1998.

Vargas, Laura (pseudonym). Interview with author. Montebello, Calif., November 14, 2004.

Archival Collections

University of Arizona, University of Arizona Library
  Department of Special Collections
  Southwest Folklore Center Manuscript Collection
University of California, Los Angeles
  Charles E. Young Research Library, Department of Special Collections
    Guy S. Endore Papers 279
    Alice Greenfield McGrath Collection 1490
    Carey McWilliams Collection 1243
    Sleepy Lagoon Defense Committee 107
  Chicano Studies Research Library
    Ron López Papers 0003

California State University, Long Beach, University Library, Department of Special
    Collections
    Rosie the Riveter Revisited: Women and the World War II Work Experience
Huntington Library
    John Anson Ford Papers
Southern California Library for Social Studies and Research
    Robert W. Kenney Papers
    Ben Margolis Papers
    Alice Greenfield McGrath Papers
Stanford University, Green Library, Special Collections
    Bert Corona Papers M0238

Periodicals and Newspapers

Akron Beacon Journal
Arizona Republic
California Eagle
Colliers
Daily Aztec
Eastside Journal
The Independent
La Causa
Corazón de Aztlán
CounterPunch (online)
The Crisis
Guardian Unlimited
The Gully Online Magazine
La Opinión
Latina
Life
Los Angeles Daily News
Los Angeles Examiner
Los Angeles Herald-Express
Los Angeles Magazine
Los Angeles Times
Lowrider
The New Republic
Newsday
Newsweek
New York Daily News
New York Times

Pittsburgh Courier
Rolling Stone
Saint Paul Pioneer Press
San Francisco Chronicle
Santa Cruz Sentinel
Sensation
Survey Monthly
Time
Toronto Star
Wall Street Journal
Washington Times
WorkingForChange (online)

Published Sources

Acuña, Rudy. *A Mexican American Chronicle*. New York: American Book Company, 1971.

———. *Occupied America: A History of Chicanos*. New York: Harper and Row, 1988.

Adler, Patricia Rae. "The 1943 Zoot-Suit Riots: Brief Episode in a Long Conflict." In *The Mexican-Americans: An Awakening Minority*, edited by Manuel P. Servín, 124–42. Beverly Hills, Calif.: Glencoe Press, 1970.

Alarcón, Norma. "Chicana Feminism: In the Tracks of 'the' Native Woman." *Cultural Studies* 4, no. 3 (1990): 248–56.

———. "Chicana's Feminist Literature: A Re-vision through Malintzín/or Malintzín: Putting Flesh Back on the Object." In *This Bridge Called My Back: Writings by Radical Women of Color*, edited by Cherríe Moraga and Gloria Anzaldúa, 182–90. New York: Kitchen Table Women of Color Press, 1983.

———. "Making *Familia* from Scratch: Split Subjectivities in the Work of Helena María Viramontes and Cherríe Moraga." In *Chicana Creativity and Criticism: Charting New Frontiers in American Literature*, edited by María Herrera-Sobek and Helena María Viramontes, 147–59. Houston: Arte Público Press, 1988.

———. "Traddutora, Traditora: A Paradigmatic Figure of Chicana Feminism." *Cultural Critique* 13 (1989): 57–87.

Alarcón, Norma, Caren Kaplan, and Minoo Moallem. "Introduction: Between Woman and Nation." In *Between Woman and Nation: Nationalisms, Transnational Feminisms, and the State*, edited by Caren Kaplan, Norma Alarcón, and Minoo Moallem, 1–16. Durham, N.C.: Duke University Press, 1999.

Alcalá, Rita Cano. "From Chingada to Chingona: La Malinche Redefined or, A Long Line of Hermanas." *Aztlán* 26, no. 2 (2001): 33–61.

Alcoff, Linda, and Laura Gray. "Survivor Discourse: Transgression or Recuperation?" *Signs*, 18, no. 2 (1993): 260–90.

Alexander, M. Jacqui. "Not Just (Any) Body Can Be a Citizen: The Politics of Law, Sexuality and Postcoloniality in Trinidad and Tobago and the Bahamas." *Feminist Review*, no. 48 (1994): 5–23.

———. *Pedagogies of Crossing: Meditations on Feminism, Sexual Politics, Memory, and the Sacred*. Durham, N.C.: Duke University Press, 2005.

Almaguer, Tomás. "Chicano Men: A Cartography of Homosexual Identity and Behavior." *Differences* 3, no. 2 (1991): 75–100.

Althusser, Louis. "Ideology and Ideological State Apparatuses (Notes towards an Investigation)." In *Lenin and Philosophy*. Translated by Ben Brewster. New York: Monthly Review Press, 1971.

Alurista. *Nationchild Plumaroja*. San Diego: Toltecas en Aztlán, 1972.

Alva, Javier. "The Sacred Spot." In *Aztlán: An Anthology of Mexican American Literature*, edited by Luis Valdez and Stan Steiner, 170–73. New York: Vintage Books, 1972.

Alvarez, George R. "Calo: The 'Other' Spanish." *ETC: A Review of General Semantics* 24, no. 1 (1967): 7–13.

Alvarez, Luis. "From Zoot Suits to Hip Hop: Towards a Relational Chicana/o Studies." *Latino Studies* 5, no. 1 (2007): 53–75.

———. *The Power of the Zoot: Youth Culture and Resistance during World War II*. Berkeley: University of California Press, 2008.

———. "Zoot Violence on the Home Front: Race, Riots, and Youth Culture during World War II." In *Mexican Americans and World War II*, edited by Maggie Rivas-Rodríguez, 141–75. Austin: University of Texas Press, 2005.

Amaya, Hector. "Dying American or the Violence of Citizenship: Latinos in Iraq." *Latino Studies* 5, no. 1 (2007): 3–24.

Anderson, Benedict. *Imagined Communities: Reflections on the Origin and Spread of Nationalism*. New York: Verso, 1991.

Anderson, Karen. *Wartime Women: Sex Roles, Family Relations, and the Status of Women*. Westport, Conn.: Greenwood Press, 1981.

Anzaldúa, Gloria. *Borderlands / La Frontera: The New Mestiza*. San Francisco: Aunt Lute, 1987.

Arteaga, Alfred. *Chicano Poetics: Heterotexts and Hybridities*. New York: Cambridge University Press, 1997.

Avila, Eric. *Popular Culture in the Age of White Flight: Fear and Fantasy in Suburban Los Angeles*. Berkeley: University of California Press, 2004.

Bailey, Beth, and David Farber. *The First Strange Place: The Alchemy of Race and Sex in World War II Hawaii*. Baltimore: Johns Hopkins University Press, 1992.

Balibar, Etienne, and Immanuel Wallerstein. *Race, Nation, Class: Ambiguous Identities*. London: Verso, 1991.

Banay, Ralph S. "A Psychiatrist Looks at the Zoot Suit." *Probation* 22, no. 3 (1944): 81–85.

Barajas, Frank. "The Defense Committees of Sleepy Lagoon: A Convergent Struggle against Fascism, 1942–1944." *Aztlán* 31, no. 1 (2006): 33–62.

Barker, George Carpenter. *Pachuco: An American-Spanish Argot and Its Social Functions in Tucson, Arizona.* Tucson: University of Arizona Press, 1950.

Batstone, David, and Eduardo Mendieta, eds. *The Good Citizen.* New York: Routledge, 2001.

Behdad, Ali. *A Forgetful Nation: On Immigration and Cultural Identity in the United States.* Durham, N.C.: Duke University Press, 2005.

Beiner, Ronald, ed. *Theorizing Citizenship.* Albany: State University of New York Press, 1995.

Bell, Shannon. "Finding the Male within and Taking Him Cruising: Drag-King-for-a-Day." In *The Third Sex,* edited by Arthur Kroker and Marilouise Kroker, 89–103. New York: St. Martin's Press, 1993.

Benhabib, Seyla. *The Rights of Others: Aliens, Residents, and Citizens.* Cambridge: Cambridge University Press, 2004.

Berk-Seligson, Susan. "A Sociolinguistic View of the Mexican-American Speech Community," *Latin American Research Review* 15, No. 2 (1980): 65–110.

Bérubé, Allan. *Coming out under Fire: The History of Gay Men and Women in World War II.* New York: Free Press, 1990.

———. "Marching to a Different Drummer: Lesbian and Gay GIs in World War II." In *Powers of Desire: The Politics of Sexuality,* edited by Ann Snitow, Christine Stansell, and Sharon Thompson, 88–99. New York: Monthly Review Press, 1983.

Bettie, Julie. "Women without Class: *Chicas, Cholas,* Trash, and the Presence/Absence of Class Identity." *Signs* 26, no. 1 (2000): 1–35.

———. *Women without Class: Girls, Race, and Identity.* Berkeley: University of California Press, 2003.

Bhabha, Homi K. *The Location of Culture.* New York: Routledge, 1994.

———, ed. *Nation and Narration.* London: Routledge, 1990.

Blackman, Inge, and Kathryn Perry, "Skirting the Issue: Lesbian Fashion for the 1990s." *Feminist Review* 34 (1990): 67–78.

Blea, Irene. *La Chicana and the Intersection of Race, Class, and Gender.* New York: Praeger, 1992.

Bogardus, Emory S. "Gangs of Mexican-American Youth." *Sociology and Social Research* 28, no. 1 (1943): 55–66.

———. *The Mexican in the United States.* New York: Jerome S. Ozer, 1971.

Bordo, Susan R. "The Body and the Reproduction of Femininity: A Feminist Approach of Foucault." In *Gender/Body/Knowledge: Feminist Reconstructions of*

Being and Knowing, edited by Alison M. Jaggar and Susan R. Bordo, 13–33. New Brunswick, N.J.: Rutgers University Press, 1989.

Boris, Eileen. "'You Wouldn't Want One of 'Em Dancing with Your Wife': Racialized Bodies on the Job in World War II." *American Quarterly* 50, no. 1 (1998): 77–108.

Bosniak, Linda. *The Citizen and the Alien: Dilemmas of Contemporary Membership.* Princeton, N.J.: Princeton University Press, 2006.

Bourdieu, Pierre. *Distinction: A Social Critique of the Judgement of Taste.* Translated by Richard Nice. Cambridge, Mass.: Harvard University Press, 1984.

———. *Photography: A Middle-Brow Art.* Translated by Shaun Whiteside. Stanford, Calif.: Stanford University Press, 1990.

Bowen, John R. *Why the French Don't Like Headscarves: Islam, the State, and Public Space.* Princeton, N.J.: Princeton University Press, 2007.

Braddy, Haldeen. "The Pachucos and Their Argot." *Southern Folklore Quarterly* 24, no. 4 (December 1960): 255–71.

Brady, Mary Pat. *Extinct Lands, Temporal Geographies: Chicana Literature and the Urgency of Space.* Durham, N.C.: Duke University Press, 2002.

———. "'Full of Empty': Creating the Southwest as 'Terra Incognita.'" In *Nineteenth-century Geographies: The Transformation of Space from the Victorian Age to the American Century,* edited by Ronald Thomas and Helena Michie, 251–64. New Brunswick, N.J.: Rutgers University Press, 2002.

Brown, Monica. *Gang Nation: Delinquent Citizens in Puerto Rican, Chicano, and Chicana Narratives.* Minneapolis: University of Minnesota Press, 2002.

Brown, Wendy. *States of Injury: Power and Freedom in Late Modernity.* Princeton, N.J.: Princeton University Press, 1995.

Broyles-González, Yolanda. *El Teatro Campesino: Theater in the Chicano Movement.* Austin: University of Texas Press, 1994.

Brubaker, Rogers. *Nationalism Reframed: Nationhood and the National Question in the New Europe.* Cambridge: Cambridge University Press, 1996.

Brubaker, William Rogers, ed. *Immigration and the Politics of Citizenship in Europe and North America.* Lanham, Md.: University Press of America, 1989.

Bruce-Novoa, Juan. *Chicano Authors: Inquiry by Interview.* Austin: University of Texas Press, 1980.

———. *Chicano Poetry: A Response to Chaos.* Austin: University of Texas Press, 1982.

Burciaga, José Antonio. *Restless Serpents.* Menlo Park, Calif.: Diseños Literarios, 1976.

Burgess, Ernest W. "The Effect of War on the American Family." *American Journal of Sociology* 48, no. 3 (1942): 343–52.

Butler, Judith. *Antigone's Claim: Kinship between Life and Death.* New York: Columbia University Press, 2000.

————. *Bodies That Matter: On the Discursive Limits of "Sex."* New York: Routledge, 1993.

————. *Gender Trouble: Feminism and the Subversion of Identity.* New York: Routledge, 1990.

Calhoun, Craig. *Nationalism.* Minneapolis: University of Minnesota Press, 1997.

Calloway, Cab. *Of Minnie the Moocher and Me.* New York: Thomas Y. Crowell, 1976.

Campbell, D'Ann. *Women at War with America: Private Lives in a Patriotic Era.* Cambridge, Mass.: Harvard University Press, 1984.

Candelaria, Cordelia. "La Malinche, Feminist Prototype." *Frontiers* 5, no. 2 (1980): 1–6.

Case, Sue-Ellen. "Toward a Butch-Femme Aesthetic." In *Making a Spectacle: Feminist Essays on Contemporary Women's Theater,* edited by Lynda Hart, 282–99. Ann Arbor: University of Michigan Press, 1989.

Castellano, Olivia. "Estos Vatos with Their Intellectual Conversation." *Imagine* 1, no. 1 (Summer 1984): 48.

Chabram-Dernersesian, Angie. "I Throw Punches for My Race, but I Don't Want to Be a Man: Writing Us—Chica-nos (Girl, Us) / Chicanas—into the Movement Script." In *Cultural Studies,* edited by Lawrence Grossberg, Carey Nelson, and Paula Treichler, 81–95. New York: Routledge, 1992.

Chafe, William Henry. *The American Woman: Her Changing Social, Economic, and Political Roles, 1920–1970.* New York: Oxford University Press, 1972.

Chatterjee, Partha. *The Nation and Its Fragments: Colonial and Postcolonial Histories.* Princeton, N.J.: Princeton University Press, 1993.

Chauncey, George. *Gay New York: Gender, Urban Culture, and the Making of the Gay Male World, 1890–1940.* New York: Basic Books, 1994.

Chávez, Ernesto. *¡Mi Raza Primero! (My People First!): Nationalism, Identity, and Insurgency in the Chicano Movement in Los Angeles, 1966–1978.* Berkeley: University of California Press, 2002.

Chibnall, Steve. "Whistle and Zoot: The Changing Meaning of a Suit of Clothes." *History Workshop* 20 (Autumn 1985): 56–81.

Clark, Kenneth B., and James Barker. "The Zoot Effect in Personality: A Race Riot Participant." *Journal of Abnormal and Social Psychology* 40, no. 2 (April 1945): 143–48.

Coltharp, Lurline. "Invitation to the Dance: Spanish in the El Paso Underworld." In *Texas Studies in Bilingualism: Spanish, French, German, Czech, Polish, Serbian, and Norwegian in the Southwest,* edited by Glenn G. Gilbert, 7–17. Berlin: Walter de Gruyter, 1970.

Coltharp, Lurline. *The Tongue of the Tirilones: A Linguistic Study of a Criminal Argot.* Tuscaloosa: University of Alabama Press, 1965.

Corona, Bert. "Chicano Scholars and Public Issues in the United States in the Eighties." In *History, Culture, and Society: Chicano Studies in the 1980s.* Edited by Mario T. García, Francisco Lomeli, Mario Barrera, Edward Escobar, and John García. Ypsilanti: Bilingual Press/Editorial Bilingüe, 1983.

Cosgrove, Stuart. "The Zoot Suit and Style Warfare." *History Workshop Journal* 18 (1984): 77–91.

Costello, John. *Virtue under Fire: How World War II Changed Our Social and Sexual Attitudes.* Boston: Little, Brown, 1985.

Cotera, Marta. "Our Feminist Heritage." In *Chicana Feminist Thought: The Basic Historical Writings,* edited by Alma M. García, 41–44. New York: Routledge, 1997.

Crane, Diana. *Fashion and Its Social Agendas: Class, Gender, and Identity in Clothing.* Chicago: University of Chicago Press, 2000.

Cvetkovich, Ann. *An Archive of Feelings: Trauma, Sexuality, and Lesbian Public Cultures.* Durham, N.C.: Duke University Press, 2003.

Dabakis, Melissa. "Gendered Labor: Norman Rockwell's *Rosie the Riveter* and the Discourses of Wartime Womanhood." In *Gender and American History since 1890,* edited by Barbara Melosh, 182–204. New York: Routledge, 1993.

Daniels, Douglas Henry. "Los Angeles Zoot: Race 'Riot,' the Pachuco, and Black Music Culture." *Journal of African American History* 87 (Winter 2002): 98–118.

Davenport, Walter. "Swing It, Swing Shift!" *Colliers* 110, no. 8 (August 1942): 24–29.

Davis, Lisa E. "The Butch as Drag Artiste: Greenwich Village in the Roaring Forties." In *The Persistent Desire: A Femme-Butch Reader,* edited by Joan Nestle, 45–53. Boston: Alyson Publications, 1992.

Day, Mark. "The Pertinence of the 'Sleepy Lagoon' Case." *Journal of Mexican American History* 4 (1974): 71–75.

De Genova, Nicholas. *Working the Boundaries: Race, Space, and "Illegality" in Mexican Chicago.* Durham, N.C.: Duke University Press, 2005.

Delano, Page Dougherty. "Making Up for War: Sexuality and Citizenship in Wartime Culture." *Feminist Studies* 26, no. 1 (2000): 33–68.

de Lauretis, Teresa. *The Practice of Love: Lesbian Sexuality and Perverse Desire.* Bloomington: Indiana University Press, 1994.

Del Castillo, Adelaida R. "Malintzín Tenepal: A Preliminary Look into a New Perspective." *Encuentro Femenil* 1, no. 2 (1974): 58–77.

del Fuego, Laura. *Maravilla.* Encino, Calif.: Floricanto Press, 1989.

D'Emilio, John. *Sexual Politics, Sexual Communities: The Making of a Homosexual Minority in the United States, 1940–1970.* 2nd ed. Chicago: University of Chicago Press, 1998.

Derian, James Der. "9/11: Before, After, and In Between." In *Understanding September 11*, edited by Craig Calhoun, Paul Price, and Ashley Timmer, 177–90. New York: New Press, 2002.

Díaz del Castillo, Bernal. *The Conquest of New Spain*. Translated by J. M. Cohen. Baltimore: Penguin, 1983.

Duggan, Lisa. *The Twilight of Equality? Neoliberalism, Cultural Politics, and the Attack on Democracy*. Boston: Beacon Press, 2003.

Durán, Marcus. "Retrato de un Bato Loco." In *Voices of Aztlán: Chicano Literature of Today*, edited by Dorothy E. Harth and Lewis M. Baldwin, 49–51. New York: Mentor, 1974.

Ehrenreich, Barbara. *Fear of Falling: The Inner Life of the Middle Class*. New York: Pantheon Books, 1989.

———. "Prison Abuse: Feminism's Assumptions Upended." *Los Angeles Times*, May 16, 2004.

"El Hijo Desobediente." In *Pachuco: An American-Spanish Argot and Its Social Functions in Tucson, Arizona*, by George Carpenter Barker, 37–39. Tucson: University of Arizona Press, 1950.

Elshtain, Jean Bethke. *Public Man/Private Woman: Women in Social and Political Thought*. Princeton, N.J.: Princeton University Press, 1981.

Enstad, Nan. *Ladies of Labor, Girls of Adventure: Working Women, Popular Culture, and Labor Politics at the Turn of the Twentieth Century*. New York: Columbia University Press, 1999.

Erenberg, Lewis A., and Susan E. Hirsch, eds. *The War in American Culture: Society and Consciousness during World War II*. Chicago: University of Chicago Press, 1996.

Escobar, Edward J. *Race, Police, and the Making of a Political Identity: Mexican Americans and the Los Angeles Police Department, 1900–1945*. Berkeley: University of California Press, 1999.

———. "Zoot-Suiters and Cops: Chicano Youth and the Los Angeles Police Department during World War II." In *The War in American Culture: Society and Consciousness during World War II*, edited by Lewis A. Erenberg and Susan E. Hirsch, 284–309. Chicago: University of Chicago Press, 1996.

Escobedo, Elizabeth R. "The Pachuca Panic: Sexual and Cultural Battlegrounds in World War II Los Angeles." *Western Historical Quarterly* 38, no. 2 (2007): 133–56.

España-Maram, Linda N. "Brown 'Hordes' in McIntosh Suits: Filipinos, Taxi Dance Halls, and Performing the Immigrant Body in Los Angeles, 1930s-1940s." In *Generations of Youth: Youth Cultures and History in Twentieth-Century America*, edited by Joe Austin and Michael Nevin Willard, 118–35. New York: New York University Press, 1998.

Espinoza, Dionne. "'Revolutionary Sisters': Women's Solidarity and Collective Identification among Chicana Brown Berets in East Los Angeles, 1967–1970." *Aztlán* 26, no. 1 (Spring 2001): 17–58.

———. "'Tanto Tiempo Disfrutamos...': Revisiting the Gender and Sexual Politics of Chicana/o Youth Culture in East Los Angeles in the 1960s." In *Velvet Barrios: Popular Culture and Chicana/o Sexualities*, edited Alicia Gaspar de Alba, 89–106. New York: Palgrave Macmillan, 2003.

Evans, Jessica, and Stuart Hall, eds., *Visual Culture: The Reader*. London: Sage Publications, 1999.

Faderman, Lillian. *Odd Girls and Twilight Lovers: A History of Lesbian Life in Twentieth-Century America*. New York: Columbia University Press, 1991.

Fishman, Sarah. *The Battle for Children: World War II, Youth Crime, and Juvenile Justice in Twentieth-Century France*. Cambridge, Mass.: Harvard University Press, 2002.

Fitzgerald Keith. *The Face of the Nation: Immigration, the State, and the National Identity*. Stanford, Calif.: Stanford University Press, 1996.

Flores, William V., and Rina Benmayor. *Latino Cultural Citizenship: Claiming Identity, Space, and Rights*. Boston: Beacon Press, 1997.

Foley, Neil. *The White Scourge: Mexicans, Blacks, and Poor Whites in Texas Cotton Culture*. Berkeley: University of California Press, 1997.

Ford, John Anson. *Thirty Explosive Years in Los Angeles County*. San Marino, Calif.: Huntington Library, 1961.

Fraiman, Susan. *Cool Men and the Second Sex*. New York: Columbia University Press, 2003.

Frank, Thomas. *The Conquest of Cool: Business Culture, Counterculture, and the Rise of Hip Consumerism*. Chicago: University of Chicago Press, 1997.

Franklin, Benjamin. "The German Language in Pennsylvania." In *Language Loyalties: A Source Book on the Official English Controversy*, edited by James Crawford, 18–19. Chicago: University of Chicago Press, 1992.

Fraser, Nancy. "Rethinking the Public Sphere." *Social Text* 25, no. 26 (1994): 56–90.

Frazier, E. Franklin. "Ethnic and Minority Groups in Wartime, with Special Reference to the Negro." *American Journal of Sociology* 48, no. 3 (1942): 369–77.

Fregoso, Rosa-Linda. *The Bronze Screen: Chicana and Chicano Film Culture*. Minneapolis: University of Minnesota Press, 1993.

———. "Homegirls, *Cholas*, and *Pachucas* in Cinema: Taking over the Public Sphere." *California History* 74, no. 3 (1995): 316–27.

———. *MeXicana Encounters: The Making of Social Identities on the Borderlands*. Berkeley: University of California Press, 2005.

————. "Re-Imagining Chicana Urban Identities in the Public Sphere, *Cool Chuca Style*." In *Between Women and Nation: Nationalisms, Transnational Feminisms, and the State*, edited by Caren Kaplan, Norma Alarcón, and Minoo Moallem, 72–91. Durham, N.C.: Duke University Press, 1999.

Freud, Sigmund. *Beyond the Pleasure Principle and Other Writings*. Translated by John Reddick. London: Penguin Books, 2003.

Fuentes, Dagoberto, and José A. López. *Barrio Language Dictionary: First Dictionary of Caló*. La Puente, Calif.: Sunburst Enterprises, 1974.

Gaarder, Alfred Bruce. "Notes on Some Spanish Terms in the Southwest." *Hispania* 27, no. 3 (1944): 330–34.

Gaines, Jane. "War, Women, and Lipstick: Fan Mags in the Forties," *Heresies* 5, No. 2 (1985): 42–47.

Gal, Susan. "Language, Gender, and Power: An Anthropological Review." In *Gender Articulated: Language and the Socially Constructed Self*, edited by Kira Hall and Mary Bucholtz, 169–82. New York: Routledge, 1995.

Galindo, D. Letticia. "Caló and Taboo Language Use among Chicanas: A Description of Linguistic Appropriation and Innovation." In *Speaking Chicana: Voice, Power, and Identity*, edited by D. Letticia Galindo and María Dolores Gonzáles, Tucson: University of Arizona Press, 1999.

————. "Capturing Chicano Voices: An Interdisciplinary Approach." In *Cultural Performances: Proceedings of the Third Berkeley Women and Language Conference*, edited by Mary Bucholtz, A. C. Liang, Laurel A. Sutton, and Caitlin Hines, 320–31. Berkeley: Berkeley Women and Language Group, University of California, 1994.

————. "Dispelling the Male-Only Myth: Chicanas and Caló." *The Bilingual Review / La Revista Bilingüe* 17, no. 1 (1992): 3–35.

————. "The Language of Gangs, Drugs, and Prison Life among Chicanas." *Latino Studies Journal* 4, no. 3 (1993): 23–43.

————. "Perceptions of Pachuquismo and Use of Calo/Pachuco Spanish by Various Chicana Women." *La Red/The Net*, no. 48 (1981): 2, 10.

Garber, Marjorie. *Vested Interests: Cross-Dressing and the Cultural Anxiety*. New York: Routledge, 1992.

García, Alma M., ed. *Chicana Feminist Thought: The Basic Historical Writings*. New York: Routledge, 1997.

García, Mario T. "Americans All: The Mexican American Generation and the Politics of Wartime, 1941–45." In *The Mexican American Experience: An Interdisciplinary Anthology*, edited by Rodolfo O. de la Garza, Frank D. Bean, Charles M. Bonjean, Ricardo Romo, and Rodolfo Alvarez, 201–12. Austin: University of Texas Press, 1985.

————. *Memories of Chicano History: The Life and Narrative of Bert Corona*. Berkeley: University of California Press, 1994.

———. *Mexican Americans: Leadership, Ideology, and Identity, 1930–1960.* New Haven, Conn.: Yale University Press, 1989.

García, Matt. *A World of Its Own: Race, Labor, and Citrus in the Making of Greater Los Angeles, 1900–1970.* Chapel Hill: University of North Carolina Press, 2001.

Garza, Carmen Lomas. *Un Pedacito de Mi Corazón /A Piece of My Heart: The Art of Carmen Lomas Garza.* New York: New Press, 1981.

Garza, Daniel. "Saturday Belongs to the Palomía." In *The Chicanos: Mexican American Voices,* edited by Ed Ludwig and James Santibanez, 25–30. Baltimore: Penguin, 1971.

Gaspar de Alba, Alicia. *Chicano Art, Inside/Outside the Master's House: Cultural Politics and the CARA Exhibition.* Austin: University of Texas Press, 1998.

Gellner, Ernest. *Nationalism.* New York: New York University Press, 1997.

Gilroy, Paul. "It's a Family Affair." In *Black Popular Culture: A Project by Michelle Wallace,* edited by Gina Dent, 303–16. Seattle: Bay Press, 1992.

Gluck, Sherna Berger. *Rosie the Riveter Revisited: Women, the War, and Social Change.* Boston: Twayne Publishers, 1987.

Golden, Hyman E., Frank O'Leary, and Morris Lipsius. *Dictionary of American Underworld Lingo.* New York: Twayne Publishers, 1950.

Goldman, Shifra M., and Tomás Ybarra-Frausto. "The Political and Social Contexts of Chicano Art." In *Chicano Art: Resistance and Affirmation, 1965–1985,* edited by Richard Griswold del Castillo, Teresa McKenna, and Yvonne Yarbro-Bejarano, 83–95. Los Angeles: Wight Art Gallery, University of California, 1991.

Gonzáles, Rodolfo. "Chicano Nationalism: The Key to Unity for La Raza." In *A Documentary History of the Mexican Americans,* edited by Wayne Moquin and Charles Van Doren, 378–82. New York: Praeger Publishers, 1971.

———. *I Am Joaquin / Yo Soy Joaquín.* New York: Bantam Books, 1971.

González, Rafael Jesus. "Pachuco: The Birth of a Creole Language." *Arizona Quarterly* 23, no. 4 (1967): 343–56.

Grajeda, Rafael. "The Pachuco in Chicano Poetry: The Process of Legend Creation." *Revista Chicano-Riqueña* 8, no. 4 (1980): 45–58.

Granado, Virginia. "Para Mi Jefe." *De Colores* 1, no. 2 (spring 1974): 37.

Green, George K. "Calo, Pachuco, and Lunfardo: Certain Homogeneous Tendencies in Vernacular Spanish." In *Research Issues and Problems in United States Spanish: Latin American and Southwestern Varieties,* edited by Jacob L. Ornstein-Galicia, George K. Green, and Dennis J. Bixler-Márquez, 243–49. Brownsville, Texas: Pan American University, 1988.

Griffith, Beatrice. *American Me.* Westport, Conn.: Greenwood Press, 1947.

———. "The Pachuco Patois." *Common Ground* 7, no. 4 (1947): 77–84.

Griswold del Castillo, Richard. *César Chávez: A Triumph of Spirit.* Norman: University of Oklahoma Press, 1995.

Griswold del Castillo, Richard, and Arnoldo de León. *North to Aztlán: A History of Mexican Americans in the United States.* New York: Twayne Publishers, 1996.

Griswold del Castillo, Richard, Teresa McKenna, and Yvonne Yarbro-Bejarano, eds. *Chicano Art: Resistance and Affirmation, 1965–1985.* Los Angeles: Wight Art Gallery, University of California, 1991.

Halberstam, Judith. *Female Masculinity.* Durham, N.C.: Duke University Press, 1998.

Hall, Stuart. "The Work of Representation." In *Representation: Cultural Representations and Signifying Practices,* edited by Stuart Hall, 13–74. London: Sage Publications, 1997.

Haraway, Donna. *Simians, Cyborgs, and Women: The Reinvention of Nature.* New York: Routledge, 1991.

Hartmann, Heidi. "The Family as the Locus of Gender, Class, and Political Struggle: The Example of Housework." In *Feminism and Methodology,* edited by Sandra Harding, 109–34. Bloomington: Indiana University Press, 1987.

Hartmann, Susan. "Prescriptions for Penelope: Literature on Women's Obligations to Returning World War II Veterans." *Women's Studies* 5, no. 3 (1978): 223–39.

Hebdige, Dick. *Subculture: The Meaning of Style.* London: Routledge, 1989.

Henstell, Bruce. "The Zoot Suit: One Fashion That Was Really a Riot." *Los Angeles Magazine* 23, no. 4 (April 1978): 218–24.

Hernández, Inés. "Para Teresa." In *Infinite Divisions: An Anthology of Chicana Literature,* edited by Tey Diana Rebolledo and Eliana S. Rivero, 330–33. Tucson: University of Arizona Press, 1993.

———. "Para Teresa." In *Siete Poetas.* Tucson: Scorpion Press, 1978.

Hernández-Chávez, Eduardo, Andrew D. Cohen, and Anthony F. Beltramo, *El Lenguaje de los Chicanos: Regional and Social Characteristics Used by Mexican Americans.* Arlington, Va.: Center for Applied Linguistics, 1975.

Herrera-Sobek, María. *The Mexican Corrido: A Feminist Analysis.* Bloomington: Indiana University Press, 1993.

———. "The Street Scene: Metaphoric Strategies in Two Contemporary Chicana Poets." In *Chicana (W)rites: On Word and Film,* edited by María Herrera-Sobek and Helena María Viramontes, 147–69. Berkeley, Calif.: Third Woman Press, 1995.

———. "The Treacherous Woman Archetype: A Structuring Agent in the Corrido." *Aztlán* 13, nos. 1–2 (1982): 135–48.

Higonnet, Margaret, et al., eds. *Behind the Lines: Gender and the Two World Wars.* New Haven, Conn.: Yale University Press, 1987.

Hinojos, Francisco G. "Notes on the Pachuco: Stereotypes, History and Dialect." *Atisbos: Journal of Chicano Research* (1975): 53–65.

Hollibaugh, Amber, and Cherríe Moraga. "What We're Rollin around in Bed with: Sexual Silences in Feminism." In *Powers of Desire: The Politics of Sexuality*, edited by Ann Snitow, Christine Stansell, and Sharon Thompson, 394–405. New York: Monthly Review Press, 1983.

Hondagneu-Sotelo, Pierrette, and Michael A. Messner. "Gender Displays and Men's Power: 'The New Man' and the Mexican Immigrant Man." In *Theorizing Masculinities*, edited by Harry Brod and Michael Kaufman, 200–218. Thousand Oaks, Calif.: Sage, 1994.

Honey, Maureen. *Creating Rosie the Riveter: Class, Gender, and Propaganda during World War II*. Amherst: University of Massachusetts Press, 1984.

Huaco-Nuzum, Carmen. "Mi Familia / My Family." *Aztlán* 23, no. 1 (1998): 141–53.

Humphrey, Norman David. "The Stereotype and the Social Types of Mexican-American Youths." *Journal of Social Psychology* 22 (1945): 69–78.

Huntington, Samuel P. *Who Are We? The Challenges to America's Identity*. New York: Simon and Schuster, 2004.

Hurtado, Aída. *Voicing Chicana Feminisms: Young Women Speak Out on Sexuality and Identity*. New York: New York University Press, 2003.

Hutter, Harriett S. "El Milagrucho: A Linguistic Commentary on a Pachuco Text." *Hispania* 67, no. 2 (May 1984): 256–61.

Johnson, Gaye Theresa. "Constellations of Struggle: Luisa Moreno, Charlotta Bass, and the Legacy for Ethnic Studies." *Aztlán* 33, no. 1 (spring 2008): 155–72.

Joppke, Christian, ed. *Challenge to the Nation-State: Immigration in Western Europe and the United States*. Oxford: Oxford University Press, 1998.

Keaton, Trica Danielle. *Muslim Girls and the Other France: Race, Identity Politics, and Social Exclusion*. Bloomington: Indiana University Press, 2006.

Kelley, Robin D. G. *Race Rebels: Culture, Politics, and the Black Working Class*. New York: Free Press, 1994.

Kennedy, David M. *Freedom from Fear: The American People in Depression and War, 1929–1945*. New York: Oxford University Press, 1999.

Kennedy, Elizabeth Lapovsky, and Madeline Davis. *Boots of Leather, Slippers of Gold: The History of a Lesbian Community*. New York: Penguin, 1993.

———. " 'They Was No One to Mess With': The Construction of the Butch Role in the Lesbian Community of the 1940s and 1950s." In *The Persistent Desire: A Femme-Butch Reader*, edited by Joan Nestle, 62–79. Boston: Alyson Publications, 1992.

Kerber, Linda K. "Separate Spheres, Female Worlds, Woman's Place: The Rhetoric of Women's History." *Journal of American History* 75, no. 1 (1988): 9–39.

Kessler-Harris, Alice. *Out to Work: A History of Wage-Earning Women in the United States.* New York: Oxford University Press, 1982.

Kohn, Hans. *The Idea of Nationalism: A Study in Its Origins and Background.* New Brunswick, N.J.: Transaction Publishers, 2005.

Lacan, Jacques. "The Mirror Stage as Formative of the Function of the I as Revealed in Psychoanalytic Experience." In *Écrits*, translated by Alan Sheridan, 1–7. New York: W. W. Norton, 1977.

Lakoff, Robin Tolmach. *Language and Woman's Place: Text and Commentaries.* Edited by Mary Bucholtz. New York: Oxford University Press, 2004.

———. *Talking Power: The Politics of Language in Our Lives.* New York: Basic Books, 1990.

Leal, Luis. "Mexican American Literature: A Historical Perspective." In *Modern Chicano Writers: A Collection of Critical Essays*, edited by Joseph Sommers and Tomás Ybarra-Frausto, 1830 Englewood Cliffs, N.J.: Prentice-Hall, 1979.

Leland, John. *Hip: The History.* New York: HarperCollins, 2004.

Lewis, Reina, and Katrina Rolley. "Ad(dressing) the Dyke: Lesbian Looks and Lesbians Looking." In *Outlooks: Lesbian and Gay Sexualities and Visual Cultures*, edited Peter Horne and Reina Lewis, 178–90. New York: Routledge, 1996.

Leyva, Yolanda Chávez. "Listening to the Silences in Latina/Chicana Lesbian History." In *Living Chicana Theory*, edited by Carla Trujillo, 429–34. Berkeley, Calif.: Third Woman Press, 1998.

Limón, José. *Mexican Ballads, Chicano Poems: History and Influence in Mexican-American Social Poetry.* Berkeley: University of California Press, 1992.

Lingeman, Richard R. *Don't You Know There's a War On?: The American Home Front, 1941–1945.* New York: Capricorn Books, 1976.

Lipsitz, George. *American Studies in a Moment of Danger.* Minneapolis: University of Minnesota Press, 2001.

———. "Not Just Another Social Movement: Poster Art and the Movimiento Chicano." In *Chicano Graphic Art in California*, edited by Chon A. Noriega, 71–89. Santa Barbara, Calif.: University Art Museum, 2001.

———. *Rainbow at Midnight: Labor and Culture in the 1940s.* Urbana: University of Illinois Press, 1994.

———. *Time Passages: Collective Memory and American Popular Culture.* Minneapolis: University of Minnesota Press, 1990.

Livia, Anna. "'I Ought to Throw a Buick at You': Fictional Representations of Butch/Femme Speech." In *Gender Articulated: Language and the Socially Constructed Self*, edited by Kira Hall and Mary Bucholtz, 245–77. New York: Routledge, 1995.

Lloyd, David. "Nationalisms against the State." In *The Politics of Culture in the Shadow of Capital*, edited by Lisa Lowe and David Lloyd, 173–97. Durham, N.C.: Duke University Press, 1997.

Lowe, Lisa. *Immigrant Acts: On Asian American Cultural Politics.* Durham, N.C.: Duke University Press, 1996.

Luckenbill, Dan. *The Pachuco Era: Catalog of an Exhibit.* Los Angeles: Regents of the University of California, 1990.

Luibhéid, Eithne. *Entry Denied: Controlling Sexuality at the Border.* Minneapolis: University of Minnesota Press, 2002.

MacAdams, Lewis. *Birth of the Cool: Beat, Bebop, and the American Avant-Garde.* New York: Free Press, 2001.

Macías, Anthony. "Bringing Music to the People: Race, Urban Culture, and Municipal Politics in Postwar Los Angeles." *American Quarterly* 56, no. 3 (2004): 693–717.

———. *Mexican American Mojo: Popular Music, Dance, and Urban Culture in Los Angeles, 1935–1968.* Durham, N.C.: Duke University Press, 2008.

Madrid-Barela, Arturo. "In Search of the Authentic Pachuco: An Interpretative Essay." *Aztlán* 4, no. 1 (1974): 31–60.

Mahmood, Saba. *The Politics of Piety: The Islamic Revival and the Feminist Subject.* Princeton, N.J.: Princeton University Press, 2004.

Mailer, Norman. "The White Negro." In *Keeping Time: Readings in Jazz History,* edited by Robert Walser, 242–46. New York: Oxford University Press, 1999.

Majors, Richard, and Janice Mancini Bilson. *Cool Pose: The Dilemmas of Black Manhood in America.* New York: Lexington Books, 1992.

Malcolm X. *The Autobiography of Malcolm X.* New York: Ballantine Books, 1964.

Márez, Curtis. "Brown: The Politics of Working-Class Chicano Style." *Social Text* 48, vol. 14, no. 3 (1996): 109–32.

Mariscal, George. *Brown-eyed Children of the Sun: Lessons from the Chicano Movement, 1965–1975.* Albuquerque: University of New Mexico Press, 2005.

———. "Homeland Security, Militarism, and the Future of Latinos and Latinas in the United States." *Radical History Review* 93 (2005): 39–52.

Marshall, T. H., and Tom Bottomore. *Citizenship and Social Class.* London: Pluto Press, 1992.

Mazón, Maurico. *The Zoot-Suit Riots: The Psychology of Symbolic Annihilation.* Austin: University of Texas Press, 1984.

McAlister, Melani. *Epic Encounters: Culture, Media, and U.S. Interests in the Middle East since 1945.* Berkeley: University of California Press, 2005.

McClintock, Anne. "Family Feuds: Gender, Nationalism and the Family." *Feminist Review,* no. 44 (1993): 61–80.

McGrath, Alice, and Michael Balter. *The Education of Alice McGrath: Oral History Transcript.* Los Angeles: UCLA Oral History Program, 1987.

McRobbie, Angela. "Settling Accounts with Subcultures: A Feminist Critique." *Screen Education* 34 (1980): 37–49.

McWilliams, Carey. *North from Mexico: The Spanish-Speaking People of the United States.* New York: Praeger, 1990.

Medovoi, Leerom. *Rebels: Youth and the Cold War Origins of Identity.* Durham, N.C.: Duke University Press, 2005.

Meier, Matt S., and Feliciano Ribera. *Mexican Americans/American Mexicans: From Conquistadores to Chicanos.* New York: Hill and Wang, 1972.

Mendoza-Denton, Norma. "The Anguish of Normative Gender: Sociolinguistic Studies among U.S. Latinas." In *Language and Woman's Place: Text and Commentaries,* edited by Mary Bucholtz, 260–68. New York: Oxford University Press, 2004.

———. "Fighting Words: Latina Girls, Gangs, and Language Attitudes." In *Speaking Chicana: Voice, Power, and Identity,* edited by D. Letticia Galindo and María Dolores Gonzáles, 39–56. Tucson: University of Arizona Press, 1999.

———. *Homegirls: Language and Cultural Practice among Latina Youth Gangs.* Maiden, Mass.: Blackwell Publishing, 2008.

———. "Language Attitudes and Gang Affiliation among California Latina Girls." In *Cultural Performances: Proceedings of the Third Berkeley Women and Language Conference,* edited by Mary Bucholtz, A. C. Liang, Laurel A. Sutton, and Caitlin Hines, 478–86. Berkeley: Berkeley Women and Language Group, University of California, 1994.

———. "'Muy Macha': Gender and Ideology in Gang-Girls' Discourse about Makeup." *Ethnos* 61, nos. 1–2 (1996): 47–63.

———. "Turn-Initial *No:* Collaborative Opposition among Latina Adolescents." In *Reinventing Identities: The Gendered Self in Discourse,* edited by Mary Bucholtz, A. C. Liang, and Laurel A. Sutton, 274–92. New York: Oxford University Press, 1999.

Mercer, Kobena. *Welcome to the Jungle: New Positions in Black Cultural Studies.* New York: Routledge, 1994.

Meyer, Leisa D. *Creating G. I. Jane: Sexuality and Power in the Women's Army Corps during World War II.* New York: Columbia University Press, 1996.

Mezzrow, Milton "Mezz," and Bernard Wolfe. *Really the Blues.* New York: Random House, 1946.

Milkman, Ruth. *Women, Work, and Protest: A Century of U.S. Women's Labor History.* Boston: Routledge and Kegan Paul, 1985.

Miranda, Marie "Keta." *Homegirls in the Public Sphere.* Austin: University of Texas Press, 2003.

Mirandé, Alfredo. "The Chicano Family: A Reanalysis of Conflicting Views." *Journal of Marriage and the Family* 39 (1977): 747–56.

———. *Gringo Justice.* Notre Dame, Ind.: University of Notre Dame Press, 1987.

Molina, Natalia. *Fit to Be Citzens? Public Health and Race in Los Angeles, 1879–1939.* Berkeley: University of California Press, 2006.

Montejano, David. *Anglos and Mexicans in the Making of Texas, 1836–1986.* Austin: University of Texas Press, 1987.

Montoya, José. "El Louie." In *Literatura Chicana: Texto y contexto,* edited by Antonia Castañeda Shular, Tomás Ybarra-Frausto, and Joseph Sommers, 173–76. Englewood Cliffs, N.J.: Prentice-Hall, 1972.

———. *Pachuco Art: A Historical Update.* Sacramento, Calif.: RCAF, 1977.

———. "Los Vatos." In *El Espejo / The Mirror: Selected Mexican American Literature,* edited by Octavio Romano-V, 186–87. Berkeley: Quinto Sol Publications, 1969.

Moore, Joan W. *Going Down to the Barrio: Homeboys and Homegirls in Change.* Philadelphia: Temple University Press, 1991.

Moore, Joan W., and Alfredo Cuéllar. *Mexican Americans.* Englewood Cliffs, N.J.: Prentice-Hall, 1970.

Moore, Joan W., with Robert García, Carlos García, Luis Cerda, and Frank Valencia. *Homeboys: Gangs, Drugs, and Prison in the Barrios of Los Angeles.* Philadelphia: Temple University Press, 1978.

Moraga, Cherríe. *Giving Up the Ghost.* Los Angeles: West End Press, 1986.

———. *The Last Generation: Prose and Poetry.* Boston: South End Press, 1993.

———. "Later She Met Joyce." In *Loving in the War Years: lo que nunca pasó los labios,* 19–21. Boston: South End Press, 1983.

———. *Loving in the War Years: lo que nunca pasó por los labios.* Boston: South End Press, 1983.

Moreno, Raquel. *El Milagrucho. El Grito* 4, no. 3 (1971): 64–66.

Morín, Raúl. *Among the Valiant: Mexican Americans in WWII and Korea.* Alhambra, Calif.: Borden Publishing, 1966.

Mulvey, Laura. "Visual Pleasure and Narrative Cinema." *Screen* 16, no. 3 (1975): 6–18.

Muñoz, Carlos Jr. *Youth, Identity, Power: The Chicano Movement.* London: Verso Press, 1989.

Muñoz, José Esteban. *Disidentifications: Queers of Color and the Performance of Politics.* Minneapolis: University of Minnesota Press, 1999.

Murray, Yxta Maya. *Locas.* New York: Grove Press, 1997.

Nash, Gerald. *The American West Transformed: The Impact of the Second World War.* Bloomington: Indiana University Press, 1985.

Navarro, J. L. "East Los Angeles: Passing Time." In *Aztlán: An Anthology of Mexican American Literature,* edited by Luis Valdez and Stan Steiner, 163–70. New York: Vintage Books, 1972.

————. "To a Dead Lowrider." In *Aztlán: An Anthology of Mexican American Literature*, edited by Luis Valdez and Stan Steiner, 337–39. New York: Vintage Books, 1972.

Nestle, Joan. *A Restricted Country*. Ithaca, N.Y.: Firebrand Books, 1987.

Ngai, Mae M. *Impossible Subjects: Illegal Aliens and the Making of Modern America*. Princeton, N.J.: Princeton University Press, 2004.

Nieto-Gómez, Ana. "Chicana Feminism." In *Chicana Feminist Thought: The Basic Historical Writings*, edited by Alma M. García, 52–57. New York: Routledge, 1997.

————. "La Femenista." In *Chicana Feminist Thought: The Basic Historical Writings*, edited by Alma M. García, 86–92. New York: Routledge, 1997.

Noriega, Chon. "'American Family': Mi Casa Es Su Casa." *Chronicle of Higher Education*, March 8, 2002, http://web-lexis-nexis.com (visited September 9, 2005).

————. "Fashion Crimes." *Aztlán* 26, no. 1 (2001): 1–13.

Oboler, Suzanne, ed. *Latinos and Citizenship: The Dilemma of Belonging*. New York: Palgrave Macmillan, 2006.

Odem, Mary E. *Delinquent Daughters: Protecting and Policing Adolescent Female Sexuality in the United States*. Chapel Hill: University of North Carolina Press, 1995.

Omi, Michael, and Howard Winant. *Racial Formation in the United States, from the 1960s to the 1990s*. New York: Routledge, 1994.

Ong, Aihwa. "Cultural Citizenship as Subject-Making: Immigrants Negotiate Racial and Cultural Boundaries in the United States." *Current Anthropology* 37, no. 5 (1996): 737–63.

————. *Flexible Citizenship: The Cultural Logics of Transnationality*. Durham, N.C.: Duke University Press, 1999.

————. *Neoliberalism as Exception: Mutations in Citizenship and Sovereignty*. Durham, N.C.: Duke University Press, 2006.

Ornstein-Galicia, Jacob. "Chicano Caló: Description and Review of a Border Variety." *Hispanic Journal of Behavioral Sciences* 9, no. 4 (1987): 359–73.

Orona-Córdova, Roberta. "*Zoot Suit* and the Pachuco Phenomenon: An Interview with Luis Valdez." *Revista Chicano-Riqueña* 11, no. 1 (1983): 95–111.

Oropeza, Lorena. ¡*Raza Sí*! ¡*Guerra No*! *Chicano Protest and Patriotism during the Viet Nam War Era*. Berkeley: University of California Press, 2005.

Orozco, Cynthia E. "Beyond Machismo, La Familia, and Ladies Auxiliaries: A Historiography of Mexican-Origin Women's Participation in Voluntary Associations and Politics in the United States, 1870–1990." *Perspectives in Mexican American Studies* 5 (1995): 1–34.

Ortega, Adolfo. *Caló Tapestry*. Berkeley: Editorial Justa Publications, 1977.

Ortner, Sherry B. "Preliminary Notes on Class and Culture." In *Recapturing Anthropology: Working in the Present*, edited by Richard G. Fox, 163–89. Santa Fe, N.M.: School of American Research, 1991.

Pagán, Eduardo Obregón. *Murder at the Sleepy Lagoon: Zoot Suits, Race, and Riot in Wartime L.A.* Chapel Hill: University of North Carolina Press, 2003.

Paz, Octavio. *The Labyrinth of Solitude and Other Writings*. Translated by Lysander Kemp, Yara Milos, and Rachel Phillips Belash. New York: Grove Press, 1985.

Peiss, Kathy L. *Cheap Amusements: Working Women and Leisure in New York City, 1880–1920*. Philadelphia: Temple University Press, 1985.

Pérez, Emma. "Sexuality and Discourse: Notes from a Chicana Survivor." In *Chicana Lesbians: The Girls Our Mothers Warned Us About*, edited by Carla Trujillo, 159–84. Berkeley: Third Woman Press, 1991.

Pérez, Laura Elisa. "*El desorden*, Nationalism, and Chicana/o Aesthetics." In *Between Woman and Nation: Nationalisms, Transnational Feminisms, and the State*, edited by Caren Kaplan, Norma Alarcón, and Minoo Moallem, 19–46. Durham, N.C.: Duke University Press, 1999.

Pérez-Torres, Rafael. "Refiguring Aztlán." In *Postcolonial Theory and the United States: Race, Ethnicity, and Literature*, edited by Amritjit Singh and Peter Schmidt, 103–21. Jackson: University of Mississippi Press, 2000.

Perrett, Geoffrey. *Days of Sadness, Years of Triumph: The American People, 1939–1945*. New York: Coward, McCann and Geoghegan, 1973.

Pin-Fat, Veronique, and Maria Stern. "The Scripting of Private Jessica Lynch: Biopolitics, Gender, and the 'Feminization' of the U.S. Military." *Alternatives: Global, Local, Political* 30, no. 1 (2005): 25–54.

Polkinhorn, Harry, Alfredo Velasco, and Malcolm Lambert. *El libro de caló: The Dictionary of Chicano Slang*. Oakland, Calif.: Floricanto Press, 1986.

Ponce, Mary Helen. *Hoyt Street: An Autobiography*. Albuquerque: University of New Mexico Press, 1993.

———. *The Wedding*. Houston: Arte Público Press, 1989.

Post, Emily. *Etiquette: The Blue Book of Social Usage*. New York: Funk and Wagnalls, 1942.

Poutain, Dick, and David Robins. *Cool Rules: Anatomy of an Attitude*. London: Reaktion Books, 2000.

Pratt, Mary Louise. *Imperial Eyes: Travel Writing and Transculturation*. New York: Routledge, 1992.

Puar, Jasbir K. "On Torture: Abu Ghraib." *Radical History Review* 93 (2005): 13–38.

Puar, Jasbir K., and Amit S. Rai. "Monster, Terrorist, Fag: The War on Terrorism and the Production of Docile Patriots." *Social Text* 72, vol. 20, no. 3 (2002): 117–48.

Quiñonez, Naomi. "Rosita the Riveter: Welding Tradition with Wartime Transformations." In *Mexican Americans and World War II*, edited by Maggie Rivas-Rodríguez, 245–68. Austin: University of Texas Press, 2005.

Ramírez, Catherine S. "Crimes of Fashion: The Pachuca and Chicana Style Politics." *Meridians* 2, no. 2 (2002): 1–35.

raúlsalinas. *Un Trip through the Mind Jail y Otras Excursions*. Houston: Arte Público Press, 1999.

———. "A Trip through the Mind Jail." In *Aztlán: An Anthology of Mexican American Literature*, edited by Luis Valdez and Stan Steiner, 339–44. New York: Vintage Books, 1972.

Rechy, John. "El Paso del Norte." In *Literatura chicana: Texto y contexto / Chicano Literature: Text and Context*, edited by Antonia Castañeda Shular, Tomás Ybarra-Frausto, and Joseph Sommers. Englewood Cliffs, N.J.: Prentice-Hall, 1972.

Reckless, Walter C. "The Impact of War on Crime, Delinquency, and Prostitution." *American Journal of Sociology* 48, no. 3 (1942): 378–86.

Redl, Fritz. "Zoot Suits: An Interpretation." *Survey Midmonthly* 79, no. 10 (October 1943): 259–62.

Rendón, Armando B. *Chicano Manifesto: The History and Aspirations of the Second Largest Minority in America*. New York: Collier Books, 1971.

Rivas-Rodríguez, Maggie, ed. *Mexican Americans and World War II*. Austin: University of Texas Press, 2005.

Rivera, Tomás. "On the Road to Texas: Pete Fonseca." In *Aztlán: An Anthology of Mexican American Literature*, edited by Luis Valdez and Stan Steiner, 146–54. New York: Vintage Books, 1972.

Rodríguez, Luis J. "Expresiones de mi barrio/Barrio Expressions," *El Grito* 6, no. 4 (1973): 20–25.

Rodríguez, Richard T. "Serial Kinship: Representing La Familia in Early Chicano Publications." *Aztlán* 27, no. 1 (2002): 123–38.

———. "The Verse of the Godfather: Signifying Family and Nationalism in Chicano Rap and Hip-Hop Culture." In *Velvet Barrios: Popular Culture and Chicana/o Sexualities*, edited by Alicia Gaspar de Alba, 107–22. New York: Palgrave Macmillan, 2003.

Romano-V., Octavio. "The Historical and Intellectual Presence of Mexican-Americans." *El Grito* 2, no. 2 (1969): 32–46.

Romo, Ricardo. *East Los Angeles: History of a Barrio*. Austin: University of Texas Press, 1983.

Rosaldo, Renato. "The Borders of Belonging: Nation and Citizen in the Hinterlands." In *Cultural Citizenship in Island Southeast Asia: Nation and Belonging in the Hinterlands*, edited by Renato Rosaldo, 1–15. Berkeley: University of California Press, 2003.

————. "Cultural Citizenship and Educational Democracy." *Cultural Anthropology* 9, no. 3 (1994): 402–11.

————. *Culture and Truth: The Remaking of Social Analysis.* Boston: Beacon Press, 1989.

Rosales, Francisco A. *Chicano! The History of the Mexican American Civil Rights Movement.* Houston: Arte Público Press, 1996.

Rosensweig, Jay B. *Caló: Gutter Spanish.* New York: E. P. Dutton, 1973.

Rubin, Gayle. "Of Catamites and Kings: Reflections on Butch, Gender, and Boundaries." In *The Persistent Desire: A Femme-Butch Reader,* edited by Joan Nestle, 466–82. Boston: Alyson Publications, 1992.

————. "The Traffic in Women: Notes on the 'Political Economy' of Sex." In *Toward an Anthropology of Women,* edited by Rayna R. Reiter, 157–210. New York: Monthly Review Press, 1975.

Ruiz, Mona, with Geoff Boucher. *Two Badges: The Lives of Mona Ruiz.* Houston: Arte Público Press, 1997.

Ruiz, Vicki L. *Cannery Women, Cannery Lives: Mexican Women, Unionization, and the California Food Processing Industry, 1930–1950.* Albuquerque: University of New Mexico Press, 1987.

————. "The Flapper and the Chaperone: Historical Memory among Mexican-American Women." In *Seeking Common Ground: Multidisciplinary Studies of Immigrant Women in the United States,* edited by Donna Gabaccia, 141–57. Westport, Conn.: Greenwood Press, 1992.

————. *From Out of the Shadows: Mexican Women in Twentieth-Century America.* New York: Oxford University Press, 1998.

————. "'Star Struck': Acculturation, Adolescence, and the Mexican American Woman, 1920–1950." In *Building with Our Hands: New Directions in Chicana Studies,* edited by Adela de la Torre and Beatríz M. Pesquera, 109–29. Berkeley: University of California Press, 1993.

————. "Una Mujer sin Fronteras: Luisa Moreno and Latina Labor Activism." *Pacific Historical Review* 73, no. 1 (2004): 1–20.

Rupp, Leila J. *Mobilizing Women for War: German and American Propaganda, 1939–1945.* Princeton, N.J.: Princeton University Press, 1978.

Saldaña-Portillo, María Josefina. *The Revolutionary Imagination in the Americas and the Age of Development.* Durham, N.C.: Duke University Press, 2003.

Saldívar, José David. *The Dialectics of Our America: Genealogy, Cultural Critique, and Literary History.* Durham, N.C.: Duke University Press, 1991.

Saldívar, Ramón. *The Borderlands of Culture: Américo Paredes and the Transnational Imaginary.* Durham, N.C.: Duke University Press, 2006.

Saldívar-Hull, Sonia. *Feminism on the Border: Chicana Gender Politics and Literature.* Berkeley: University of California Press, 2000.

Sánchez, George J. *Becoming Mexican American: Ethnicity, Culture, and Identity in Chicano Los Angeles, 1900–1945.* New York: Oxford University Press, 1993.

———. "'Go After the Women': Americanization and the Mexican Immigrant Woman, 1915–1929." In *Unequal Sisters: A Multicultural Reader in U.S. Women's History,* edited by Ellen Carol DuBois and Vicki L. Ruiz, 250–63. New York: Routledge, 1990.

Sánchez, Marta Ester. *Contemporary Chicana Poetry: A Critical Approach to an Emerging Literature.* Berkeley: University of California Press, 1985.

———. *"Shakin' up" Race and Gender: Intercultural Connections in Puerto Rican, African American, and Chicano Narratives and Culture (1965–1995).* Austin: University of Texas Press, 2006.

Sánchez, Ricardo. *Canto y Grito Mi Liberación: The Liberation of a Chicano Mind Soul.* Pullman: Washington State University Press, 1978.

Sánchez, Rosaura. *Chicano Discourse: Socio-Historic Perspectives.* Houston: Arte Público Press, 1994.

———. "Chicano Spanish: Varieties, Styles and Functions." In *Chicano Speech in the Bilingual Classroom,* edited by Dennis J. Bixler-Márquez and Jacob Ornstein-Galicia, 55–68. New York: Peter Lang, 1988.

Sanchez, Thomas. *Zoot Suit Murders.* New York: Vintage Books, 1978.

Sanchez-Tranquilino, Marcos. "Mano a Mano: An Essay on the Representation of the Zoot Suit and Its Misrepresentation by Octavio Paz." *Los Angeles Institute of Contemporary Art* 46 (1987): 34–42.

Sanchez-Tranquilino, Marcos, and John Tagg. "The Pachuco's Flayed Hide: The Museum, Identity, and Buenas Garras." In *Chicano Art: Resistance and Affirmation,* edited by Richard Griswold del Castillo, Teresa McKenna, and Yvonne Yarbro-Bejarano, 97–108. Los Angeles: Wight Art Gallery, University of California, Los Angeles, 1991.

San Miguel, Guadalupe. *"Let All of Them Take Heed": Mexican Americans and the Campaign for Educational Equality in Texas, 1910–1981.* Austin: University of Texas Press, 1987.

Santillán, Richard. "Rosita the Riveter: Midwest Mexican American Women during World War II, 1941–1945." *Perspectives in Mexican American Studies* 2 (1989): 115–47.

Schalet, Amy, Geoffrey Hunt, and Karen Joe-Laidler. "Respectability and Autonomy: The Articulation and Meaning of Sexuality among the Girls in the Gang." *Journal of Contemporary Ethnography* 32, no. 1 (2003): 108–43.

Scott, James C. *Domination and the Arts of Resistance: Hidden Transcripts.* New Haven, Conn.: Yale University Press, 1990.

Scott, Joan W. *The Politics of the Veil.* Princeton, N.J.: Princeton University Press, 2007.

———. "Symptomatic Politics: The Banning of Islamic Head Scarves in French Public Schools." *French Politics, Culture and Society* 23, no. 3 (2005): 106–28.

Scott, Joan W., and Debra Keates, eds. *Going Public: Feminism and the Shifting Boundaries of the Private Sphere.* Urbana: University of Illinois Press, 2004.

Scott, Robin F. "The Zoot-Suit Riots." In *The Mexican-Americans: An Awakening Minority,* edited by Manuel P. Servín, 116–24. Beverly Hills: Glencoe Press, 1970.

Servín, Manuel P. "World War II and the Mexican-American." In *The Mexican-Americans: An Awakening Minority,* edited by Manuel P. Servín, 99. Beverly Hills: Glencoe Press, 1970.

Shack, William A. *Harlem in Montmartre: A Paris Jazz Story between the Great Wars.* Berkeley: University of California Press, 2001.

Shuck, Peter H. "The Re-Evaluation of American Citizenship." In *Challenge to the Nation-State: Immigration in Western Europe and the United States,* edited by Christian Joppke, 191–230. Oxford: Oxford University Press, 1998.

Shular, Antonia Castañeda, Tomás Ybarra-Frausto, and Joseph Sommers, eds. *Literatura chicana: texto y contexto / Chicano Literature: Text and Context.* Englewood Cliffs, N.J.: Prentice-Hall, 1972.

Sikes, Gini. *8 Ball Chicks: A Year in the Violent World of Girl Gangsters.* New York: Anchor Books, 1997.

Smith, Anthony D. *National Identity.* Reno: University of Nevada Press, 1991.

———. *Nationalism and Modernism: A Critical Survey of Recent Theories of Nations and Nationalism.* London: Routledge, 1998.

Stansell, Christine. *City of Women: Sex and Class in New York, 1789–1860.* Urbana: University of Illinois Press, 1987.

Stearns, Peter N. *American Cool: Constructing a Twentieth-Century Emotional Style.* New York: New York University Press, 1994.

Stegner, Wallace. *One Nation.* Boston: Houghton Mifflin Company, 1945.

Steiner, Stan. *La Raza: The Mexican Americans.* New York: Harper and Row, 1969.

Sturken, Marita, and Lisa Cartwright. *Practices of Looking: An Introduction to Visual Culture.* New York: Oxford University Press, 2001.

Suárez, Mario. "Kid Zopilote." *Arizona Quarterly* 3, no. 2 (1947): 130–37.

Tafolla, Carmen. *Sonnets to Human Beings and Other Selected Works.* Santa Monica, Calif.: Lalo Press, 1992.

Takaki, Ronald. *Double Victory: A Multicultural History of America in World War II.* Boston: Little, Brown, 2000.

Thompson, Robert Farris. "An Aesthetic of the Cool." *African Arts* 7, no. 1 (1973): 40–91.

Tuck, Ruth. *Not with the Fist.* New York: Arno Press, 1946.

Turner, Ralph H., and Samuel J. Surace. "Zoot-Suiters and Mexicans: Symbols in Crowd Behavior." *American Journal of Sociology* 62, no. 1 (1956): 14–20.

Tyler, Bruce M. "Black Jive and White Repression." *Journal of Ethnic Studies* 16, no. 4 (Winter 1989): 31–66.

Valdez, Luis. *Zoot Suit and Other Plays.* Houston: Arte Público Press, 1992.

Valdez, Luis, and Stan Steiner, eds. *Aztlán: An Anthology of Mexican American Literature.* New York: Vintage Books, 1972.

Veblen, Thorstein. *Theory of the Leisure Class.* New Brunswick, N.J.: Transaction Publishers, 1992.

Vigil, Evangelina. *Thirty an' Seen a Lot.* Berkeley: Third Woman Press, 1982.

Villanueva, Tino. *Hay Otra Voz: Poems (1968–1971).* New York: Coleccíon Mensaje, 1972.

Villarreal, José Antonio. *Pocho.* New York: Anchor Books, 1959.

Villarreal, Rudolfo C. *Arizona's Hispanic Flyboys, 1941–1945.* Lincoln, Neb.: Writers Club Press, 2002.

Walton, Frank L. *Thread of Victory: The Conversion and Conservation of Textiles, Clothing and Leather for the World's Biggest War Program.* New York: Fairchild Publishing, 1945.

White, Shane, and Graham White. *Stylin': African American Expressive Culture from Its Beginnings to the Zoot Suit.* Ithaca, N.Y.: Cornell University Press, 1998.

Williams, Raymond. *Keywords: A Vocabulary of Culture and Society.* New York: Oxford University Press, 1983.

Winter, Ella. "Are Children Worse in Wartime?" *Colliers,* March 1943, 52–55.

Wyatt, David. *Five Fires: Race, Catastrophe, and the Shaping of California.* Reading, Mass.: Addison-Wesley, 1997.

Yarbro-Bejarano, Yvonne. "The Female Subject in Chicano Theatre: Sexuality, 'Race,' and Class." *Theatre Journal* 38, no. 4 (1986): 389–407.

———. *The Wounded Heart: Writing on Cherríe Moraga.* Austin: University of Texas Press, 2001.

Yuval-Davis, Nira, and Floya Anthias, eds. *Women-Nation-State.* Houndsmill: Macmillan, 1989.

Zavella, Patricia. "The Problematic Relationship of Feminism and Chicana Studies." *Women's Studies* 17 (1989): 25–36.

———. *Women's Work and Chicano Families: Cannery Workers of the Santa Clara Valley.* Ithaca, N.Y.: Cornell University Press, 1987.

Zinn, Maxine Baca. "Political Familism: Toward Sex Role Equality in Chicano Families." In *The Chicano Studies Reader: An Anthology of Aztlán, 1970–2000,* edited by Chon Noriega, Eric R. Avila, Karen Mary Davalos, Chela Sandoval, and Rafael Pérez-Torres, 455–72. Los Angeles: UCLA Chicano Studies Research Center, 2001.

Zolberg, Aristide R. *A Nation by Design: Immigration Policy in the Fashioning of America*. New York: Russell Sage Foundation, 2006.

Dissertations, Theses, and Unpublished Papers

Alvarez, Luis. "The Power of the Zoot: Race, Community, and Resistance in American Youth Culture, 1940–1945." Ph.D. diss., University of Texas at Austin, 2001.

Chávez, Marisela Rodríguez. "Despierten hermanas y hermanos! Women, the Chicano Movement, and Chicana Feminisms in California, 1966–1981." Ph.D. diss., Stanford University, 2004.

Cummings, Laura Lee. "Que siga el corrido: Tucson Pachucos and Their Times." Ph.D. diss., University of Arizona, 1994.

De Lorca, Lou. "The Reality of a Myth: A Historical View of the Pachuco in East Los Angeles." Master's thesis, California State University, Dominguez Hills, 1997.

Domer, Marilyn. "The Zoot-Suit Riot: A Culmination of Social Tension in Los Angeles." Master's thesis, Claremont Graduate School, 1955.

Escobedo, Elizabeth. "Mexican American Home Front: The Politics of Gender, Culture and Community in World War II Los Angeles." Ph.D. diss., University of Washington, 2004.

Gaytán, David Rojas. "Pachucos and the Wartime Mexican Angeleno Press." Master's thesis, California State University, Hayward, 1996.

Green, Susan Marie. "'Give It Your Best!' The Zoot Suit Riots of 1943." Master's thesis, University of Minnesota, 1995.

Jones, Solomon J. "The Government Riots of Los Angeles, June 1943." Master's thesis, University of California, Los Angeles, 1969.

Katz, Linda Fine. "The Evolution of the Pachuco Language and Culture." Master's thesis, University of California, Los Angeles, 1974.

Ramírez, Catherine Sue. "The Pachuca in Chicana/o Art, Literature, and History: Reexamining Nation, Cultural Nationalism, and Resistance." Ph.D. diss., University of California, Berkeley, 2000.

Rodríguez, Richard T. "Reimagined Communities: Family, Masculinity, and Nationalism in Chicano Cultural Production." Ph.D. diss., University of California, Santa Cruz, 2000.

Rosales, Karla E. "Papis, Dykes, Daddies: A Study of Chicana and Latina Self-Identified Butch Lesbians." Master's thesis, San Francisco State University, 2001.

Sine, Don Thomas. "Zoot Suit Riots of Los Angeles, 1943: A New Perspective." Master's thesis, California State University, Long Beach, 1976.

Zamora, Bernice B. Ortíz. "Mythopoeia of Chicano Poetry: An Introduction to Cultural Archetypes." Ph.D. diss., Stanford University, 1986.

Music and Films

Anders, Allison. *Mi Vida Loca*. Home Box Office, 1994.

Gilbert, L. Wolfe, and Bob O'Brien. "A Zoot Suit (for My Sunday Gal)." http://lyricsplayground.com (visited January 4, 2007).

Rosales, Karla E. *Mind If I Call You Sir? A Discussion between Latina Butches and Female-to-Male Transgendered Latinos*. San Francisco: Sticky Girl Productions, 2004.

Salas, Miguel. "El Bracero y La Pachuca." *Pachuco Boogie, featuring Don Tosti*. El Cerrito, Calif.: Arhoolie Productions, 2002.

Tosti, Don (Edmundo Martínez Tostado). *Pachuco Boogie, featuring Don Tosti*. El Cerrito, Calif.: Arhoolie Productions, 2002.

Tovares, Joseph. *The American Experience: Zoot Suit Riots*. Boston: WGBH Educational Foundation, 2001.

Valdez, Luis. *Zoot Suit*. Universal Pictures, 1981.

INDEX

Abu Ghraib, 144

Adventures of Kiki and El Cruiser, The (Cisneros), 9–10, 13

African Americans, 2, 57, 83, 88, 176 n. 99, 190 n. 83; vernacular English of, 88, 91, 92

Aguilar, Bertha: characterization in *Zoot Suit*, 104, 105, 106; court testimony of, 87, 100–103, 183 n. 101

Althusser, Louis, on "state apparatus," xiv, 149 nn. 5–6

Alurista (poet), 26–27, 120

American home front: after 9/11, 137–47; in World War II era, xiv, 9, 20, 40, 63, 67; xenophobia on, 64, 88, 140

Americanization, 18, 26, 42, 61; "American identity" and, 45, 50, 58, 88, 94, 185 n. 5. *See also* nationalism

American studies, 23

Angeleno press, 18, 26, 27, 28, 36; pachuca in, 38–39, 57, 63, 70–73, 83, 86, 88, 98, 103, 117

Ayres report, 63

Aztecs, 6, 12, 38

Aztlán, 12; *Plan Espiritual de Aztlán*, 113

baby boomers, 91, 153 n. 38

Baca, Dora, 34; court testimony of, 102, 104, 182 n. 85, 183 n. 114

Baca, Judith F., xvii, xviii–xix, xx, 15, 122–23, 124, 132, 134–35, 136, 157 n. 69

Barrios, Dora, 29, 30, 162 n. 25, 182 n. 85

Bright, John, 31

Brown Berets, 103, 115

Brown v. Board of Education, 14

Calloway, Cabell ("Cab"), 4, 88

caló (pachuco slang), xii–xiv; masculinity and, 91–94; origins of, 83–87

carnalismo, 113, 119, 187 n. 39

Castellano, Olivia, 120

cha-cha, xx, 150 n. 11

Chávez, César, 112

Chávez, Delia ("Dee"), 25, 28, 47, 48, 49, 50, 51–52, 59, 189 n. 71

Chicana/Chicano: identity of, xvii, 8, 13, 16, 17, 22–23, 26, 85, 107, 109, 113, 123, 134, 160 n. 109; as term, xxv, 12

Chicana/Chicano Studies, xxi, 8, 9, 13, 28, 56; intellectuals and writers, 84, 89, 109

Chicana feminism, 7–8, 12, 155 n. 51; cultural production and, 51, 79, 111, 114, 133

Chicanismo, 21, 28, 113

Chicano family: in artistic production, 118–19, 131–34, 146; ideology of, 113–15, 117

Chicano movement (cultural production), ix, xiv, xv, xvii; feminist critiques of, 7–9; pachuca imagery in, 23, 58, 80–81, 94, 110, 119–36, 153

Catherine S. Ramírez is an associate professor of American studies at the University of California, Santa Cruz.

Library of Congress Cataloging-in-Publication Data
Ramírez, Catherine Sue
The woman in the zoot suit: gender, nationalism, and the
cultural politics of memory / Catherine S. Ramírez.
p. cm.
Includes bibliographical references and index.
ISBN 978-0-8223-4286-1 (cloth : alk. paper)
ISBN 978-0-8223-4303-5 (pbk. : alk. paper)
1. Mexican American women—California—Los Angeles—
Ethnic identity. 2. Mexican American women—California—
Los Angeles—Social conditions. 3. Mexican American
women—History—20th century. 4. Mexican American
women—Social conditions. 5. Zoot Suit Riots, Los Angeles,
Calif., 1943. I. Title.
E184.M5R329 2009
979.4'94052—dc22   2008041777